LIBERAL PARTY POLITICS IN BRITAIN

LIBERAL PARTY POLITICS IN BRITAIN

by

Arthur Cyr

With a foreword by Michael Steed

TRANSACTION INC
New Brunswick, New Jersey 08903

First published in the U.S.A. by Transaction Inc.,
New Brunswick, New Jersey 08903

© Arthur Cyr 1977

Library of Congress Cataloging in Publication Data
Cyr, Arthur I   1945-
   Liberal party politics in Britain.
   1.   Liberal Party (Gt. Brit.) – History.
I.   Title.
JN1129.L32C92   329.9'41   76-702

ISBN 0-87855-145-X

Printed in the United Kingdom.

CONTENTS

TABLES AND FIGURES

To Betty

FOREWORD

The British Liberal Party is a puzzle to political science. The traditional view from British universities has been of a United Kingdom with a stable well-functioning system of government, which in turn reflects a strong executive, clear lines of accountability to the electorate through parliamentary majorities based on a two-party system and a simple, socio-economic basis of voting behaviour. The Liberal Party has obstinately refused to fit into this picture: a denial of the class basis of voting and an irrelevancy in the power politics of Westminster. For a while, after it sank to third-party status in the early twenties, it was easy to regard it as a quaint survival, en route to an inevitable grave, and conveniently to ignore it wherever it belied a preferred interpretation of British politics. Latterly, as political scientists have caught up with the party's persistent presence, several explanations of why people vote Liberal have been offered. But the view that the party itself is an anomaly has been maintained, even though the pattern of one small and two large parties is the most enduring in British political history. There is, as yet, no authoritative contemporary British work on the Liberal Party.

Things might have been different if British academic tradition had been more aware of the similarities with other European political systems. There is a family of liberal parties in Western Europe, possessing in common a descent from the nineteenth century movements of political emancipation and each a defender of individualistic values in a collectivist age, though they differ markedly in some other respects. But while the European liberal parties have themselves recognized this affinity and have been loosely linked for more than half a century (in the *Entente*

Internationale des Partis Radicaux et des Parties Démocratiques similaires (1924), then the Liberal International (1947), now supplemented by the Federation of Liberal and Democratic Parties of the European Community (1976)), most political scientists have preferred to focus on a dichotomy between the continental multi-party systems and the simpler party systems of the English-speaking world. Arthur Cyr, coming from another country in the Anglo-Saxon mould, is no exception. He, therefore, accepts the challenge which would not pose itself in a European context: how to explain the role of the British Liberal Party in what on the face of it is a two-party system.

Americans examining British politics have all too often done so through the eyes of their own country. Since the totally different two-party system of the United States has thrown up several short-lived third-party movements, it has been all too easy – and misleading – for them to see Britain's permanent third-party in similar protest or safety-valve terms. Cyr avoids this view (if he has a geographical context, it is the English-speaking parliamentary systems, or old Commonwealth). He places his interpretation firmly in the context of the view of Great Britain's political system expounded in Samuel Beer's classic, *Modern British Politics*. Beer wrote very much in terms of a two-party system, but one which in its ideology and interest articulation is totally unlike the American model. Tracing the development of political ideas and conflicts in Britain, he shows how the Liberal Party fell into decline with the eclipse of its particular style of politics and leaves no place for the modern survival of Liberal-Radical politics in the collectivist age.

Arthur Cyr takes Beer's analysis a step further and sees the Liberal Party as reflecting a dimension of individualism versus collectivism which the class-based conflict of the two main parties obscures. Its presence, in fact, is the corollary of the nature of the division between its two big partners. If they were differently defined – for instance, loose coalitions on the American style – there would be no need for a Liberal Party. Its fortunes, therefore, are intimately linked to the two class-collectivist parties and the way their view of politics adequately covers changes in society. The Liberal Party does not represent a class, or section, nor a developed ideology; it is quintessentially a vehicle of certain ideas, and a certain style of politics.

This view is skilfully woven into the material on the Liberal Party in these pages. In discussing the party's heritage (Chapter 1), the policies it has emphasized in recent years (Chapter 3), the internal structure of the party (Chapter 4), its voting base (Chapter 6) and the reasons why its activists get involved in it (Chapter 7), he shows the relevance of this theme, and thus demonstrates that the Liberal Party has a coherence and consistency, despite many appearances to the contrary. He concludes with an interesting hypothesis about the relationship between the Liberal electoral revival and the changing style of pressure group politics.

The idea that the Liberal Party is, or ought to be, a different sort of political party, which could provide a home for those engaged in liberal and humanitarian politics outside a party framework, and which could be a base from which a new, broader progressive movement would be launched, was very much Jo Grimond's. It has much in common with Arthur Cyr's analysis. Cyr tends to concentrate on the Grimond years, and the two or three immediately following. The bulk of the material that he has researched comes from the nineteen-sixties, and much of the book carries the perspective of those years. The developments through which the party has since passed tend to confirm Cyr's findings – indeed the community politics strategy adopted by the party in 1970 made its role much more specifically what Cyr sees it as having been. But the electoral successes of the 1973/74 period, together with developments in the British political system, brought out questions about what sort of role such a party could play in British politics, and exposed contradictions inside the Liberal Party which undermined any role it would have wished to play.

The June 1970 general election saw a bad slump in the Liberal vote, conforming to the so far invariable pattern that the Liberal Party loses ground when a Labour

Government is in office. But although the Liberal vote dropped by 3% in comparable constituencies, it rose against the trend in one-seventh of them and jumped by more than ten per cent in four – Birmingham Ladywood; Liverpool, Wavertree; Rochdale; and Southport. The common factor was a well-entrenched local Liberal councillor as candidate, and these results were a striking testimony to the willingness of people to vote Liberal in return for municipal service. It was also a striking break with the usual electoral pattern: normally a national movement of votes in British elections relentlessly overrides the appeal of a local candidate. This in turn has reflected the solidification of British politics on a national, class-defined basis. These results were a glimpse of the more personal politics in which the Liberal Party would be more at home; they also seemed to offer a wedge to prise open the domination of the two main parties. But the brutal political fact was that the party was back to only six MPs, three of them elected with hairsbreadth margins, and none (for the first time ever) from outside the Celtic Fringe.

The next two years were a black period for the party. Jeremy Thorpe lost his wife in tragic circumstances and understandably took a less active role as leader for a period. He also moved into business activities, as a director of a fringe bank – a decision which was to lead to later problems. The Heath government rapidly lost popularity as it failed to halt rising inflation; the promise of being able to do so was, in the opinion of many, the main reason that it had won the election. It was also following policies in housing and industrial relations which aroused bitter opposition. Nationally, the Liberal Party failed to make any impact in response, whilst the Housing Finance Bill and Industrial Relations Bill galvanised and united the Labour Party. There was some hope among Liberals that they would benefit from facing a Conservative Government. But the electoral record was appalling. The May 1971 local election Liberal vote was the lowest for fifteen years, and the May 1972 results showed only a small recovery – except for Liverpool where vigorous local campaigning was producing a remarkable series of Liberal gains. In the first two years of the 1970 parliament, there were fifteen by-elections. The Liberal Party did not even contest eight of them, and in the seven that it did it averaged a mere 9%. These seven were, of course, the half in which the party expected to be stronger (and in due course Liberal candidates were to take 22% of the votes cast in them in February 1974).

Not surprisingly, there was internal dissension and a search for scapegoats. Thorpe was probably saved from criticism by the memory of the bitter disputes of the 1967/8 period, and the loss of his wife. There was some attempt to put the blame on the Young Liberals (and a separate sour dispute about the party's stance on the Middle East which got enmeshed with controversy over the Young Liberals). The 1971 assembly was a particularly divided occasion.

But this period also saw the groundwork prepared for the surge of Liberal support that was to follow. There was an important shift in the emphasis of the Young Liberal and activist wings of the party. In the nineteen-sixties it had been international idealism which had aroused them most – their greatest victory had been in leading the Liberal Party's growing opposition to the British Government's support for American involvement in Vietnam, and another area of major emphasis was racial politics in Southern Africa. In this they reflected both the youthful concerns of the time, and the long-standing emphasis of the Liberal Party itself. Whether it was Gladstone denouncing the Bulgarian massacres, or Clement Davies exposing the hypocrisy of the Labour Government's expulsion of Seretse Khama from Bechuanaland in 1951, or David Steel's leadership of the opposition to the effectively racialist Commonwealth Immigration Act of 1968, it has become traditional for Liberal leaders to make a name by taking up an issue of principle in the international field. The Young Liberal activists thus fitted well into a strand of British Liberalism (which helps to explain why they were at home within the Liberal Party).

But in 1970, the Young Liberals switched their efforts to the domestic political strategy of the party and, forging an alliance with a number of Liberal councillors, were able to persuade the post-election assembly to adopt a resolution on what was termed Community Politics. This success reflects the fact that by this stage it would be more accurate to talk of a Radical activist wing, including the Young Liberals, many of whose members were outside the Young Liberals as such. It later centred around a Radical Bulletin Group, which echoed the Radical Reform Group of twenty years earlier and which maintained through a newsletter and regular seminars a point of contact and inspiration within the party. It is always hard to evaluate the importance of a loosely-organized internal pressure group like this, and Radical Bulletin may well have been at least as much an expression of what was happening as a cause. But within a couple of years, ex-Young Liberals of the sixties, local councillors, party members primarily engaged in outside pressure groups or voluntary organizations and others were co-operating together under the banner of Community Politics.

The actual resolution adopted in 1970 stressed a dual approach to politics. It proclaimed that the party should continue to work inside established political institutions (parliamentary and local government) but that at the same time it should be working directly, with people, to achieve changes in society. In the latter way more genuine democracy and popular participation could be created (as well as the desirable changes) than by seeking to make the changes from above. This fits very clearly with the style of politics developed by the late Wallace Lawler in Birmingham, which Cyr describes on pp 251-3, and more generally from the voluntarism he discusses on p 259ff. The emphasis on democracy and the concern with people in communities, rather than as classes or sections, was developed out of previous Liberal ideas. But the emphasis on direct action (and even, though this was to be a source of much dispute, possibly on direct non-violent illegal action) and the deliberate de-emphasis on parliamentary democracy was a marked shift away from traditional Liberal priorities. In some respects it was the resurgence of a more Radical approach to politics over the Liberal approach in the sense used by Cyr in Chapter 1. The strategy was never given wholehearted support by the parliamentary leadership but at local levels it inspired more general and systematic activity. Quite contrary to the one-time distaste for party politics in local government (see p. 136), local elections were seen as means by which Liberals could mobilize support, not just for electoral purposes, but in order to secure the community involvement they sought.

The tide turned nationally suddenly in mid-1972. By good chance a by-election occurred in Rochdale, one Labour-held seat which the Liberals could hope to gain. Another pending by-election, in a safe Conservative suburban London seat, Sutton & Cheam, where the Liberals had taken a mere 6% of the votes in the 1971 local elections, was seized upon by Trevor Jones, the main architect of the Liberal advance in Liverpool, as the place where he would show that his methods could win a parliamentary seat. The 1972 assembly met in a self-induced confident mood, and made a success of procedural reforms designed to make it easier for delegates to be involved in formulating policy – a reversal of the shift towards more managed assemblies made in 1960 and an interesting case of practising inside the party the policies of participation it was promoting. There followed the anticipated gain of Rochdale, and stupendous victory at Sutton & Cheam where the Liberal vote shot up to 53.6%. There was widespread criticism that this result had been achieved by debasing politics to the level of litter clearance and broken paving stones – but Trevor Jones's methods had paid off.

There followed the Liberal Party's annus mirabilis. In 1973 six English by-elections were fought; the lowest vote scored was 36.5%, and three elected Liberal MPs. In May the Liverpool Liberals almost took outright control of the city council, an achievement which made the nine Liberal councillors in Birmingham, which Cyr looks at on p. 252, look very small meat indeed. At the same time in Scotland, the SNP outshone Liberals at by-elections, gaining a safe Labour seat in the heart of Glasgow, and at a by-election in Lincoln a rebel Labour MP trounced his official opponent by a five to two majority. The external verities of British party politics seemed about to slip away and if not everywhere in Britain, in most of the country the Liberals were well-placed to take advantage. The community politics strategy was producing (or so it seemed) new Liberal councillors in hitherto forlorn territory, and enabling the party to build a much more solid organizational base.

The sudden explosion of Liberal support in 1972-3 came during a period of discontent with a Conservative Government; the two lesser peaks of 1958 and 1962 had done so as well, and it was tempting to see this as the third of a kind. Certainly many commentators at the time did so, expecting it would melt away as a general election drew near just as the previous two had done. But there were important differences. Liberal support had risen steadily during the 1955 and 1959 parliaments, culminating in a peak. The party had not produced these two revivals by its own efforts. Jo Grimond's arrival as leader and the organizational improvements in the party came after the first revival was well under way; the spate of policy-making in the early sixties which Cyr examines in chapter 3 was mostly published after the voting trend had started to move downwards again. This time, with the element of good luck over the timing of the Rochdale by-election, the explosion had come after a lean period and followed both the adoption of a considered strategy and hard work.

The premature dissolution of February 1974 offered another change from the pattern. The previous revivals had died away some time before general elections fell due and the modest Liberal advances at the 1959 and 1964 general elections reflected a level of support much lower than had been achieved a year or two earlier. So firmly was the idea held that voting Liberal was for many a by-election only protest, it was widely assumed in early 1974 that the announcement of an election would send by-election Liberal voters back to their Tory and Labour homes.

However, the February 1974 campaign went the Liberals' way. The increased strength of the party on the ground enabled it to put up more candidates than at any time for forty-five years; this alone ensured that its total vote would rise. The two larger party leaderships concentrated on attacking each other, and ignored the Liberals until it was so late that turning to attack them only increased their credibility. The result was a total Liberal vote of six million, and if there had been time to put up a candidate in every seat it would have been nearer to seven million.

This achievement demands explanation. On the face of it, the circumstances of the campaign were exactly those likely to crush the Liberal Party. A government, challenged by a powerful interest group, was using the weapon of dissolution to appeal to the country; the direct chain of accountability from government to people was on full display and the two-party system fighting on home ground. Yet it was the two-party system which was the loser, as both major parties sunk to their lowest share of the popular vote for over forty years. The precise circumstances of the election – a clash between a Conservative Government which had tried to trap the unions by a partisan law and a National Union of Mineworkers egged on by militants to defy the elected government – seemed pre-eminently class-divisive. Twenty years earlier, and perhaps even ten, this would inevitably have polarised the electorate on the basis of partisan class-loyalties; the minor, non-class parties would have been rendered irrelevant.

Yet class politics lost, the Liberals being the beneficiaries in England and Wales and the Scottish National Party the main one in Scotland. This gives powerful support to one of the themes which Arthur Cyr develops in chapter 8, the steady decline in class feeling. That the February 1974 clash failed to relight the fires of social conflict is witness to how far the decline had gone. The Liberal and Nationalist gains were much the greatest among young voters, those least affected by a declining antagonism.

The Liberal Party played its part in gathering the harvest. In a highly skilled television campaign fought entirely from his own constituency in the West Country (the distance from London probably adding to a tactical stance outside the two-party battle), Jeremy Thorpe projected an appeal of sweet reasonableness and moderation. If there was a centre-ground between the two major parties he was aiming to fill it. As a tactic, it certainly seemed to have paid off.

Yet there was an essential contradiction between this successful tactic, and the party's declared community politics strategy. The latter saw the Liberal Party as the vehicle of a radical, popular, democratic movement against the British political establishment, embodied in the two major parties. The former saw the Liberal Party lying between them, combining the best of the more progressive Conservatives and the social democratic wing of the Labour Party (one of whose leading members, Christopher Mayhew MP, was soon after to break away to join the Liberal Party). The contradiction was not generally felt so starkly among Liberals, but it was — and still is — nonetheless there. The build-up to the 1974 election had owed more, so it seemed, to the community politics strategy — Liverpool and Sutton & Cheam were essential stages on the route to the credibility which Jeremy Thorpe projected in February 1974. But the votes garnered in 1974 were won on a national basis, and local effort — in contrast to 1970 — counted for little. Indeed the worst results in England came from Liverpool. The massive six million vote left the Liberal Party with many question marks about how it had got to that position, and how it should go further.

But the outcome of the February 1974 election had placed the Liberal Party in a situation where it had to act, or react, fast. No party had an overall majority of seats, and with its massive vote the Liberal Party was in a real sense the moral victor — both the two main parties having suffered enormous losses of votes. But no Liberal initiative was taken until four days after the election, when a suggestion of an all-party coalition fell flat. Instead the Labour Party at once offered to form a minority government; Mr Heath invited Mr Thorpe to go and see him, which he did. There followed a weekend of non-negotiations, since it became clear that the Conservatives were not contemplating an offer of coalition on terms which the Liberals could conceivably accept. But by meeting and talking with the Conservative

Prime Minister, the Liberal leader allowed it to appear that
he was considering a deal. He had not consulted his
colleagues beforehand, and the Liberal Party was
completely unprepared for any concerted consideration of
possible arrangements with another party. There was a
flood of protest from members of the party when it seemed
that a Tory/Liberal deal was in prospect; by the time he
saw Heath, Thorpe was aware of this feeling and the
Liberal MPs meeting two days later confirmed that no
agreement was possible. Heath resigned, a Labour
Government sneaked into office and the election result was
made to appear as if it was in some sense a Labour victory.

This is the nearest the Liberal Party has come to real
power since the Liberal Ministers resigned from the
National Government in 1932. The opportunity presented
was badly bungled; why?

There are many reasons. Hardly anyone in British politics
in early 1974 was prepared for a situation of no overall
majority, and for the politics of coalition-formation or inter-
party arrangements (John Pardoe, chairman of the party's
Standing Committee was the only prominent Liberal
exception to this lack of foresight).[1] The election results were
reported, as they came in, in two-party system terms, and it
took a while for their significance to sink in. For trivial but in
a fast moving situation all-important reasons, the Liberal
Party was badly placed to adjust and act quickly. Most
Liberal MPs sit for fairly remote rural constituencies, which
declare their results fairly late. The composition and size of
the Parliamentary Liberal Party is not, therefore, known
until the leaderships of the other two parties know both their
own individual results and the approximate overall result.
The Liberal Party is, therefore, badly placed tactically on
the day following a British general election.

The Labour Party seized a tactical initiative; Harold
Wilson alone seems to have thought clearly or quickly that
Friday afternoon.[2] Ignoring the overall composition of the
new House of Commons, and the votes cast in the election, he
in effect claimed a victory which no one else, by their actions,
was able later to do. This ruled out, in advance, any
Labour/Liberal arrangement. Electorally and politically,

the Liberal Party would have had to explore such an arrangement before it could treat with the Conservative Party. The mood of the party was particularly radical, following the build-up of the previous three years and an election fought against an incumbent Conservative Government. The majority of Liberal MPs held seats against Conservative opponents with the support of would-be Labour voters – and an overwhelming majority of the seats which the party was well-placed to capture depended on getting such second preference Labour votes. The only justification for considering any coalition or arrangement for conditional support from the backbenches with the Conservative Party could have been that Labour had refused such a deal. By Friday evening, it would have needed very clear thinking, astuteness, a solid base in his own party and luck for any Liberal leader to have taken a successful initiative.

Nevertheless, the facts that Jeremy Thorpe and his parliamentary colleagues allowed themselves to be outmanouevred by both Wilson and Heath, and that he was made to look as if he might have wanted a coalition with Heath, undermined his standing (which had been extremely high following the election campaign) for the brief 1974 parliament. That in turn limited the freedom of action of the Liberal MPs to exploit their parliamentary position during that period, a position which was also limited by the simple mathematics of the composition of the Commons. Although in the country the Liberals seemed to hold the balance of power (which of course they clearly did in votes cast), the fourteen MPs plus either large party did not form an overall majority in the House.

However, relevant as these reasons are to why the Liberals fluffed their chances both in the days following the election and during the life of the short parliament, there were much more fundamental problems which the situation revealed. There was the essential dilemma of what role the Liberal Party would have liked to play. The party had not sought coalition when it had held the balance of power twice in the twenties, and had unhappy memories of two peacetime coalitions (1918-22, 1931-2). Yet if it is to act as a real political party and seek executive power, the logic of both its voting position and of its demand for proportional representation is that it should do so in coalition. That was also the attitude of its voters, as evidenced by several opinion polls taken during the summer of 1974. One survey, undertaken for the *Observer* by *Business Decisions* in July showed that 92% of Liberal voters wanted some form of coalition if the party held the balance of power again, and only 4% wanted it to refuse any coalition.

Yet the sort of role implied in a preparedness to bargain with one or both of the two larger parties contradicted the posture implied in the community politics strategy. During 1974 there were radical activists who argued that the dual approach meant that the party could both seek executive political power in co-operation with another party, and seek to change the political system through direct community action. But a mood of distrust of coalition-mongering, mixed with a fear of betrayal of the basis of the party's recent progress, was more common. This was accentuated by the short-term political fact that, with an anti-coalition minority Labour Government, any talk of coalition or power-sharing arrangements implied working with the Conservative Party, or a Conservative-dominated all-party Government of National Unity (since the bulk of the Labour party would have refused such an arrangement).

Consequently any move by the Liberal Party during 1974 risked splitting the party – as the reaction to an ill-judged party political broadcast by David Steel, the chief whip, in June showed. This problem, inherent in the psychology and history of the party, was made far worse by the Liberal Party's structural inadequacies.

Arthur Cyr examines the Liberal Party structure in chapter 4 from the point of view of the light it throws on the character of British Liberalism, mentioning the bitter rows inside the party during 1967/8 (see pp 167-9). Both the diffuseness of structure which he discerns, and the particular battle of 1967/8 reflect a long existing weakness in the party structure, which had got considerably worse in the ten years up to 1974.

Up to the First World War, the Liberal Party was a

parliamentary caucus party in the strict sense. The extra-parliamentary National Liberal Federation exercised some influence at periods, in particular during the 1890s, but the party was essentially embodied in its MPs and parliamentary leadership, and the structure which underpinned them was composed of constituency associations looking to their own MPs and a Liberal Central Association controlled by the Chief Whip. For twenty years following the Asquith/Lloyd George split of 1916, there was structural chaos, and the Liberal Party existed more as a concept envelopping several organizations, both in and out of parliament, and sometimes in intense rivalry with each other, than as a body.

At a convention in 1936, the Liberal Party adopted for the first time a constitution. But the structure laid down therein was confined, exclusively until 1946 and mainly until 1969, to organs of what was termed the Liberal Party Organization. Deference to the idea that it was improper for a party to limit the freedom of its MPs, the old representative principle, left the structural relationship of the MPs to the party unclear, and in a real sense the organizational parts of the 1936 constitution existed within a wider, unwritten constitution in which the primacy of the party leader was clear, but his precise authority and the lines of communication to and from him highly debatable. In 1946 the problems this produced led to the creation of the Liberal Party Committee, formed by a complex process which mixed election with nomination by the leader. The ingenious but cumbrous basis of this committee could have made it an effective shadow cabinet which at the same time was in charge of the party. But it never seems to have worked that way, though it did act as a channel of communication between the parliamentary and non-parliamentary wings of the party.

The reality was that for a quarter of a century after 1936 the party was so small that the formal structure was less important than the handful of leading Liberals who operated it. Cyr describes in chapter 4, the establishment, or élite, which ran the party during the latter part of these

years (as also during the earlier part), and the key people
he mentions – Frank Byers and Mark Bonham Carter –
characteristically combined ability, parliamentary
experience, the personal confidence of Grimond as leader
and elected office within the party's structure. There were
tensions and squabbles in those years, as Cyr points out,
but the closeness and effectiveness of this ruling group
allowed central management of the party in a manner
which its constitution, written or unwritten, did not
guarantee. They were aided by the small numbers of people
involved in the party, and the personal standing of Jo
Grimond, its leader.

With the party's expansion, problems were bound to
arise. The difficulties that Grimond experienced in 1965
(see p. 171) were symptomatic of increasingly poor
communications. A bigger party could not be run as a club.
The newer, younger members created a new situation,
quite apart from their numbers. They reflected the
democratic mood of the time, Grimond's own talk of
participation and democracy and of course an old Radical-
Liberal tradition. In addition many of them were to become
local councillors in urban areas, more qualified to speak as
representatives for the bulk of the Liberal vote in urban
England than the Liberal MPs who tended to represent
rural Celtic Fringe constituencies. The British electoral
system not only distorts representation of parties; it is also,
as in this case, liable to distort the geographical balance of a
party so that the urban English majority were simply
unrepresented.

The party structure these new activists found, that of the
Liberal Party Organization, was the most open and
democratic of the British political parties. But from the
1964 and 1966 elections onwards, it found itself
increasingly relegated to an inferior status by the
parliamentary leadership. The new chief whip from 1964,
Eric Lubbock, and the new leader from 1967, Jeremy
Thorpe, were both contemptous of the elected bodies and
officers of the party. The chief whip had previously
exercised a key liaison role between the MPs and the rest of
the party; Lubbock preferred to spend his Saturdays in his

constituency and his weekdays in the Commons, ignoring the party. Another factor which coincidentally made things worse was the growing nationalist mood in Scotland and Wales; the Scottish and Welsh Liberal MPs, usually in the majority, increasingly looked simply to their own Scottish and Welsh Liberal parties, which in turn detached themselves somewhat from the British level of the party. Most regional parties in England, however, had no MPs of their own to look to. The diffuse structure of the party was badly placed to take a new leader in 1967, whoever he was.

In fact, as Cyr describes, the manner of Thorpe's election made things worse, revealing a gulf between the twelve Liberal MPs and the rest of the party and what he not unfairly calls a war ensued for eighteen months. The end of that war in June 1968 left the structural problem totally unresolved. A reform of the party's constitution in 1969 incorporated the unwritten constitution into the formal document but attempts to change the main structure of the party were defeated. The Liberal Party Committee (which Thorpe had simply ceased to convene) was buried and replaced by the Standing Committee, whose meetings, however, neither leader nor chief whip normally attended.

Meanwhile, members of the party recruited in the Grimond era, followed by those who came in through the Young Liberals of the 'Red Guards' period, became increasingly important in the party – running the regional parties, in the assembly, in the council and in the executive committee. The adoption of the community politics strategy in part reflects this. After the 1970 election, with only six MPs and not one outside the rural Celtic fringe, the party was more than ever before embodied in its extra-parliamentary organs and officers

If there had been any major policy or strategy differences in the party it is extremely difficult to see how they could have been settled during this period. By distancing itself from the rest of the party, the parliamentary party lost only a little of its power of political initiative and of the authority it exercised to the country at large. But it forfeited much of the power which Grimond and his associates had had fifteen years earlier to mould the strategy of the party and ensure that its resources were utilised for that strategy. At the same time the other officers of the party were limited in their effectiveness because they could not dispute the primacy of the parliamentary arena, and no one wanted to be responsible for reviving the public disputation of 1967/8. Yet it was notable that during the summer of 1973, when the community politics idea came under attack in the press and from other parties, the main public defendants were the president, the chairman and the immediate ex-chairman of the party (himself a former MP, and now once again an MP), not the parliamentary leadership.

That was the background, complicated first by the high standing with which Thorpe emerged from the election campaign, and then by the distrust of his motives in seeing Heath, with which the Liberal Party faced the situation of 1974. Arthur Cyr places this situation in the context of a tension between a party elite prepared to consider coalition to achieve power and a section of the party membership strongly opposed to it (p. 171). No doubt there is an inherent tension of this sort; those likely to take office in a coalition are more aware of the power that it offers, and those who are distant are more aware of the danger of compromise. But the gap in communication inside the Liberal Party in 1974 meant that much more than that tension was involved, and if communications had been better both certain MPs and many rank and file might have found there was more common ground in their perception of the situation. Cyr refers to the resolution passed by the assembly in September 1974; having been myself involved in the drafting of the text of that resolution, I would record a personal impression of the situation. Anticipating trouble from the reactions to hints of coalition which the press had been reporting, Jeremy Thorpe chose himself to tie his hands in a speech before the relevant debate opened, severely limiting the party's willingness to enter into coalition. If he, or other MPs, had been more willing to manouevre by involving themselves in the process leading to the drafting of the resolution, they would almost certainly have secured a more free hand.

That is a small example of the poor communications and

the detachment of the parliamentary leadership from the party which weakened its impact in 1974. But there were more profound weaknesses. Firstly, in its failure to think through any strategy of exercising parliamentary power; for too many, the beguiling success of the community politics strategy in 1972/3 had lead to an overestimation of the party's capacity to gather support and win power in its own way, and an underestimation of the importance of what happens in parliament. Secondly, in a failure to develop an internal structure to fit the party's desire to be a democratic movement operating simultaneously at different levels. If the precise circumstances had been rather more favourable in the days following the February election, the party would have found it difficult to agree on how to grasp the opportunity.

In consequence, it is perhaps surprising that the Liberal vote did not drop more in the October 1974 election. By putting up candidates in a hundred extra constituencies the true decline (from 6.1 million to 4.8 million votes in seats fought both times) was partly disguised. With John Pardoe as an increasingly effective main spokesman, the party fought in favour of an incomes policy to deal with the inflationary pressures which it foresaw. Both the other two parties opposed the need for an incomes policy. Within twelve months, the elected Labour Government had come to accept one and, at time of writing, it has proved effective for a period of two years and may be prolonged further. Although it did not use his precise method, the Labour government in 1976 even adopted the Pardoe suggestion of using the tax system to make the policy work. In concentrating on the problem of inflation, and offering the sort of policy which the opinion polls suggested would have most public support, the Liberal Party made some worthwhile use of the position which its February advance had given it. But the uncertainties of the previous seven months seemed to illustrate all too clearly the need for the election to produce a government and the party was unable to decide just what to offer in this respect. The two-party system had trapped it and prevented any further advance.

In the months following the October 1974 election, the

party drifted. It entered 1975 with a more widely spread base of active members than at any time in recent years. But the costs of two elections, and declining income (something suffered by all three parties, and leading to the setting up in 1975 of a committee to enquire into the need for state financial support to political parties) were producing problems with its central organization which demanded attention. Whereas 1973 (with the first elections following local government reorganization) and 1974 had seen an excess of elections, 1975 saw the least since the war. But in the few local elections that did take place (in the English metropolitan boroughs) and in the single parliamentary by-election, the Liberal vote dropped badly. But in the absence of any substantial electoral test, there was little sense of how well the party was faring with its voters. The referendum on British membership of the European Community came and went, the Liberal Party playing its part, but without making any particular impact. The 1975 assembly was rated a reasonable success, though there were muted criticisms of Thorpe's leadership which made many of the press headlines. The year ended and, as far as the Liberal Party was concerned, little had happened.

Then, during the first half of 1976, the party went through a convulsion whose true import is not easy to judge so soon after the event. But since it led directly to a change of leader, accompanied by an important change in the way the party's leader is elected, it certainly had significant political consequences.

On 29 January, Jeremy Thorpe's none too secure position as leader was struck two blows. Norman Scott, a man charged with minor offences used the protection of court proceedings to allege a homosexual affair with Thorpe. And the much delayed Department of Trade report on the collapse of the bank of which Thorpe had been a director was published. The latter was described by *The Times* as 'one of the most disturbing documents ever to emerge' from the Department's inspectors, making 'devastating criticisms' of the central figure in the episode whose personal friendship with Thorpe had brought the Liberal leader on to the board of directors; it referred to

Thorpe's role as 'a cautionary tale for any leading politician'.[3] In the weeks that were to come, many Liberals continued to regard this affair as reflecting much more seriously on their leader than the question of a past sexual liaison.

But the press fastened on to the Scott affair. In the following months they were rewarded by a series of good news stories, as evidence of payments of money to Scott (in which Thorpe's personal friends were involved) came to light, a disappeared former Liberal MP, Peter Bessell, was discovered in California, and Scott appeared as a witness in another court case with wild stories of alleged attempts to silence him. Inuendo, allegation and assumption were leant credence by earlier attempts to conceal or withhold information. Thorpe steadfastly denied anything more than a casual acquaintanceship with Scott, whom he had aided as a constituent, and denied all knowledge of what had evidently been an elaborate attempt to stop Scott from talking. As with the Watergate affair, it was the constant stream of fresh disclosure about this cover-up which was damaging and which turned the question into one of Thorpe's credibility. In May Peter Bessell announced that he had been lying to protect Thorpe, and three days later the *Sunday Times* published, at Thorpe's request, two letters to Scott, about whose content there had been speculation. They revealed nothing specifically damaging, but indicated a closeness between the two men which did not correspond well with Thorpe's earlier denials. The following day he resigned, blaming a press 'campaign of denigration'. Press interest in Scott ceased, and the several unanswered questions about the affair were forgotten.

It was a stupid, tragic, trivial story out of which no one emerged with credit. The press had undoubtedly hounded Thorpe, and clearly their real interest lay in the original allegation of homosexuality. The *Daily Mirror* and *Daily Mail* each made the affair their main news story on thirteen different days. This national interest could not but affect the party, and Liberal MPs were free with their comments, which were duly well publicised. Several of them evidently considered that there were other, much more substantial

reasons why Thorpe should retire from the leadership and
found themselves accordingly making ambiguous or barbed
statements about their loyalty to him over the Scott affair.
Thorpe's own line of vigorous denial gave the cue to other
Liberal spokesmen who were lead thence, willingly or
unwillingly, into implying that what had passed between
Thorpe and Scott fifteen years earlier actually mattered.
The Liberal Party had only in July 1975 decided to back
the Campaign for Homosexual Equality's demand for the
removal of all discriminatory legislation against
homosexuals, and in general the Liberal Party has been by
far the most sympathetic to the Campaign's case on such
questions. But because of the official position of total denial
of Scott's allegation, no Liberal could simply state that the
leader's sexuality did not matter without appearing to
throw more doubt on his veracity. The result was that the
Liberal Party endured the massive publicity in much
confusion. In by-elections in March and a major round of
local elections in May (when the gains of 1973 were being
defended) the party suffered a big loss of support, including
its position as the largest party on the Liverpool council.
There was considerable relief, but much sympathy for him,
when Thorpe ended the agony with his resignation.

In retrospect, the affair was of such little consequence
that it is a wonder that it held such fascination for press,
party and public. Perhaps its most serious aspect is as an
example of the power of the media to make news. Though
some debate was made about the willingness of the public
to accept a political leader with suspect sexual relations, in
truth it established nothing on this score. Because of
Thorpe's steadfast denial, no one knew whether
homosexuality in a leading political figure would have
proved acceptable. But in May 1976, the Liberal Party was
left without a leader.

By chance, the party was at an advanced stage of
considering proposals whereby the leader should in future
be elected by the whole membership of the Liberal Party;
indeed the precise constitutional amendment to enable this
was in print for publication in the *Liberal News* on the day
following Thorpe's resignation. It was agreed to ask Jo

Grimond to return as acting leader while a special meeting of the assembly was summoned to consider the new rules. This was done; they were approved and the party moved to a contest between the two candidates nominated, John Pardoe and David Steel. After a three-week campaign, which did much to re-establish the party's self-respect after the earlier imbroglio, Steel emerged triumphant by a clear but not crushing majority.

David Steel has used this clear command of the party's membership to establish a style of quiet but firm leadership. The quietness was subject to some criticism from the media at the time of the party's 1976 assembly in Llandudno. But Steel emerged triumphant from that assembly following a speech which was heralded as combining political realism with the intellectual thrust that Jo Grimond used to show. He has yet to find a way, though, of working easily with the organs of the party outside Parliament.

The method by which David Steel was elected is itself of great interest. By deciding to have the party leader elected by the whole party, the Liberals moved dramatically from the method of hurried choice by twelve MPs used in 1967. The demand for this more democratic method reflected the growing strength in the party of the newer members described above. They were determined to apply within the party the sort of participatory democracy that they were preaching in government and industry. Although there was some initial resistance, in the end the Liberal MPs accepted the change willingly provided that they kept a certain role at the nomination stage. The resultant system, balancing the election by the party membership with a special role for MPs, is a cunning mixing of parliamentary and mass-party influences, of traditional Liberal and Radical ideas about democracy. That of itself should help to produce a leadership more in touch with the whole party, and so mend the division of the Thorpe years. Liberals also hope that the public use of a highly open and democratic system, in which over sixty thousand members cast votes this time, will also of itself commend the party's democratic attitudes. Cyr's point about the party's structure exemplifying its view of politics is abundantly proved.

As for the contest between Pardoe and Steel, there was no great political debate. The failure of the campaign to bring out any policy differences argues for the coherence of the Liberal Party's policy attitudes. There were striking differences in the styles of the two contestants; Steel's victory was a choice of someone who was regarded as more effective by fellow parliamentarians and by the press. Pardoe made a bold bid to offer the party what he saw as a dramatically different strategy, mobilising the discontent with Britain's national failures to become the instrument of constitutional change. But Steel stressed that he agreed with all the relevant policies of constitutional reform. Pardoe's strategy was really a mixture of self-confidence in his own ability to make Liberal policy sound more excitingly different and of a certain stance towards the British parliamentary system. He argued that the Liberals could not convince people of the need for political reform unless they were prepared to be much more disrespectful of parliament. The majority of the Radical activist wing responded to Pardoe but several leading Radicals backed Steel. The result showed that in the grass-roots membership of the party there was rather more of a desire to work effectively inside the parliamentary system than some of Pardoe's supporters wanted, but for most it was probably a choice of personalities. Pardoe's pugnacious style and his wilder statements did not go down with the party's rank-and-file (and maybe would not have done with the electorate) so they preferred David Steel, whose impeccable Liberal principles inspired widespread respect. In so doing they decided that, at any rate for the next few years, the British Liberal Party would continue to try to work for a variety of policies on several fronts rather than attempt a dash for power by staking all on a particular issue.

It is a pity for political science that Pardoe did not win since he would have offered an experiment in whether the adoption of an aggressive, populist style could have enabled the Liberal Party to break out of its third-party role. If the past is any guide it is otherwise not likely to gain any ground so long as Labour remains in government. Yet the future never resembles the past exactly and there are several new factors present in the late seventies which may give the Liberal Party a new chance.

The prospect of direct election of the European parliament offers the British Liberal Party a significance on the European stage, and in the long run political habits acquired from other states in which coalitions are acceptable to large parties may have a profound impact in Britain. The idea of coalition as a proper form of majority government in Britain is gaining ground, and there is now more widespread support for reform of the Westminster electoral system than at any time for over fifty years. At the same time both direct elections and the proposal for devolved assemblies in Scotland and Wales have raised the issue of proportional representation more immediately. The current strength of the Scottish Nationalists and Ulster parties makes it more likely that situations of no overall majority in the Commons, even with the present-voting system, will recur. The Liberal MPs have shown that they can exploit the pivotal position this gives them in the present House by voting for the second reading of the Scotland & Wales Bill and then, because the Government was unwilling to make any of a number of concessions they demanded, against the guillotine motion. The devolution issue ought to offer an obvious role to the only party which is genuinely and unitedly in favour of devolution throughout Britain – though unreconciled differences between Scottish Liberal views and English regionalists remain a weakness.

Internally the party's central organisation is in a weak state, especially in financial resources. But in bringing in an outsider, Hugh Jones, to take over the new post of Secretary-General of the Party, the party hopes to rectify this weakness. The grass-roots organisation is stronger: on the simple measure of the number of affiliated associations the party's position is indicated by the record number of 457 (out of 516 constituencies in England) at the end of December 1975 and the same number in December 1976 (compared with the highest figure of 436 for England and Wales in July 1963 recorded by Cyr in table 4-1). Since David Steel became leader, the Liberal electoral record has varied – of six by-elections, there were four rather bad results, one fair and one extremely good. This unevenness, reflected also in local government by-elections, indicates that the party's electoral base is much lower than the votes recorded twice in 1974, but its potential is, if anything, still greater.

The biggest factor favouring its electoral future is still the youthfulness of the 1974 Liberal vote. This brings its prospects into the context in which Cyr places his analysis of the party's role: the strength and relevance of class politics. The youthful vote of 1974, as also for the two Nationalist parties, reflected the steady reduction in political saliency of class feelings among newer voters. But if, for social or economic or other reasons outside the Liberal Party's influence, class as a determinant of political issues and loyalties were to revive, the party would have to fight to keep its place in the political system – though as the expression of certain humanitarian and individualistic values it would be bound to have some role. If, however, class continues to decline, it will be the two class-based parties which have to fight to defend an ageing electoral base, and the role of the Liberal Party in British politics will expand.

Michael Steed
March 1977

1 At the 1973 assembly, Pardoe had succeeded, against the wishes of some parliamentary colleagues, in committing the party to consider the implications of holding the balance of power. This never happened. During the February 1974 election, the official briefing to candidates dodged the question as follows: *What happens in this situation is surely a matter for the other two parties. In the light of the suggestions of the other parties the Liberal M.P.s will have to decide whether to support one particular party in Government or, if such an arrangement is unsatisfactory from the Liberal point of view, whether to vote for every piece of legislation according to its merits.*

2 D.E. Butler & D. Kavanagh *The British General Election of February 1974* London, 1974, p 257.

3 *The Times* 30 January 1976.

INTRODUCTION

The British Liberal Party played a prominent role in the two general elections of 1974. In the February polling, the party received 19·3 per cent of the vote, by far the most it has secured in any general election since the Second World War. This surge, combined with the fact that neither of the two major parties held a majority of House of Commons seats, led to considerable speculation concerning possible coalition government and a basic party realignment in Britain. Unfortunately for the Liberals, however, their rising expectations were frustrated in October. To be sure, the Liberal vote of 18·3 per cent remained comparatively high, but there was some slippage from the February peak, even though the party offered a larger number of candidates. More important, the impression of momentum was lost, while coalition speculation was brought to a halt by the formation of a Labour Government with a narrow but clear majority.

As a result, anticipation within the party of an enormous improvement in political position was disappointed. It was not the first time this had happened in recent years, only the latest. Veteran Liberals naturally recalled the period of a decade before, when – under the leadership of Jo Grimond – electoral gains had been smaller but hopes and expectations even higher. That era also ended in disappointment, with dissipation of Liberal strength, inability to build on early gains, and total failure to approach the basic goal of fundamental party realignment in Britain.

Even though electoral revival may have been frustrated, questions about the position and role of the Liberal Party linger. The continued existence of the party appears, at least on the surface, to be anomalous. The Liberals have for decades been a small third party, powerfully overshadowed by the Tories and Labour, lacking access to large national interest groups, philosophically out of tune with the dominant themes of the nation's politics, and not always taken seriously by a majority of the electorate. The frustration of earlier revivals has served to underline the point that the Liberal Party is considerably weaker than the Tories or Labour, has not been able to approach their levels of popular support in elections of recent memory, and may not be able to maintain even its current position for long. Nevertheless, while the Liberals have not been able to manage an electoral revival powerful enough to create basic party realignment, they have been able to avoid extinction. The party continues to exist, despite all the serious problems attending status as a small third party in the British political system, and has experienced two recent periods of substantially increased support. More generally, there has been a post-war 'revival' of the party in the sense that over the last two decades it has managed to avoid a repetition of the situation in the early and mid 1950s, when it appeared to be on the verge of passing out of existence.

The study which follows is an attempt to analyse the modern Liberal Party and place it within the context of the broader British political environment. It addresses the paradoxical issue that the party has been unable to achieve a position of national power, yet continues to exist and periodically draws new support. Aside from clarification concerning the position of the party, a related goal of the study is to use the party's recent history to highlight broader associated political and social changes taking place in Britain. Appropriately, given the different dimensions of the party's revival, a variety of approaches and techniques are employed in analysis. Evidence used ranges from hard quantitative data to information of a very impressionistic nature.

A basic thesis of the study is that the Liberal Party's revival is significant for reasons which transcend its small size and particular failures. There are indications that the dominance of two well-disciplined political parties, Conservative and Labour, is breaking down. The strength of these two parties, and the intensity of the conflict between them, was one of the defining qualities of British politics in this century. Currently, however, political individualism seems to have become much more important than it was in earlier decades. These developments in turn appear to be associated with a declining significance of class conceptions in determining political behaviour. Various diverse but related changes in the character of political conflict and competition indicate that a more general Liberal revival, transcending the small party, has been taking place. Patterns of political life in Britain are, at least partially, moving in directions which resemble nineteenth-century Liberal and Radical politics, rather than twentieth-century collectivist politics. Nevertheless, this does not mean that the Liberal Party is likely to profit directly from this important development in any dramatic manner. Rather, the growth of Liberalism makes all political parties increasingly insecure in their support from activists and voters. A central feature of Liberalism is lack of strong commitment to political parties in the modern, collectivist sense. The recent erratic course of electoral support for the Liberal Party is therefore fully consistent with a more generally developing Liberal revival.

Use of these terms – Liberal, Radical and collectivist – implies the fact that this study relies very heavily on the broad conceptual categorization and analysis of British party politics developed by Professor Samuel Beer. Indeed, an initial incentive for undertaking this work on the Liberals was that the party seems to reject the themes and trends characteristic of what Beer defines as modern collectivist politics in Britain. The recent history of the party has provided a basis for developing the argument that Britain appears to be entering a new, post-collectivist phase of politics. Throughout the course of the study, there is reference to Beer's conceptual insights. Appropriately, reliance upon his work is especially strong in the earlier sections, where the historical background of Liberalism, and the principal features of modern collectivism, are outlined.

Comparatively more attention is devoted to the Liberal Party revival under Jo Grimond than to the more recent gains under Jeremy Thorpe. Several considerations lie behind this approach. First, the earlier period was a much livelier one within the party. A large number of new activists were attracted, including a group of writers and scholars who undertook a redefinition and updating of traditional Liberal policy. Second, Grimond's personal impact as leader, both within the party and throughout the country, appears to have been greater than that which Thorpe achieved. Third, the earlier revival was more pivotal in terms of the broader political system. It was during this time that the nationalist parties began to gain significant momentum, that Tory and Labour moved detectably towards Liberal policy directions, and striking growth in electoral volatility became apparent.

Partly because of the importance of the Grimond period, the analysis which follows is not strictly chronological. Rather, in summary form, it may be divided into three general perspectives, each of which is useful to understanding the position of the Liberal Party and developments in the broader political system. First, as noted above, with the electoral revival under Grimond the party also experienced a revival in ideas and policy. Well-drafted policy statements were published, written by activists newly drawn to the party. The liveliness of the policy development within the party contrasted with a more general tone and atmosphere of self-doubt and political malaise which appeared to afflict Britain at approximately the same time, making Liberal efforts especially notable. Second, structurally the Liberal Party has been diffuse, with a positive hostility to internal hierarchy and discipline. Opposition by rank-and-file members has frustrated efforts by the party élite to impose tighter control and organization. Clearly, a major appeal of the party has been to activists who reject not only abstract conceptions of class, but explicit efforts to establish internal structure and limit the independence of members. This feature of the Liberal Party has been a distinct handicap in political competition with the Tory and Labour Parties, which are not only much larger, but have retained disciplined organizations even as their electoral positions have become more unpredictable.

The third perspective reveals that, sociologically, the Liberal Party's revivals signal broader changes taking place within the British electorate and society. The first revival of the party provided comparatively early evidence that class considerations were declining in electoral influence. This trend has led to increasing volatility within the electorate, rendering the Conservative and Labour bases of support much less reliable. The weakening of the class division has permitted the re-emergence of regional issues, reflected in growing support for the Welsh and, especially, the Scottish nationalists. Party politics itself is being rejected by increasing numbers of activists, who are devoting their energies to non-party voluntary associations. The small parties and voluntary associations, in turn, address problems of sections of the country and sectors of society which are peripheral to the calculus of collectivist politics. In total, these three main themes of the analysis – the intellectual, structural and sociological aspects of the Liberal revival – help to explain both the role of the party, which has appeared to be so out of tune with the dominant motif of British politics, and broader changes taking place in Britain.

The themes and arguments developed in the study, as well as the evidence used in their support, reflect the co-operation of a large number of British Liberals who supplied a range of written materials, patiently submitted to lengthy personal interviews and responded to written enquiries. Almost without exception, they were anxious to help, and generous with their time. Many were hospitable well beyond the requirements of formal courtesy. The total number is far too great to list individually, but some should be cited for their special assistance. Mr Awdry, the librarian of the National Liberal Club in London, provided a fund of important party literature, and served as a ready source of anecdote and party history. Ron Arnold of the Liberal Research Department, Evelyn Hill of the Liberal Publications Department, and Robert Gibbs and Chris Paice of the Liberal Information Department were always cordial in helping with numerous requests, and were also accommodating in finding scarce office space for a visiting

American researcher. A number of prominent past and present party leaders and activists discussed their own roles and their views of the party's place in British politics, and they are mentioned with thanks: Lord Avebury; Lord Banks; Lord Beaumont; Professor Max Beloff; Peter Bessell; the Hon, Mark Bonham Carter; Lord Byers; Pratap Chitnis; the Rt Hon. Jo Grimond, MP; Richard Holme; the late Sidney Hope; Russell Johnston, MP; the late Alasdair Mackenzie; Dennis Minnis; John Pardoe, MP; Lady Seear; Hugh Tinker; and Richard Wainwright, MP. Michael Steed has not only provided a Foreword; he has also reviewed the study with care and his reactions have been incorporated in the interpretation of several important points. I am particularly grateful for his aid.

The Frank Knox Memorial Fellowship Fund of Harvard University supported an academic year's research in England. While there, a variety of organizations were of assistance: the University of London and the London School of Economics and Political Science provided access to their libraries; more specific information needs were met by the library of the London National Liberal Club, the Liberal Party Organization, the Conservative Central Office, Plaid Cymru, the Scottish Nationalist Party, Social Surveys (Gallup Poll) Ltd, National Opinion Polls Ltd, Imperial Chemical Industries Ltd, Rolls-Royce Ltd, and Aspro-Nicholas Ltd.

Two of the component parts of the research for this study were verbal interviews with leading and middle-level Liberals, and a written questionnaire circulated among a broader sample of party activists. Seventy-one personal interviews were conducted. The written questionnaire was circulated within an activist sample of 157 people. It received a rate of response of about 66 per cent, or 104 returns. There are methodological problems and limitations associated with trying to come to grips with the Liberal Party in this manner, and they are outlined in the Appendix.

Academics, I hope, will find this a helpful contribution to research and analysis of British politics. British Liberals will not find here either tactical advice or unbalanced praise. However, I hope they will be able to infer that I have developed considerable goodwill for their party and affection for them. Their aid and help kept the work from becoming a burden, led me into new analytic perspectives, and make the project even more interesting than I had anticipated.

My most important debt is to Professor Beer, and it goes well beyond use of his general approach to British politics. He supervised the Ph.D. dissertation which was the initial version of this study, provided suggestions concerning revisions for publication, and throughout has served as an invaluable source of encouragement and criticism. Above all, he urged conceptual rigour combined with an effort to see the broader implications of the Liberal Party's recent history.

ARTHUR CYR
Los Angeles, California

December 1976

1

The Liberal Tradition

*'Time and again in history victory has come to a little
party with big ideas ...'*[1]
G.K. Chesterton

Since the Liberal Party's collapse after the First World
War, it has been unable to re-establish a position as one of
the main competitors for political power in Britain. The
party experienced a brief though exciting political revival
under Jo Grimond during the late 1950s and early 1960s;
and more recently under Jeremy Thorpe has enjoyed a
series of by-election victories which culminated in relatively
high (though still minority) electoral support in the two
general elections of 1974. Yet since the Second World War
the Liberals have never been able to advance beyond a
small number of MPs or a comparatively small minority of
the councillors in British local government. At the same
time, reflecting the irony with which the above quotation is
intended here, the Liberals in recent years have also played
an important role in promoting and registering broad
political and social changes in Britain.

The Liberal Party is very much a nineteenth-century
political antique in its approaches to policy, to party
discipline, and to internal structure and organization. In
each of these areas, the party reflects the individualism and
decentralization of traditional Liberalism, in contrast to the
dominant trends in modern British party and government
organization. This is precisely what makes it significant
beyond its small size, for politics in Britain is to a degree
moving away from the patterns and practices of what
Samuel Beer has termed the Collectivist Age, is coming

1 Quotation from Maisie Ward, *Gilbert Keith Chesterton*, p. 136.

instead to resemble pre-collectivist styles of nineteenth-century Liberal and Radical politics. It has been a dynamic change, overlain with considerable irony: British politics is still characterized primarily by collectivism in party structure and competition, and the development of public policy, but this very situation has encouraged the revival of Liberalism. Collectivism, because of its solidity, rigidity and formality has supplied an opening for the diffuseness, flexibility and informality of Liberalism.

The party's role as representative of the reaction against collectivism can be used as a double-edged analytic tool. First, looking inward to the Liberal Party, it provides that odd and small political formation with a coherence and consistency – and an importance in British politics. Taken by themselves, the Liberals lack the clear class or sectional bases which usually give insight into the functions of more conventional political parties. Instead, the Liberal Party's electorate is neither economically nor geographically distinct. It is a cross-section of the class spectrum, a thinly-spread national electorate only somewhat anchored in the 'Celtic Fringe' of Scotland and Wales, with residual support in the West Country. Second, looking outward to the broader political system, the Liberal Party's ironic fate of revival – but still, so far, limited revival – points significantly to important alterations in British politics as it moves into a post-collectivist period.

This role of the indistinct Liberal Party as the distinct, coherent opponent of collectivism may be divided into three planes – intellectual, structural and sociological. The analysis which follows reflects these three outlooks. Each of the perspectives on the Liberal Party addresses the most central irony of the party's revival, notably that it has been limited and contained in part by the same factors which have encouraged it. In addition, collectivism's weaknesses, to which Liberalism responds, have been based on central, solid structural foundations which have enabled its governmental calculus to survive, compromised only in part. Collectivism's weaknesses rest on a foundation of strength; Liberalism's virtues are a function of inherent fragility.

Intellectually, the party's revival is masked by the comparatively limited electoral gains under Grimond and Thorpe. Qualitative impressiveness, that is, has been only partially reflected in quantitative gains in parliamentary elections, local elections, or even the more fluid area of public opinion polls. In the late 1950s and early 1960s the party's growth in popular support, combined with the more important personal appeal of the leader, Jo Grimond, drew a group of talented policy advisers. They, in turn, were able to help in providing the Liberals with coherent policy statements. Specifically, the Liberals were able to bring traditional party policy up to date and define relevant proposals in such fields as taxation, industrial affairs, consumer protection, social services, and local and regional government reform.

During the same period that increased attention and votes were drawn to the Liberal Party, the two larger parties moved several notches toward Liberal policy positions on some of these issues. Liberal doctrine was not precisely reflected in the statements of Tory and Labour, but it did have an echo. Presumably the two major parties were responding to the same popular currents which were carrying the Liberals forward. Unfortunately for the Grimond loyalists and planners, this blurring of policy differences meant also that the Liberal Party was separated from the potentially profitable aura of originality. In the meantime, the main parties have retained their important advantages of political credibility as potential Governments, close ties with powerful national economic producer groups, and their still-formidable national electoral constituencies. Moreover, the party under Thorpe did not pursue the effort at policy definition.

Structurally, the corollary of the individualism and localism of Liberal Party doctrine is a positive hostility to party discipline and central direction. Hence, the party has never been able to muster the sort of self-control and internal co-ordination which are requisite to make the most of limited political opportunities. Good Liberals apply the notion of hostility to collectivism to internal party affairs as well, to the despair of more sophisticated members of the elite and the detriment of national political revival. Yet an important attraction for many of the party's activists is precisely this lack of rigid structure.

Sociologically, the revival of the Liberal Party is related to very significant political changes in modern Britain. First, the party's revival appears to be one indication of the more general decline of class as the main determinant of the ways in which people vote. Second, it has been correlated with an impressive growth in the number, strength and visibility of voluntary social-service and reform associations. In a sense, this represents a return to the past, because the nineteenth century was a time of important non-party organizations of this type. For Liberal Party loyalists, party remains a phenomenon which must not subordinate the individual. For many other Liberals, however, party itself is unimportant. The flexibility, and normally specific-issue focus, of voluntary groups make them appealing to activists concerned with a wide range of social, economic and political problems. Third, the increasing strength of the Scottish and Welsh nationalist parties indicates that regional concerns are becoming more important, and more generally that the two major parties have had their electoral dominance reduced.

This blossoming of voluntarism and regionalism seems clearly related inversely to the decline of class politics in the collectivist sense. With the weakening of the basic horizontal political cleavage across the nation, attention is freed to focus on new tensions – the vertical divisions between regions of unequal prosperity, the new and more subtle horizontal division between the affluent majority and the pockets of poverty which continue to exist. It is precisely these concerns which are addressed by the Liberal Party, as well as the nationalist parties and the voluntary associations. More broadly still, the Liberal revival *qua* decline of class voting has bred a new volatility in the British electorate, which seems to be in the process of developing less predictable, more unstable, patterns and becoming therefore more American.

These various changes, analytically separable into three planes but all related to the Liberal Party, are important to understanding current British politics and the direction in which those politics appear to be moving. Nevertheless, the Liberal Party may not profit from further development of these trends of change. Even if Liberal patterns continue to grow, as they appear to be doing, both among activists and within the electorate, they are unlikely to lead to a consistent revival of the party. Rather, all parties eventually will be deprived of the possibility of the disciplined and solid electorates upon which Labour and Tory could rely in the Collectivist Age.

Liberalism: Individualism and Conservatism

An essential first step to analysis is clear definition of the two generally antagonistic conceptions, Liberalism and collectivism. This may be done through presentation of historical background, with attention to the nineteenth-century Liberal Age in British politics and the development of the Collectivist Age in the twentieth century. Additionally, an appropriate way to begin illustration of how Liberalism replies to collectivism is through discussion of the specific problems, shortcomings and limitations of the latter.

As an initial *caveat*, it must be noted that Liberalism and collectivism are not to be confused, as political doctrines and practical approaches to politics, with the more general philosophical conceptions of 'liberalism' or the equally general social biases of 'conservatism' which have been significant in British political history.[2] Even at the height of the Collectivist Age, Britain has remained a 'liberal' state in its respect for the formal rights of the individual; even at the height of the Liberal Age, Britain was a profoundly 'conservative' society, differentiated and divided into various social and economic strata, with tension and

2 In this discussion, 'liberal' and 'liberalism' refer to the conceptions of natural rights and liberties held by Locke and Lockean liberals, as well as to the variety of Continental liberal parties; 'Liberal' and 'Liberalism' refer to the British Liberal Party, its members and the specific programmes and attitudes associated with it, including the non-party service and reform associations discussed in the text.

conflict among them.

The adherents of the nineteenth-century Liberal Party could reach back to a strongly established liberal philosophy in order to bolster their party commitment. Nevertheless, simply because liberalism, understood as legal guarantees of the rights of the individual, was so broadly accepted, it was not associated with a particular party. Rather, the political culture generally is identified with the development of this perspective. John Locke, the 'soul of liberalism', is not linked exclusively or even directly to the historical Liberal Party. In consequence, the party was not in a position to profit from ties to these more generally recognized values. In some contrast with the situation elsewhere in Europe, the Liberal Party could fade from the scene without significant impact on well-established civil protections of the rights of citizens.

At the same time, the nineteenth-century Liberals did represent a distinctive departure from earlier British political parties. Reflecting the fact that new demands were growing within the nation for broader and more extensive popular representation, Liberalism emphasized individual political freedom. In contrast to the older Whig and Tory parties, with their hierarchical and aristocratic conceptions of social life and political competition, and very limited views of representation, the Liberals focused attention upon the individual citizen. Just as the Liberals rejected these earlier themes, so they would later oppose the theories of class conflict associated with the Labour Party. Following from this general approach, the Liberals favoured broad and comparatively unstructured political representation. The suffrage should be extensive, based on the rationale that equal individuals all deserved a meaningful voice in politics and government. Liberal individualism also led to pressures to remove various forms of special privilege which had been considered not only acceptable but natural to Whigs and Tories in earlier periods.[3]

These early Liberals, however, were not democrats in

3 Samuel Beer, *British Politics in The Collectivist Age*, p. 37. This book, Beer's primary work, is drawn upon heavily for the historical discussion in this chapter.

any direct or simple majoritarian sense. Rather, they accepted the proposition that some citizens were more worthy than others, and therefore more deserving of political influence and power. Their contribution was in the new measurements of worth which they employed. Property, for the Liberals, was the principal means for determining the competence and intelligence of citizens, and hence their desirability as voters. To the Liberals, the safeguarding of property was an important function of public policy. In this sense, therefore, they believed in a sort of social hierarchy; but it is important to emphasize that their conception was strikingly different from earlier ones. Reflecting the market principles of Liberal economics, their society was one in which men's positions could be changed radically through the acquisition of material wealth. Tory and Whig notions about society, and the standing of people within it, were much more static and unchanging, with position determined by birth and continuing affiliation with family and a range of corporate bodies. Liberal individualism, on the other hand, conceived of a more fluid, open social milieu. Far from advocating an end to discrimination, Liberals favoured it. What they promoted was change in the basis for discrimination. Liberals generally favoured property qualifications for the franchise, but combined this with belief in equality both in imposing such regulations and in the size of electoral districts.[4]

Liberals had a middle-class bias, but again it contrasted with older ideas about class and degree in British politics. Theoretically, their social environment was not only more fluid, but also simpler. While Liberals did not accept total individualism or an unlimited conception of the rights of citizens, they did reject the complex notions of hierarchy characteristic of earlier, more aristocratic periods in British politics. Liberals normally conceived of only three general levels in society – upper, middle and lower. In this context, emphasis was given to the middle class as particularly representative of the best interests of all of society. As Macaulay wrote: 'The middle class, that brave, honest and

4 *Ibid.*, p. 34.

stout-hearted class, which is as anxious for the maintenance of order and the security of society, as it is hostile to corruption and oppression'.[5] The middle class was viewed as the stratum most likely to oppose special privileges and to favour the use of competition to bring about an equitable distribution of justice and wealth.

It is not surprising that British Liberals, within their individualism, explicitly favoured a particular class or feared giving too much power to a working class viewed as uneducated and therefore unqualified for the franchise. As noted above, the dominance of Liberal politics in the nineteenth century should not be allowed to suggest that British society was losing its fundamental conservatism, traditionalism and differentiation. The basis of representation and political competition has changed and evolved over the span of British history, but there has been a consistency in the separation of different social groups and orders. Even comparatively extreme individualists among the Liberals were affected by the broad currents of social conservatism in the nation.[6]

The relationship between class and the Liberals provides important insights for understanding the later history of the party. The general Liberal bias toward the middle class was reflected in practical political behaviour. Liberals were not only extremely rigid in principle in opposing the granting of political power to the lower class, they refused to become more flexible even when this would have been in their interest. Later in the nineteenth century, as substantial sectors of the working-class population acquired the franchise and began to move toward an impact on political parties and government policy, it proved impossible for their representatives to participate within the framework of the Liberal Party. Liberal co-operation with the Labour Party and trade union elements was always feeble and reluctantly undertaken. Liberals throughout the various echelons of the party refused to accept working-class activists as equals. This was a significant factor in bringing about the abrupt collapse of the Liberals from

5 *Ibid.*, p. 36.
6 *Ibid.*, p. 35.

national political power after the First World War, and their inability to carve out a more substantial electoral base in the years since.[7]

Liberal theories of representation had an important bearing not only on class discrimination within the party, but also on the structure of the party and its relationships with other organizations. Liberal theory argued that the ideal political environment should be one of individualism, and the party was characterized by considerable internal freedom and independence. Members of Parliament, it was believed, as well as the constituents who elected them, should be as unencumbered as possible by external restraints and influences on the exercise of judgment. Parliamentary behaviour, therefore, should be based on coalitions which are inherently temporary, formed to achieve a particular change or goal. To be sure, party was viewed as important, both for MPs and the broader political system. In theory, however, its role was to help protect processes of election and government from illegitimate external influences, primarily the disliked 'interests'.[8] The conception of party as a continuing, reasonably independent political formation first gained broad acceptance during the early nineteenth century. The basic appeal to Liberals, however, was that it served as a buffer between direct influence by outside groups and individuals, including electors, upon representatives. Far from being democrats, many Liberals saw party organization mainly as a device which made it possible to take unpopular decisions, without immediate fear of defeat or recall by their constituents. These ideas, of course, contrast markedly with the much more powerful role given to party organization and discipline in Whig and especially, later, collectivist politics.[9]

Liberal distrust of organization also applied to economic interest groups. Again, the situation contrasts with what came later, after the advent of collectivist politics and the

7 This important topic is discussed in more detail below. See, e.g., *ibid.*, pp. 146 ff.

8 *Ibid.*, p. 38.

9 *Ibid.*, p. 39.

important and legitimate role given collectivism to inclusive, structured interest groups of producers and consumers. Public policy was not conceived by the Liberals as being inevitably a partial result, at least, of the interplay between organized interest groups, but rather as best achieved through decisions unfettered by such forces.[10] Because interest groups were alien to Liberalism, the party was not closely identified with them. In fact, the British economy in the nineteenth century had not yet begun to develop the very large industrial and commercial combinations which have been so typical of more recent decades. As a result, practical political considerations did not conflict sharply with philosophical predispositions.[11]

The British Liberals' distrust of organized interests reflects a strong current in American political theory. Concerning party, it is fair to say that the British Liberals were more favourably disposed than those prominent and influential early American leaders who regarded 'party' and 'faction' as interchangeable concepts. As we have seen, Liberals saw party as functional, not as a strongly organized and disciplined structure for popular representation, but rather as a useful source of protection for MPs. Regarding established interest groups, however, both British Liberals and their American counterparts had strong reservations and suspicions. Interests compromised individualism, and at the same time promoted divisions among a wide variety of groups within the polity, without any compensating gains or benefits. This relates to the broader point that American political culture has been characterized by Liberal, and related Radical, conceptions of government, society and proper political competition. More organic notions of hierarchy and natural division within society, so typical of British politics in Tory, Whig and collectivist conceptions, have been absent from the American milieu. British Liberals appear to have sensed that their political norms were in fact much more congenial to the American than the British environment: Cobden, the

10. *Ibid.*, p. 33.

11 See *ibid.*, pp. 61 ff. on the representation of interests during the Liberal and Radical periods.

Liberal leader and writer, saw in America a hopeful vision of what Britain could become in the future.[12]

The secondary importance of party in the context of a fundamentally individualist philosophy may be seen in the influential role accorded alternative structures for popular political and social participation. The Liberals were not only advocates of a limited and restrained conception of party, but also of active voluntary associations. As discussed below, such formations were used to provide social services and, more dramatically, to agitate for a range of specific reforms. Clearly in tune with Liberal philosophy, they were for that very reason only informally linked with the Liberal Party.[13]

This leads into an important, much more general observation about these nineteenth-century Liberals. It would be a serious error to argue that the Liberals were against political and social reform because of their faith in the free market and the middle-class, and suspicion of fostering dangerous concentrations of power or enfranchising a working-class viewed as unworthy. The nineteenth-century Liberals did not preach unrestrained competition, nor did they view competition as being entirely an atomistic force. Rather, numbers of Liberals favoured wide varieties of specific reforms, and competition was considered essentially a unifying force. In a dramatic affirmation, Macaulay emotionally declared that economic growth was not worth the cost of imposing economic misery on the population at large.[14]

Liberal economics was seen generally as a vehicle for bringing affluence to the population as a whole, not as a divider which would entrench wealth and leave the mass of the people in poverty. The notion of international unity through competition was articulated by Liberals in their doctrine of free trade. It was viewed as something which would breed, through the very process of economic interchange between states, an international community of people who felt accustomed to one another because they

12 *Ibid.*, p. 37.
13 *Ibid.*, pp. 43-5.
14 Guido de Ruggiero, *The History of European Liberalism*, p. 141.

had dealt with one another in the market place.[15] A very intense, unco-ordinated atomism was not, therefore, the dominant characteristic of English Liberals. Where Liberalism did seem to favour extreme individualism, it was connected with the conviction that it would – as in free trade – lead to a transcendent unity.

Radicalism

The growth of Radicalism within the Liberal Party later in the nineteenth century introduced strident advocates of much more far-reaching reform. Radicals were informed neither by the middle-class bias typical of Liberal politicians nor by the sense of automaticity present in the market of Liberal economists. Instead, echoing the atomism which Louis Hartz has stressed as the excitement and bane of American politics, Radicals were intense advocates of majority rule.[16] Beer has emphasized this as the prime quality differentiating them from Liberals. He describes a 'fundamental' difference between 'Liberal and Old Whig parliamentarism' and 'Radical direct democracy'. For the Radicals, obvious and simple majority rule should decide as many major questions as possible.[17]

The majoritarianism of the English and American Radicals was never total. But the majority, while not justified in doing anything and everything, was considered to be the best agent for discerning the proper course of public action. Most important of all, it was seen as a means of combating the organized 'interests' which were, for the Radical, the enemies of good, just government. In this opposition to permanent, structured interest groups, which differs from the more moderate unease of Liberals, Radicals stood in sharp contrast with the themes of collectivism, whether that collectivism is seen as organic and emotional, or administrative and organizational. Though more willing than Liberals to use the State positively for social reform, the intense individualism of Radicals was an ultimate rejection

15 *Ibid.*, p. 129.
16 The reference is to Louis Hartz, *The Liberal Tradition in America*.
17 Beer, *op. cit.*, p. 41.

of, an ultimate moving away from, the sociology of collectivism. Members of the population, in their role as citizens, were free to combine to try to sway the policies of government; and the levelling democracy of the Radical model of society removed limits on both the scope and membership of such reformist groups.[18]

On a local level, the spread of Radicalism created an atmosphere very different from that to which older Liberals were accustomed. There was a streak of moral fervour in Liberalism, but its intensity was overshadowed by the near-fanaticism of some Radicals. One member of the Leeds Liberal Association has left a memoir of his own very personal reaction to the clash between old-line Liberals and the new breed of Radical over the issue of candidate selection:[19]

> On all sides I heard extreme opinions expressed by men whose faces and names were quite unfamiliar to me, and I found to my dismay that the more extreme the opinions, the warmer was their reception by these representative Liberals. They would hardly listen to their old leaders, who had grown grey in fighting the battles of Liberalism. They treated with contumely any words of soberness or moderation. They applauded even speakers who were palpably selfish or insincere. As I listened to that debate, my eyes were opened, and I realized the fact that a great revolution had been suddenly and silently wrought, and that the control of the Liberal party had, in great measure, passed out of the hands of its old leaders into those of the men who managed the new 'machine'.

This new movement was deeply troubling and offensive to more traditional Liberals. For them, Radicalism's morality was either an erroneous celebration of mob rule, or completely absent in what was seen as a power grab. M. Ostrogorski, the historian, did not approve of what he witnessed; he wrote that Radicalism had abandoned 'moral power' and 'philosophy' in favour of becoming a 'physical force' interested in 'discipline' and a highly political control

18 *Ibid.*, p. 42.
19 H.J. Hanham, *Elections and Party Management*, p. 126.

of party organization. The differences in style and doctrine between Liberals and Radicals were significant, yet there were some unchanging features of the Liberal Age. Among them were the importance of non-party associations and the role of party discipline and organization.

Voluntary Groups

British Liberals believed that desirable change came through encouraging freedom rather than building structures. They resisted the latter, and worked for the former through the support of various voluntary associations outside of the party and the Government for the pursuit of political reform and the provision of social services. The voluntarism of the Liberals, as well as the later Radicals, was informed by an emotional moralism. The spirit of methodist evangelism, spread by Wesley in the revival of the eighteenth century, as well as by nineteenth-century Nonconformist reformism, set the tone for many such Liberal movements. The existence of slavery, a major focus of religious reformers, was also one of the first sources of success for the proliferating Liberal voluntary pressure groups of the time. Ostrogorski described the intensity of feeling which animated this particular movement, and remarked that 'Societies for the suppression of the slave-trade ... spring up on all sides'.[20]

The anti-slavery movement was followed by a number of voluntary reform associations. Some of the more prominent of these were: the Political Unions of the 1830s; O'Connell's Catholic Association; the London Workingmen's Association and the Chartist groups; the Short Time Committees for the Ten Hours Bill (1840s); the Liberation Society (1853); the National Reform League (1865); and the National Education League (1869).[21] One of the most important of the voluntary groups active during this period was the Anti-Corn Law League. Through an immense public relations campaign, the Anti-Corn Law

20 M. Ostrogorski, *Democracy and the Organisation of Political Parties*, vol. 1, p. 28.

21 Beer, *op. cit.*, p. 44.

Leaguers were able to win public opinion to their side against protectionism. Only the shock of a bad Irish harvest was needed to bring them legislative victory. For Ostrogorski, it was the first and greatest example of a political association achieving a legislative victory through persuasion of the public conscience.[22] Similar victories had been won by the Political Unions in their extension of the suffrage, and by the Catholic Association in the Act of Emancipation in 1829. In each of these cases, however, moral argument was diluted by an implied threat of force and intimidation. The Anti-Corn Law League, in contrast, won its victory through the sheer massiveness of its effort, outside of the structures of Parliament, to persuade public opinion at the grass roots.[23]

During the Liberal Age, voluntary associations grew not only as tools for pressuring government, but also as institutions for voluntary charity. The poverty and squalor which accompanied the industrialism of the nineteenth century led to an increase in the number of associations concerned with poverty as a specific evil. Their proliferation led to the creation, in 1869, of the Charity Organization Society, a body whose purpose was co-ordination between otherwise separate voluntary efforts.[24]

These sorts of voluntary associations served as models of approaches to philanthropy which could be emulated by public legislation. This was a feature of at least some of the programme passed in the House of Commons by the activist Liberal Government which took office in 1906. Most of the health and welfare measures passed during this period were inspired by programmes already in operation which had been developed by charitable organizations and voluntary associations in earlier years. Specifically, the health and unemployment insurance programmes of the Liberal Government were partly based on methods used by

22 Ostrogorski, *op. cit.*, p. 131.

23 'The Protectionists tried to counteract the League by the same methods, by founding associations, but they lacked vitality and spontaneity; the farmers attended the meetings of these associations as if by compulsion; the stewards and agents of the landlords used to come to their houses and fetch them to the meetings.' [*Ibid.*, p. 132.]

24 Lord Beveridge, *Voluntary Action*, pp. 125-6.

the Friendly Societies which had grown in England. The Government's school meals programme for poor children was modelled on a service first developed by the Liverpool Food Association. The legal innovation of the Government in probation for convicted criminals amounted to a public recognition of the work which had been carried on privately by the Police Court Missionaries. Beyond this, the Liberal Government had a desire to employ voluntary organizations in the provision of at least part of some state services because they could provide a flexible supplement, taking account of particular needs as well as augmenting existing manpower. Workers in the probation service, for example, were not direct employees of the State.[25]

These voluntary groups were 'associations' in the strict meaning of that term. That is, they were collections of volunteering individuals, with none of the aspects of tradition, legal bond, class or occupational loyalty, economic self-interest, or other more communal ties which have held British political formations together both before and since the Liberal period.[26] Often they were formed to pass only one particular measure, make one particular change. After they had accomplished this purpose, they might well break up. A new effort required a new commitment. Ostrogorski observed that each was a 'provisional organization', designed to last only until the triumph of the 'cause which had called it into life'.[27]

Party Structure

The compliment of strong voluntary activism was weak party organization. As described earlier, uncompromised Liberals saw party as a loose and secondary association of MPs. They joined together because they agreed with one another on issues, not because they were delegates of their geographical constituencies or because they were bound by some collective sense of party or class which transcended them in their role as independent MPs. The honourable

25 Anthony Forder, *Social Services in England and Wales*, pp. 4-6.
26 Beer, *op. cit.*, pp. 44-5.
27 Ostrogorski, *op. cit.*, p. 133.

MP and the responsible constituency voter were both defined in terms of independence from broader ties. Organizationally, there was a congruence with Liberal philosophy to make the theme of the period that of 'the golden age of the private MP'.[28] Parliamentary majorities were shifting and relatively uncertain. The First Reform Act of 1832 freed the MP from Whig forms of patronage, and before the Second Reform Act of 1867 MPs were unhindered by more modern forms of party control. There is a striking contrast between the strong discipline and the powerful national organization of the major parties in the twentieth century, and the insignificance of party structures in the middle of the nineteenth. Party managers had difficulty influencing their fellow members. There was, to be sure, extra-parliamentary organization, and it became very extensive after 1832. It served as a means for mobilization of support to elect candidates, but these nineteenth-century constituency associations neither nominated candidates nor disciplined representatives in Parliament.[29]

The Radicals, simply because they were direct majoritarians, were in favour of much stronger and more permanent party organization as a tool for registering the influence of the majority. Liberals saw structure as a barrier to freedom; Radicals saw it as a way of implementing democracy. Radicals consequently were leaders of efforts to create mass popular party formations which operated outside the confines of legislative politics.[30] The widening of the suffrage in 1867 paved the way for the extensive organization of the voting population which would have an influential role in party affairs. In that year, Joseph Chamberlain's Birmingham association formed itself along the lines of popular suffrage, unqualified by property limitations. On the national level, this popular thrust resulted in the formation of the National Liberal Federation in 1877. Its purpose, according to the 1887 report of the Federation, was 'the direct participation of all

28 Beer, *op. cit.*, pp. 38-9.
29 *Ibid.*, pp. 50-1; Hanham, *op. cit.*, p. 347.
30 Beer, pp. 43-4.

members of the party in the formation and direction of policy and in the selection of those particular measures of reform in which priority shall be given'.[31]

Liberal Collapse

The Liberal Party was able to maintain a coalition of these different elements for some decades. Nevertheless, the party experienced a sudden decline from political power and importance during the first part of the twentieth century. The most persuasive explanation for this dramatic event relates to the basic source of cleavage in collectivist politics: class. The Liberals were unable to make the efforts necessary to integrate newly enfranchised working-class sectors of the electorate and the growing trade-union movement. The social conservatism and middle-class bias characteristic of Liberals created a gulf between them and working-class elements. Moreover, Radicals fully accepted an unbiased individualist conception of society only in theory.

The other hypotheses persistently put forward to explain the Liberal disaster either do not stand up as well or do not reach broadly enough to handle fully such a major shift in British party alignments. Some analysts have suggested that the Liberals lost support because they were unable to adopt the progressive reform policies required by the times. Barbara Tuchman, in her broad survey of social and political changes in Europe in the years just before the First World War, scathingly evaluates the Liberals, condemning an alleged narrow reliance on *laissez-faire*. In her view, the last Liberal government 'had not been able to give shape to the great promise of 1906.'[32] A similar sentiment has been expressed by George Dangerfield, whose book, *The Strange Death of Liberal England*, concentrates on the demise of the party. Liberalism, in his opinion, was vaguely but unmistakably a tired, old movement by the turn of the century: 'For a nation which wanted to revive a sluggish blood by running very fast and in any direction, Liberalism

31 *Ibid.*, p. 52.
32 Barbara Tuchman, *The Proud Tower*, p. 449.

was clearly an inconvenient burden.'[33]

The reality of the last Liberal Government, however, belies this negative picture. In policy terms, the period of Liberal rule from 1906 was one of extraordinary legislative achievement, especially in the area of social reform. Liberals passed the Trades Disputes Act of 1906, the Provision of Meals Act of 1906, the Old Age Pensions Act of 1908, the Coal Mines Act of 1908, the Wages Boards Act of 1909, and the Labour Exchanges Act of 1909. They also put through the Education Bill of 1906, the four land bills of 1907, the taxation of land values in the Budget of 1909, the repeal or reduction of some food taxes, and the ending of recruitment of indentured Chinese. In 1911 came the National Insurance Act for lower-income groups, providing protection against sickness and unemployment; and in 1912 the Liberals passed a minimum wages act.[34] In terms of regulating conditions of employment, while providing broad welfare state aid, the Liberal programme is strikingly similar to the American New Deal of the 1930s. One important element in this Liberal welfare-state reformism was the presence of a number of Radical and reformist intellectuals in the party, a contrast to Continental developments. One of the distinctive qualities of the Liberals in Britain was that they carried out many of the modern welfare-state reforms which were left to socialist parties elsewhere in Europe.[35] The supply of sympathetic intellectuals enabled the activist Liberals to maintain party momentum with a continuing stream of legislation. Hence, such Liberal advocates as R.B. McCallum are on safe ground in defending the party's capacity for progressive policy innovation. He notes that, 'the Liberal Government had its philosophy for dealing with the social and socialist problem. They were not without remedies'.[36]

Another point brought up in examinations of the Liberal

---

33 George Dangerfield, *The Strange Death of Liberal England*, pp. 7-8.

34 Beer, *op. cit.*, p. 60.

35 E.J. Hobsbawm, *Labouring Men*, p. 302.

36 R.B. McCallum, *The Liberal Party from Earl Grey to Asquith*, pp. 172-3.

Party's decline is the fratricidal conflict between Asquith and Lloyd George for the leadership of the party. This personal feud created significant waves through the party; indeed divided it into two camps. One scholar who has studied the party's collapse, Trevor Wilson, puts their intra-party war at the centre of his analytical stage. According to the Wilson theory, their personal clash opened the way for the political slide of the party. The battle between their supporters was not only distracting, it weakened the party's political foundations. Once the Liberal Party had slipped to third place, it was quickly ground down between the Conservative and Labour parties and lost credibility as a potential governing party for Britain.

Certainly the quarrel split the Liberal Party structurally. In the early part of the twentieth century, there had been clear indications that the party was developing more of the concrete trappings of modern organization. The Liberal Central Association, the national headquarters controlled by the Chief Whip, had established a strong position, partly through the control of party finances. After the 1906 victory, new sources of patronage considerably enhanced its position. But the break between the two leaders, personal in 1916 when Asquith was removed as head of the wartime Coalition Government, party-wide in early 1919 when the Independent Liberals were set up to oppose the Coalition Liberals, resulted in the creation of *two* Liberal Party organizations. Right after the 1916 split, Lloyd George began to build his own political machine, and managed to collect a massive fund of campaign money to keep it alive. Asquith wrote in October 1926: 'The control of the Party has throughout been divided between two separate authorities: the Liberal Central Office and Mr Lloyd George's rival machine – the former very scantily, and the latter very richly, endowed.'[37]

Adding to the party's problems were the particular personal weaknesses of the two rival leaders: Asquith's lack of assertiveness, Lloyd George's reputation for deviousness

37 Trevor Wilson, *The Downfall of the Liberal Party 1914-1935*, pp. 354-5.

and dishonesty. The latter's bad reputation was reinforced when it was reported that he collected the bulk of his funds from the sale of honours. This became clear when the composition of the first list was made public, moving the *Nation* to state that it contained, 'its usual character of falsification of merit which belongs to its secret and evil source'.[38] Predictably, Lloyd George refused for some time to share his wealth with Liberals who did not follow him. He eventually did provide the larger party with some funds, but it is clear that he could not be accused of great generosity. In the 1924 General Election, he finally released £50,000, but his sluggishness in making this commitment reduced the number of Liberal candidates able to run. According to one analyst, this 'crippled the party beyond subsequent recovery'.[39]

To focus exclusively on the details of the Asquith/Lloyd George battle, however, limits discussion to events which were themselves in part effects of the most basic cause of Liberal collapse. The primary reason for Liberal decline was a fundamental shift in the forms of representation, and party and governmental power, in British politics. Class was becoming the basis of political representation through party. Party government and functional representation were the new collectivist structural developments. The Conservative and Labour parties were capable of adjusting to the new environment. The Liberal Party was unable to cope with changes which were so alien to its style and philosophy.

The two major parties have shown considerably more internal discipline than the Liberals. The Labour Party, for example, lacks the deference and hierarchy of the Tories, and has known great internal strife, but it has never sundered itself as the Liberals did. In 1931, when Labour Prime Minister Ramsay MacDonald formed the National Government, he could persuade only three Labour ministers – Snowden, Sankey and Thomas – and a few Labour MPs to join him in the coalition venture. The great mass of the party remained united in opposition to any co-

38 *Ibid.*, p. 122.
39 Jorgen Rasmussen, *Retrenchment and Revival*, pp. 52-3.

operation with men seen as class enemies. Through the
manoeuvre of accepting the leadership of Lloyd George for
a brief period after the First World War, the Tories were
able to drive a massive wedge through Liberal ranks. A
similar ploy in 1931 failed to break Labour solidarity.[40] The
Liberals, thanks to their individualism, lacked the
discipline to negate internal splits.

Collectivist Politics

With the development of party government, with the
discipline and unity which that title implies, a Prime
Minister and Cabinet were given a source of security of
tenure which was the reverse of the insecurity of Cabinets
during the height of the Liberal Age. Functional
representation, following the theoretical scheme set down
by Beer, 'refers to any theory that finds the community
divided into various strata, regards each of these strata as
having a certain corporate unity, and holds that they ought
to be represented in government'.[41] In the early part of the
twentieth century, British society was moving toward
increasing acceptance of a role for large 'producer groups'
of industry and labour, at the same time that such groups
were continuing to enlarge and solidify on a national scale.
When the commitment was made to greater economic
planning, the expertise of such groups became an
important lever of access for them into centres of national
governmental power.[42]

There were other, cultural reasons as well for the
growing acceptance of large organizations. The tradition of
inclusive, organic conceptions of man and society which
descended from what Beer terms Old Tory and Old Whig
times was in sympathy with the new collectivism. These old
organic formations had hardly been bureaucratic and
administrative in orientation; but in sociology, and in their
hierarchy and graded differentiations, they were not so

40 Beer, *op. cit.*, pp. 159-61.
  41 *Ibid.*, p. 71.
  42 The Tory Party was strongly committed to the planned economy
by the interwar period; see *ibid.*, pp. 292 ff.

different from the new structures. Beer makes this connection in his analysis. The new collectivist groupings and their historic predecessors contrasted with Liberal voluntary associations in being based upon considerably stronger ties than simply 'common ideas and moral judgments'. Instead of these tenuous strings, integration of a grouping – variously termed an estate, class, vocation – is a result of 'objective conditions that give its members a function and are the ground for deeply rooted, continuing – even "fixed" – interests'. In addition, the function performed is considered important for 'the community as a whole'.[43]

Because of this historical continuity, the new groups were acceptable to the Conservative Party, a political organization which traces its roots far back into the history of the nation. Moreover, both major parties had a basic receptivity to such large and inclusive organizations because each of them was based on a conception which is itself collective – class. For the Tories, the class theme was a restatement of the old idea, going back to feudal times, of the hierarchical integration of society. In the Labour Party, it was a horizontal conception of class division, bred by the establishment of a large, urban industrial working class and the adoption of a collectivist creed, Socialism, as formal party doctrine.[44]

Liberals and Radicals, in contrast, were consistent in their suspicion of, or great hostility to, organized 'interests'. The old voluntary Victorian pressure-formations were of a very different design. As a practical result of such an outlook, the party automatically repelled association with large collectivist interest groups. In consequence, a major source of finances in collectivist politics was cut off from the Liberals. Lloyd George's fund was testament to the shrewd operator's skill which he possessed, and not to any inherent Liberal Party talent for attracting money. The fund was deeply resented by his opponents in the party, not just because he refused to share it, not just because he was Lloyd George, but because they had no similar large

43 *Ibid.*, p. 71.
44 *Ibid.*, pp. 79 ff.

income of their own for their section of the party.[45]

The second major instrument of collectivist politics in the organizational sense – party government – was equally alien to the Liberal Party's political traditions. But the need for the discipline of party government is obvious once the essentials of collectivist politics have been accepted. If policy is to be consistent, discipline is necessary to provide coherence through time, both in Parliament and in party conferences. Philosophical predispositions of the Tory and Labour parties have, again, facilitated internal control. In both parties, though in different ways, class theories provide cohesion by encouraging forms of solidarity, just as they have facilitated the development of functional representation through the acceptance of administrative bureaucracy. In the Labour Party, 'Socialist Democracy' dictates that the essential source of legitimacy, and of policy as well, is the working class. This moral force, however, is channelled through the party structure. Conference resolutions set up the main parameters within which party representatives in Parliament must remain, though those representatives inevitably have and seek initiative in the details of policy. It is this very democratic aspect of the party's structure which enforces internal conformity. Party members and MPs are both pulled into the circle of obedience to party policy by the legitimacy of the party's programme. And this moral aspect is a direct result of a Socialist ideology which both inspires loyalty and provides loyalists with a sense of righteousness. The party is based on an ideology, however flexibly that doctrine might be applied in practice, which in turn gains coherence from its own starting point – class.[46]

'Tory Democracy' is also based on class, and works to enforce solidarity within the party. Here, however, in contrast to Labour ethos, the meaning of legitimacy is hierarchy rather than party democracy. In the Tory scheme, party members serve primarily to approve or veto policy, not to initiate it. That is a function reserved to the party elite, which forms a Government when the

45 Wilson, *op. cit.*, pp. 122 ff.
46 Beer, *op. cit.*, Chapter 3.

Conservative Party is victorious at the polls. The Crown, once a policy source, still serves as a symbol of the legitimacy of government to the nation. In Tory conceptions of the British Constitution, some of the aura of royal authority has been transferred fairly directly to the current chief initiator of policy, the Cabinet.[47]

In contrast, the limited Liberal efforts at discipline and organization have not been truly and firmly grounded in party philosophy, and have often been nearly invisible in party practice. The mobilization and emotion which accompanied the spread of Radicalism may have frightened older Liberals, but Radicalism itself never aspired to the kind of class solidarity of Tory or Socialist Democracy. Radicalism was based on mobilizing a majority of independent citizens, not on creating solidarity within or between classes. The very directness and intensity of its democracy encouraged suspicion of permanent, highly organized, large-scale party structures – they were too much like the hated 'interests', too likely to become narrow and self-serving.[48]

As modern national party organization began to develop after the Reform Act of 1867, the Liberal Party moved with the times. With the elaboration of formal party structures, old Liberal parliamentarism gradually faded. Beer's calculations of cohesion for each of the three main parties in the House of Commons, for both 1906 and 1908, put the Liberals ahead of the Tory and Labour parties in degree of party unity. In a more basic sense, however, modern party discipline never seems to have really overcome Liberalism's hostility to such things. The fate of the party during the Asquith/Lloyd George battle shows the fragile glass, rather than firm organic, quality of its unity. The Tories' National Union of Conservative and Unionist Associations had its roots in a party federation formed in 1867 by an initiative from the party élite, with the blessing of the leader. Disraeli saw the group as an aid in mobilizing broader sectors of the electorate. In contrast, the formation of the National Liberal Federation in 1877 was spurred by a Radical desire

47 *Ibid.*, pp. 94 ff. captures this atmosphere well.
48 *Ibid.*, pp. 39 ff.

to organize resistance against the Whig element in the
Liberal Party. The NLF helped create what party
discipline existed, but also served as a challenge to the
party leadership.[49]

Gladstone's remarkable capacity for personal leadership
enabled him to hold his diverse mass of Liberals together,
absorbing in the process the Radical challenge as well.[50]
Gladstone, however, was a great man; and the fact that his
personality was so important as a source of unity testifies to
the lack of more automatic and impersonal sources of
Liberal cohesion. The absence of clear conceptions of
authority in the party may be illustrated by turning from
the personality of the great leader to the less colourful issue
of initiation of party policy. The National Liberal
Federation was clearly a popular body of considerable
influence. Its Newcastle Programme of 1891 was directly
translated into party policy during the Liberal Government
of 1892-5. This set of proposals was the culmination of
years of Federation resolutions; yet, simultaneously, the
assent of the party leader was felt necessary to passage.
During the last period of Liberal rule, party leadership took
more of a lead while ambiguity remained a constant.
Specifically, the most impressive social legislation of the
Campbell-Bannerman and Asquith Governments seems to
have originated at the top of the party; yet, simultaneously,
much of the rest of the legislation passed was anticipated by
Federation resolutions.[51]

Class Conflict

Endemic structural weakness, however, is one thing,
sudden electoral collapse a phenomenon which is quite
different. The former is a state of affairs which has not
hampered party survival through time in the U.S.A. and

49 *Ibid.*, pp. 52, 123, and 256 ff. The last pages cited indicate that the
Liberals, before 1906-08, lagged behind the Tories somewhat in degree
of discipline, though the years after 1856 showed a steep rise in the
cohesion of both parties.

50 John Vincent, *The Formation of the Liberal Party*, pp. 237-8.

51 Beer, *op. cit.*, pp. 258-9.

other countries. The latter is, by definition, the end for a
party in terms of practical political power. This end came
remarkably, fascinatingly quickly for the Liberals. In one
decade, the Liberal Party was a dominant governing party.
In the following decade, it was rapidly, literally falling
apart around the country as the Labour Party grew in
strength and confidence. One of the most interesting
characteristics of the Liberal collapse is how quickly the
party seemed to lose any solid base of electoral support.
This was reflected in the poor showing of Independent
Liberals (i.e., those not in coalition with the Tories) in the
general election of 1922. They made unexpected gains in
sections of the country which had not previously supported
Liberals. While the party regained some lost territory in
rural Scotland, there were no comparable advances in
North Wales, Devon or Cornwall, which had been Liberal
strongholds in recent times. Party victories in rural
England, which included some seats which almost never
elected a Liberal, could be explained by discontent among
farmers concerning Coalition agricultural policy. While
there was, on balance, a Liberal gain in working-class seats,
the total was completely overshadowed by the dramatic
advances of the Labour Party.[52]

The 1923 general election, which resulted in notable
Liberal gains showed a continuing lack of Liberal connection with any distinct and consistent sector of the
electorate. Though the party gained a net of 42 seats in the
election, it did not reverse the earlier losses in its traditional
strongholds – industrial Scotland, South Wales, and the
West Riding of Yorkshire. The Liberals, continuing this
erratic pattern, again made some spectacular advances in
areas where they had formerly been weak. They gained a
number of seats which had not even gone Liberal in the
landslide year of 1906: Aylesbury, Blackpool, Chelmsford,
Chichester, Sevenoaks, Tiverton. Lloyd George thought the
results 'most surprising'. Asquith looked at the returns and
asked: 'What is the explanation for these unexpected, and
in some cases unhoped-for, victories?' Liberal campaign

53 *Ibid.*, pp. 275-80.

managers in Chichester could make no reply – they 'only knew 12 Liberals' and had not been able to find a candidate to contest the district until the very last moment.[53]

It is likely that the comparatively good Liberal showing in 1923 was mainly a reflection of unhappiness with the Conservative Government on the part of voters who normally supported the Tories, were unwilling to vote for a new and mistrusted Labour Party, and found a way out by voting Liberal. The following year, with an election held while a minority Labour Government was in office, the Liberals were literally decimated. The party was reduced from 158 to 43 MPs. The nature of the seats which they won created a most unpleasant profile of future party prospects. One of those elected was the Speaker, and 3 were university seats; these can be considered special, separate cases. Of the rest, 18 were elected mainly from agricultural areas in Scotland and Wales, and 5 of those with Tory assistance. In England, the results for Liberals were very bleak. Of the 21 seats won there, none were agricultural, which meant that the growing Labour Party might take them away or subtract enough Liberal votes for a Conservative to win. In fully 15 of the English seats won, there were no Conservative candidates. Of the 6 English seats where Liberals won in three-way races, at least 4 were taken because the Liberal candidates enjoyed considerable personal followings, not because of the automatic drawing-power of the Liberal label.[54]

The 1929 General Election, which saw the Liberals 'revive' to 59 MPs, was a disheartening result in view of the massive effort mounted by the party faithful under the leadership of Lloyd George. Again, there was evidence of lack of party identification with a consistently loyal, broad sector of the electorate. Again, it could be inferred that the Liberal Party's revival was mainly a function of voter disaffection with a Tory regime. Rather than holding and building on their 1924 base, the Liberals lost 19 of the seats won in that year, a reversal for which they compensated by gaining 35 new ones.

54 *Ibid.*, pp. 334-5.

The best systematic explanation for this unsystematic party decline returns to an element of British society which has been of maximum importance in Collectivist Age politics – class. H. Stuart Hughes, in his survey of Continental politics at the turn of the century, notes that liberal parties there were weakened by their refusal to make concessions to working-class groups in terms of actual internal party power, while they simultaneously rejected the validity of class concepts in their formal programmes and informal rhetoric.[55] In this respect, the fate of the British Liberals seems to mirror that of European liberal parties generally. In justice to the British Liberals, it should be stressed again that the party amassed an extraordinary record of legislative achievement in the years of the last Liberal Governments. Moreover, Liberals were hardly deaf to the desires of the embryonic Labour Party. The Liberals substituted the Labour draft for their own softer version of a bill to reverse the hated Taff Vale decision.[56] On a number of occasions during this period of Liberal power, Labour was the source of a proposed reform. Liberals, far from being inflexible in the face of working-class assertiveness, were sensitive to the same new, strong political elements which were expanding the Labour Party.[57]

During these years, there were particular strains which damaged Labour-Liberal relations. Industrial strife, including a 1911 incident in Liverpool in which soldiers fired on strikers, was an ever-growing problem.[58] Lloyd George's courtship of Conservatives in order to undercut Asquith in the wartime Cabinet meant that he was in debt

---

55 H. Stuart Hughes in *Contemporary Europe: A History*, pp. 12-16, echoes Samuel Beer in differentiating between liberals 'convinced of the virtues of their own class', radicals who were intensely democratic and 'like most Americans ... disliked the very idea of discussing politics in terms of class conflict'. Putting Hughes beside Beer seems to imply that Continental liberals were more explicitly class-conscious than British Liberals. Both scholars agree, however, that working-class people were effectively excluded from such formations in Britain and on the Continent.

56 Beer, *op. cit.*, p. 123.

57 *Ibid.*, p. 61.

58 Tuchman, *op. cit.*, p. 462.

to forces which would be unlikely to welcome moves toward more progressive legislation.[59] Later, the Liberal Party's hesitancy on both the land tax and capital levy worked to damage its credibility as a party of reform.[60]

These are all, however, striking examples of the broader issue of class conflict. The problems of tension between middle-class Liberals and a working-class Labour Party were both brought to a head and symbolized by the 'doormat incident' of 1917, in which Lloyd George effectively broke with the Labour leader, Arthur Henderson. Henderson was excluded from a Cabinet meeting while his suggestion that British delegates be sent to the Socialist Congress in Stockholm was evaluated. It was obviously a slap, for the Labour conference had supported sending representatives. An angry Henderson resigned from the Cabinet. Labour remained in the Coalition, but the decisive break with the Liberals had been made. Henderson occupied himself with defining a new Labour Party organization and programme. Sidney Webb aided this effort, and the views of the Fabian Society consequently found their way into a major place in party doctrine. The Labour Party, at its 1918 conference, easily reached agreement on a philosophical commitment to class-conscious Socialism and a structural emphasis on unity as necessary to victory in the class struggle. The American Ambassador at the time remarked: 'The Labour Party is already playing for supremacy'.[61]

The snubbing of Henderson dramatized at the top of the Liberal Party the problem of class conflict which had been plaguing it for some time. It centred on an unwillingness among local Liberal Associations to offer working-class candidates. Philip Poirier has discovered that, 'By 1900 it was obvious that the local Liberal associations ... were generally averse to Labour bids for seats'.[62] The Liberal-

59 Beer, *op. cit.*, pp. 137-8.
60 Catherine Cline, *Recruits to Labour – The British Labour Party 1914-1931*, pp. 45-6.
61 Beer, *op. cit.*, pp. 45-6.
61 Beer, *op. cit.*, pp. 137-9.
62 Philip Poirier, *The Advent of the British Labour Party*, p. 12.

Labour co-operation which existed at the start of the century was in reality possible only because there were so few Labour candidates at the time. A formal election accord in 1906, and an informal one in 1910, were workable because Labour was still a new, small movement. With the growth of trade unionism, and the resources which this gave the Labour Party, a clash with middle-class Liberals was unavoidable. When they were able to field large numbers of candidates, Labour did so. Beer has suggested that the Liberal Party might have stood down in 'scores, even hundreds of constituencies' in order to prevent a direct clash with Labour. But he provides his own rebuttal: 'can one conceive of the middle- and upper-class personnel of the local Liberal associations abdicating in this manner and on such a scale in favour of working-class candidates?'[63]

The national élite of the Liberal Party made some effort to create greater flexibility in local attitudes, but there was little those leaders could do given the constitution of the party. There was no way in which they could compel an association to take a particular candidate, and the Liberals lacked the ideological solidarity which stabilized the other two parties and facilitated their internal co-operation. According to F. Schnadhorst, Secretary of the National Liberal Federation, Liberals were unable to do more for a candidate than to 'earnestly bespeak for him the generous support of the Liberal Association'. Herbert Gladstone, the future Chief Whip, was quoted as early as 1892 to the effect that the 'long and short of it is that the constituencies, for social, financial, and trade reasons are extremely slow to adopt Labour candidates'.[64] Yet, as the 'doormat incident' shows, the top of the party reflected the same sort of class bias even while condemning it among the party rank-and-file.

The implications of collectivist politics in the organizational sense obviously have their role in explaining the Liberal decline. The party lacked endemic cohesion as well as steady sources of patronage. Each of these structural

63 Beer, *op. cit.*, p. 146.
64 Henry Pelling, *The Origins of the Labour Party: 1880-1900*, p. 223.

problems, however, was a function of a philosophical and psychological individualism which co-existed with practical class discrimination. The Conservative and Labour parties, accepting in theory a class-consciousness which the Liberals could accept only in practice, had both cohesion and money. The Liberals, injured by the particular ways in which they rejected and accepted class, were both divided and financially pressed.

Just as they had no class locus in their doctrine, so the Liberals quickly lost any solid base within the electorate once the broad working-class enfranchisement of 1884 redefined the nation's politics along fundamental class lines. As the Labour Party grew in strength and solidarity, alarmed middle-class voters found a home of security in the Conservative Party's class outlook. The intensity of class conflict between the two collectivist parties solidified and enlarged their constituencies. In contrast, the Liberals' lack of class conceptions not only facilitated the speedy desertion of former supporters to the two more solid coalitions on either side of them, but there was also no discernible cohesion or consistency amongst the groups of voters who remained with or came to the Liberal Party in the 1920s.

Class and associated conflicts not only built the Labour Party and demolished the Liberals, it also made the breach between Liberals and Labour especially permanent. Class had led Liberals to snub working-class candidates. Later, Labour class solidarity dictated uncompromising hostility to the Liberal Party. The brief Labour Government of 1924 was entirely dependent on Liberal support in the Commons to survive, yet there was little real consultation between the two sides. As Roy Jenkins notes in his *Asquith*, although the 'Government was absolutely dependent on Liberal votes ... many Labour members regarded the possessors of these votes as class enemies, little if any better than the Tories'.[65] Just as the Labour Party refused to follow MacDonald into coalition in 1931, so the unbending militants of the party

65 Roy Jenkins, *Asquith*, p. 502.
66 Wilson, *op. cit.*, p. 301.

refused to consider Lib-Lab in 1924, even though it meant the demise of their Government. After all, the Labour Party had decided in 1918 that it must take every opportunity to weaken the Liberals, even if this delayed Labour's coming to power. Such was the intensity and passion bred by the class war among its firm adherents.[66]

In sum, the Liberals were doubly injured by the class factor. Ironically, each injury was the reverse twist of the other. First, they rejected class as a doctrinal source of unity, either in the explicit Labour sense or the implicit Tory sense. Rather, the Liberal Party drew emotional and intellectual sustenance from opposition to class. Second, however, Liberals proved to be most class-conscious in their rejection of working-class allies as equal partners. In the elections of the 1920s, Liberals paid the cruel price for their own earlier hostility to working-class candidates and leaders. While some were adopted as candidates and accepted as Cabinet members, the snubbing of Henderson reveals their true secondary status in Liberal eyes. The Liberals were hurt by their class discrimination while earning no profit from class solidarity.

In the United States, the welfare state and regulatory reforms of the New Deal preserved the two main parties, albeit with a new majority. In Britain, similar reforms by a Liberal Government could not do the same because the social structure was less flexible, the nation's politics more clearly defined on class lines.

The Liberal Role

Given this contrast between the Liberal outlook and collectivist politics, which was instrumental in the dramatic collapse of the old Liberal Party, the growth recently of the party's strength becomes more interesting. Basic philosophical liberalism, dealing with the rights and liberties of the individual, is solidly established in British political culture and not a unique feature of the Liberal Party. At the same time, the party is closely associated historically with more specific attitudes seriously out of harmony with collectivist politics – weak party structure, emphasis on local and regional government and concerns, activism through non-party voluntary associations, and at least theoretical hostility to class politics.

With the Liberal Party's revival, the issue arises of the degree to which this is related to a more general weakening of the hold of collectivist politics in Britain. Increasing support for the party does not necessarily indicate a more general return to Liberal and Radical styles within the political system. However, in this case the party's revival of recent years does seem linked to broader changes. The chapters which follow develop the argument that the party's new strength may be understood as one indication of the breaking apart of collectivist politics, and that it is related to movements within the major parties, other small parties, and the electorate as a whole.

2

The Collectivist Reality and Liberal Advance

Collectivist Politics

The coming of the Collectivist Age might be termed a *solidification* of British politics. Sociologically, the growth of collectivist politics was founded on a new communalism in the electorate. Class-based voting led to electoral predictability, and party competition increased in intensity, reflecting the political importance of class sentiments. Organizationally, the new calculus of large national interest groups working in tandem with big administrative bureaucracy was reinforced by a new party discipline which limited the powers of the parliamentary rank-and-file.

Very different were the weaker and more informal party organizations which were a defining characteristic of the Liberal Age. The decline of parliamentarism, where MPs were free of modern party discipline in forming shifting majorities, has inevitably decreased the importance of Parliament itself. The end of parliamentarism's freedom implies discipline and control of MPs; and when he lost his independence the MP saw his prominence and importance compromised. One crucial legislative power is that of control over the nation's budget. It was, in English history, a central source of tension between Crown and Parliament, and taxing power has been a main source of leverage and influence enjoyed by the House of Commons. The degree to which the growth of Cabinet and Prime Ministerial power has reduced this and other powers of the Commons is striking. Consider the remark of Alfred Grosser, made in the context of his study of the contemporary budgetary powers of Western legislatures: 'the Congress of the United States would be at the top ... At the bottom of the ladder would be the House of Commons, whose lack of power is striking once the Chancellor of the Exchequer has revealed "his" budget to the public.'[1]

The decline in the role of Parliament has been complimented by the growth of power elsewhere – in the centrally important Cabinet, and in an expanding national bureaucracy to deal with the planning of the economy and the programme of the welfare state. A large-scale, technically competent administration is essential to provide informed preparation and staff work for decisions. In part, the greater difficulty of decision-making is a result of the larger variety of economic interest groups which have access to the instruments of government. It is also a reflection, however, of the growth of new levels of government activity in the economic planning and welfare areas in a time when technology has made all decisions more complex.

Collectivist Problems

No decision-making structure is entirely perfect, since the very effort to solve some problems tends to create others. Several very significant difficulties have resulted from collectivist administrative structures. First, there is the broad administrative paradox that efforts to create competence through building bureaucracies can undermine that very goal. Second, there is the central/local problem that decisions which seem eminently rational from a central planner's perspective may nevertheless arouse hostility within particular localities, where costs and benefits are viewed differently. Finally, there is the universality-selectivity problem of disagreement on how best to aid economically peripheral groups.

The mechanics of collectivism have required the

1 Alfred Grosser, 'The Evolution of European Parliaments', in Stephen Graubard, ed., *A New Europe?*, p. 230.

spawning of a very large bureaucracy; but, as a variety of analysts have argued, such an approach tends to be self-defeating. There is clear sensitivity to this problem in the reflections of bureaucracy's student, Max Weber. He wrote that 'Bureaucratic administration always tends to be an administration of "secret sessions"; in so far as it can, it hides its knowledge and actions from criticism.'[2] The technical expertise of administrators counters efforts at outside supervision. This is an especially telling factor in the British situation, where Parliament lacks sufficient standing committees and staff competence of the sort which give the American Congress leverage over the executive branch. A poorly informed parliament, moreover, can be an ideal aid in helping bureaucracy maintain its independence. The attempt to supervise can give a false sense of complacency to legislators and critics of bureaucracy, while masking their inability really to control decisions. Outsiders may try to impose political goals on the bureaucracy which have little or no correlation with the dictates of dispassionate administration. However, bureaucracy, as a spender of money, a consumer of other resources, and a home for careers inevitably develops its own political outlook and interests and a competitive incentive to resist control.

Related to the problem of controlling bureaucratic independence is an issue which is more directly and simply paradoxical. Aside from the independence which expertise provides and the development of political interests within a bureaucracy, the very effort to structure administrative rationality is counter-productive. Michel Crozier has written of the 'vicious circle' of bureaucracy. He has divided the paradox into four qualities typical of large administrations: (1) development of impersonal rules, which become both too rigid and too simple; (2) isolation of different strata and a concomitant group pressure on the individual for conformity; (3) centralization of decisions, which puts increasing pressure on central structures; (4)

2 Max Weber, quoted in H.H. Gerth and C. Wright Mills, eds., *From Max Weber*, p. 233.

development of parallel power relationships, which sacrifice strict and clearly defined hierarchy for special independence for some and insecurity for others whom they control.[3]

As long as a bureaucracy's routine method of operation results in the solution or at least the alleviation of problems, there is a disincentive for drastic reform. But the drag of handicaps, such as Crozier's four-fold listing, can eventually incline a bureaucracy away from this necessary competence, so that decisions are made and energies spent which have virtually no bearing on the problems to be met. Once bureaucracy departs from a rational method of means-ends calculations, the inertia of routine, combined with the protection of expertise, makes it extremely difficult to impose changes of direction from the outside. The inherent tactical advantage of inertia itself is that doing nothing will allow it to continue on its course.[4]

Harry Eckstein, in his study of the administration of the British National Health Service, has discovered a number of practical examples of the sort of problems being discussed here. Centralization of decision-making has put massive pressure on central administrators (Crozier's factor 3), which has in turn led to a constant search for simple 'costing procedures' in medical spending (factor 1), even though guidelines of this type – when applied automatically – fail to consider all the elements which should be taken into account when trying to determine the appropriate budget for a hospital. In the face of this rigidity, the strength of the central bureaucratic regime stifles protest both between different strata (factor 2), and from below within the same strata (factor 4). Eckstein, noting the force of habit within structures, observes that temporary decisions are almost impossible to change once they are made, and that there is a noticeable tendency to postpone hard decisions almost indefinitely. In the phrase of a witness before the Committee on Estimates: 'The word

---

3 Michel Crozier, *The Bureaucratic Phenomenon*, pp. 187 ff.
4 See, *e.g.*, Peter Woll, *American Bureaucracy*, pp. 161.

temporary is a term of art in the Civil Service.'[5]

This large issue of the internal contradictions of bureaucratic organizations is the most obvious and striking one connected with bureaucratic planning and administration. The irony of the paradox which is inherent in the search for administrative rationality is clear and apparent, but it is not the only type of tension which occurs. A different, less obvious and ironic difficulty results from the conflict between central and local perspectives in planning efforts. This second approach focuses on the complexity that a decision which may seem eminently rational from a national planning viewpoint, a decision which is untainted by administrative paradox in central bureaucracy, may nevertheless seem highly irrational and undesirable when examined in the light of local criteria of what is more important and what less. The issue is significant for Britain, where substantial reliance on national economic planning has developed even though there remains considerable cultural, social and economic diversity between the different regions of the nation.

In British medical-care administration – among other policy areas – centralization has led to an ignoring of the special needs of particular hospital units. The shortcoming here is clear mainly because a welfare-state function is at stake. The central decision-makers may be willing to tolerate such a situation because of administrative paradox (e.g., they like having the political power of decision-making, even if the arrangement is not sensitive to local needs; or if, in their eyes, the cost of expanding central sensitivity to local diversity clearly outweighs the benefits of such a change). Even so, however, they are not meeting their own formal criteria of providing inclusive and efficient

5 Harry Eckstein, 'Planning: The National Health Service', in Richard Rose, ed., *Policy-Making in Britain*, pp. 221-37. Theodore Marmor and David Thomas have published a strongly critical evaluation of Eckstein's book. However, their complaint is not that his general description of the structure of the health service is incorrect, but that he lacks conceptual rigour and a cross-national perspective in his analysis of bargaining between doctors and health agencies. ['Doctors, Politics and Pay Disputes: "Pressure Group Politics" Revisited', *British Journal of Political Science*, October 1972, pp. 421-42.]

welfare service. Scarcity of resources or political self-interest are clear compromises of the general welfare goal of altruism which is accepted in theory by both the centre and the localities.

The planned economy provides more instructive cases of centre *v.* local conflict, for here the goal is maximum economic efficiency rather than providing welfare. The aim is one of production rather than distribution. Human comfort is secondary rather than primary to a planner whose eye is focused on increasing output. Such an atmosphere is more conducive to centre-local clash, thanks to the hard choices required. Hard choices are necessary in the distribution of resources, too, but failure to fill needs here is a failure from both viewpoints, central and local. In the planned economy, localities may be injured by projects which make national sense to planners at the centre. An excellent – if extreme – example of this sort of problem is posed by the Beeching Report of 1963 concerning the state of the British railway system. The study advocated shutting down almost all rail lines which were not paying their way, in order to put British railways on a profitable basis. The central/local clash involved was in clear geographic, rather than less clear administrative, terms. Such lines included a major portion of the railways in both Scotland and Wales. The same decision which made eminent sense from a national criterion of increasing overall economic efficiency was disastrous for these areas. Rural rail lines which were uneconomic were also especially important to the social and economic lives of their areas. After the report was published, 'Doing a Beeching' became a slang label for any particularly wrenching or ruthless move. Nevertheless, by the late 1960s the report's recommendations had largely been implemented.[6]

The event is an instructive example of a broader phenomenon. Both Scotland and Wales have lived under the severe economic problems of declining areas; both regions have received substantial government aid. However, this assistance has not been sufficient to remove

6 Anthony Sampson, *The Anatomy of Britain*, pp. 580 ff.; Richard Caves and associates, *Britain's Economic Prospects*, p. 408.

disparities, and the administration of programmes has at times given rise to new tensions. The regions also suffer from depopulation, and other social problems which are either unique to these peripheries, or especially prominent within them.[7]

A third problem, different in turn from those of administrative paradox and central/local conflict, concerns the choice between universality and selectivity in social welfare. The centre/local disagreement is a function of economic planning; its tension results from the issue of how to determine assistance for economically peripheral areas. To the centre, national economic efficiency is the basic goal. To the periphery, such a goal may be desirable but surely not if it is asked to pay a heavy price to purchase national gains. The universality/selectivity conflict is a function of welfare-state activity; its tension results from the issue of how best to aid economically peripheral groups. The pristine model of the centrally planned economy sacrifices such groups to the prime goal of productivity. The welfare state, at least theoretically, is supposed to include them in its aid. The debate in centre/locality or centre/periphery discussion turns on whether or not either social altruism or a local economic perspective should be allowed to overcome the national economic perspective of the planners. The debate in universality/selectivity discussion turns on how best to provide benefits which have already been generally agreed upon as the policy goal.

Universal benefits refers to a system in which social services are provided uniformly to the entire population, or at least to a sector of the population which is not singled out on the basis of need. Selectivity, again as the title implies, seeks to aim available aid to those most in need. It has the administrative advantage of focusing on the very poorest, those who need help most. At the same time, it has the concomitant political disadvantage of likely unpopularity, since the loyalty of the majority is difficult to maintain. Because selective programmes usually lack support, they run two risks aside from the obvious one of outright

7 See., *e.g.*, Gavin McCrone, *Scotland's Future – The Economics of Nationalism, passim.*

abolition. First, they tend to degenerate in quality. As one poverty analyst stated categorically, 'Generally, services for the poor become poor services.'[8] Second, they tend to be turned into programmes which aid not the poor, but the comparatively prosperous majority. In other words, they are transformed from selective to non-selective vehicles of aid.[9] Universal programmes, in contrast, have the political advantage of wide popular acceptance, but combine that with the administrative disadvantage of either excluding the poor from the start or being altered to do so later on. Whether the structure chosen is broad universality or has the special differentiation of selectivity, those most in need are most likely to be neglected.

Generally, the British have sacrificed the potential administrative strengths of selectivity for the universal approach to social services. At least to some extent, they have experienced the tendency of this type of system to result in the exclusion from public benefits of some of the neediest sectors of society. An excellent example of this is the manner in which the British housing subsidy programme has worked. The Milner Holland Committee, which reported in 1965, testified that council housing – public housing owned by local units of government – in fact aided primarily the fairly well-off sectors of society. Council tenants, as well as owner-occupiers, were given large subsidies, even when they were not poor by any reasonable definition of that term. Tenants of privately owned housing, however, were excluded from the subsidy programme; yet the Milner Holland group found, on balance, that these tenants contained a higher proportion of the very poor than either of the other categories.[10]

Inferentially, this result is a reflection of the obvious point that those with higher incomes often have greater political influence than those who are less affluent, and so are able further to increase their prosperity. At the same

8 Charles I. Schottland, 'Public Assistance', in Samuel H. Beer and Richard E. Barringer, eds, *The State and the Poor*, p. 103.

9 Milton Friedman, *Capitalism and Freedom*, p. 194.

10 Caves, *op. cit.*, p. 15; Brian Lapping, *The Labour Government 1964-1970*, pp. 170-1.

time, the British housing subsidy programme is a good example of the ways in which the political ideologies which inform collectivist politics can work against the very goals to which they formally aspire. The Milner Housing Committee recommended that steps be taken to make housing subsidies more rational. The Labour Government of Harold Wilson was, however, extremely reluctant to implement the necessary changes because of important elements in party doctrine. According to Socialist ethos, landlords are automatically 'bad' and council housing 'good'. Hence, to supply, or even appear to supply, subsidies which somehow aided private landlords would create considerable turmoil within the Labour Party. The managers of the Labour Government were entirely aware of how the housing situation could be improved, but equally conscious of the political difficulty of making significant reforms in the face of the attitudes of the party rank-and-file.[11]

The Politics of Bureaucracy

Political factors are clearly in evidence in a case such as this, working obviously and strongly to deflect administrative rationality from the course it would probably take were such politics not part of the calculus. But, in fact, political influence invades administrative decision-making at all levels and in all forms of decision. It is certainly not to be slighted when examining any or all of the three types of bureaucratic tension discussed above: administrative paradox, central/local conflict, universality/ selectivity conflict. Politics in bureaucracy can be internal, a phenomenon considered in the administrative paradox. Crozier examines it specifically and in conceptual detail when he describes the development of internal isolation and parallel power relationships, and the essentially political conditions of dependence and control which result from them. More broadly, administrative organizations develop their own political goals and purposes, relying on their

11 Lapping, *op. cit.*, p. 171.

technical expertise to gain leverage. Political influence can be external too, through the impact of political parties and interest groups. The need by parties of electoral support, and the need by government of pressure-group allies in order to gain support and expertise, means that administration can be doubly affected by outside influences. First, administrative goals are defined in the light of political-electoral considerations. Second, even when this is not the case, the power and degree of access of British interest groups in collectivist politics puts them in a good position to deflect patterns of administration toward their desired end. When a particular bureaucracy lacks sufficient special expertise or political skill to protect its independence and assert its will, these external interests have an opportunity to gain access and influence.

Following Beer's analysis, a division can be made between party and interest-group influence as it relates to the welfare state and to the planned economy. To gain votes at elections, parties must successfully woo the electorate. They are required to 'bid' with 'consumer groups' for support. In modern Britain, where two large parties are fairly evenly matched and characteristically have battled fiercely for a rather small floating vote, the bidding process is obviously very intense. The bidding vehicle is the welfare state. The planned economy requires the co-operation and expert knowledge of 'producer groups', and so the Government of the day must 'bargain' with them for loyalty and assistance, keeping all the while a wary eye on its rival shadow in the opposite party. Again, because of the great amount of central planning in modern Britain, and the need for the planned economy to work well enough to provide political success, the incentive for bargaining to succeed is very great from the point of view of the political élites in power.[12]

It should not be assumed that two completely different physical populations and policy areas are implied by the labels 'consumer groups' and 'producer groups'. Rather, many of the same groups and policies are being divided

12 Beer, *op. cit.*, Chapter 12.

according to different roles. Such operations as the National Health Service do seem to be almost exclusively welfare-state functions, and their services are of such a basic nature in today's Britain that they are unlikely to be seriously compromised for reasons of economic planning. On the other hand, Beer notes that such policy fields as taxation can be viewed as falling into either social welfare or economic planning categories, depending upon which effects of tax policy are selected for examination. The difference between the two types of group, producer and consumer, is found not in their compositions but in the ways they make their influence felt. The lever of producer groups is functional representation through the executive; the lever by which consumer groups are won is party government through Parliament. The former includes access of groups directly into administrative decision-making, the latter the discipline imposed on MPs by party leadership sensitive to public opinion.[13]

There is a solidity, a rigidity to this series of arrangements which guarantees that there will be powerful opponents to virtually any alteration in major public policies. Election considerations and the self-serving influence of pressure groups constantly impose themselves over what seems to make good economic or administrative sense. For instance, an energetic government incomes policy is – at least in theory – one way to control the sort of rapid inflation which has plagued Britain in its recent history; but the hostility of trade unions to such a step has consistently prevented successive Governments from pursuing wage-control efforts for more than brief periods. Similarly, private investment, a requirement for economic health, can be encouraged through braking consumption; but through most of the fairly recent past the need to win elections has prevented British Governments from limiting consumption in a drastic manner.[14] It was this state of affairs which led Beer to suggest in a 1955 essay that British politics might be reaching such a high state of organization that movement in *any* direction in public policy innovation

13 *Ibid.*, Chapter 3.
14 *Ibid.*, pp. 421-6.

might soon require virtual unanimity among the interest groups involved. He repeated this point more explicitly in a 1969 essay in which he argued that the cost of modern British party government and functional representation is 'immobilism', 'pluralistic stagnation' – terms which describe themselves.[15]

There is no doubt that most, if not all, of the large, established economic interest groups prefer this *status quo* to the uncertainties of political decentralization. To decentralize, after all, is to disperse and multiply the doors which need opening, to require interest groups to build new avenues of access. In addition, *national* interest groups are more likely to find themselves in tune with the views of *central* – i.e., *national* – administrators than with local officials. Both public and private decision-makers on the national level are likely to have the same perspectives on economic decisions. They both are struck by the national costs and benefits of policies; particular local costs and benefits are less visible. Local councillors are likely to object strongly to industrial air and water pollution, damaged landscapes, ugly buildings and other fixtures. National bureaucrats are likely to value strongly the broad economic benefits derived from the very industries and utilities which produce obnoxious local by-products. Local councillors have to live amidst the environmental waste. National planners are charged with raising productivity. This argument is out of tune with the conventional wisdom of American party-political liberalism, at least until recently, that central government could be counted on to be more progressive, less tied to special interests and parochial habits, than local government. It is nevertheless supported by persuasive empirical evidence. Though they testified separately before the Royal Commission on Local Government in 1967, the National Chamber of Trade, Aims of Industry, and the Manchester Chamber of Commerce all concurred that the prime shortcoming of local government was the 'almost total absence' of the voice of industry and commerce on local councils. In 1959, in a

15 *Ibid*., pp. 408-9; Samuel Beer, 'The Future of British Politics: An American View', *Political Quarterly*, January/March 1955, pp. 33-42.

parallel point, the Federation of British Industries opposed the town of Halifax's attempt to take water management out of the hands of a ministerially appointed board and place it under the control of a board appointed by Halifax Council. The Federation maintained that such a board could not possibly be 'fully representative' of the local interests which they serve'[16]

Trade unions have echoed management groups in opposing devolution of regulatory authority to local government. They have expressed fears that local businessmen will have too much influence on local councils. Among other instances, this issue arose during discussions in 1963 over the advisability of the Offices, Shops and Railways Premises Act, a proposal to maintain uniform minimum working conditions. Both management and labour joined in urging that this regulation should take place through national bodies rather than entrusting its supervision to local authorities. More generally, both sides in industry seem to have reached firm *de facto* agreement that nationally uniform standards of regulation are best for them, and that this procedure is only achievable through using national institutions.[17] Naturally, thanks to established structures of functional representation, producer groups are also in a good position to influence the forms such standards assume.

These attitudes within institutions of national government, and in the groups which influence them, have important negative consequences for particular sectors of society and sections of the nation. Reviewing qualities of central/local and universality/selectivity choice will aid in making this point. Producer groups have a strong incentive to urge central perspectives in economic planning. First, producer groups themselves tend to be national in structure; thus, planning centralized in large bureaucracies in London is made to order for their influence and persuasion. Parallel structures make access easier. Second, since, as has been said, producer groups tend to have a

16 Howard Scarrow, 'Policy Pressures and Initiatives by British Local Government: The Case of Regulation in the "Public Interest" ', p. 19.

17 *Ibid.*, pp. 19-20.

national orientation as well, even without pressure from them a national focus in public planning activity is more likely to be in accord with their wishes. In a similar manner, broad-based consumer groups have an interest in securing universal welfare programmes. The bulk of the electorate is not poor. If welfare programmes were strictly selective, in simple terms, the vast majority of the population – and of the electorate – would be excluded. Universality, therefore, is the politically wise course.

Thus, the two circles are complete. Parties bid for votes through a universalist approach to the welfare state, backed by strong discipline to ensure the passage of programmes. Universality is more popular with the great majority of voters. Governments bargain with producer groups for support while relying basically on a central outlook in planning. A central perspective is the one favoured by producer groups, as well as being most likely to please *most* of the electorate. The broad influences of politics neatly reinforce administrative universality over selectivity and centrality over locality.

By definition, this general approach to public policy ensures that some sections and sectors of the nation are relegated to secondary status. Certain regions, notably Scotland and Wales, are hurt by programmes such as Beeching, which are designed to assist the economy as a whole. Universal welfare programmes tend to overlook at least some of the very poor – and, unlike selective approaches, can do so quietly from the start – as has been the experience of at least some sectors of the British housing subsidy programme. Of course, these pictures have been overdrawn for emphasis. There have been significant selective social welfare and regional development programmes, especially in more recent years. The point is that generally dominant trends in the planned economy and the welfare state have created instruments for the exclusion and frustration of some, along with subsidy and security for most.

The Liberal Role

Those left out of most of the benefits of planning because of their location or out of the subsidy of the welfare state in spite of their poverty obviously have a marked incentive for hostility to the *status quo*, and for advocacy of or sympathy with radical reform. One potential political home and base for these groups would be the Liberal Party. The party, because of its marked separation from collectivism, has been especially sensitive to the problems of both the sections and the sectors excluded from the political and administrative calculus of modern British politics and administration. Liberalism, after all, as a particularly individualistic philosophy, is consequently sensitive to diversity, and based on the desirability of autonomy. It is natural, therefore, for the good Liberal to put the needs of particular local units at the *centre* of his perspective, and to put assistance for the very needy before abstract conceptions of equality. John Stuart Mill defended a complex – some might say absurdly complex – system of proportional representation in order that every individual might be counted as an independent factor in the electoral calculator. This is the drive of a Liberal – or, more strictly and pristinely, of a Radical.[18] Very different are the rigidly egalitarian and righteous class conceptions explicit in Labour doctrine, or the natural inequality implicit in the values of any good Tory.

Yet the neglected peripheries of collectivist Britain, social and geographic, have not yet sponsored a solid, reliable, large-scale electoral revival for the Liberal Party, no matter how much they may have contributed to a more extensive revival of Liberal policy and activist styles. Several factors appear to be important here. The Liberal Party has stressed local social work and voluntarism, particularly in very recent years; but this has not rebounded directly to the benefit of the party. The poor generally are comparatively inactive politically, and their efforts are often seriously

18 The reference is to the Hare system of proportional representation, defended by Mill.

hindered by lack of political sophistication. Moreover, while the human dimension of poverty in modern Britain may be marked, the poor remain a minority of the population. They are not only a minority, but also a relatively dispersed one. Deprived sections of cities are frequently swallowed up, in electoral terms, by the more prosperous areas which surround them.

In addition, the Liberal Party has not succeeded in identifying with the peripheral regions of the nation sufficiently to establish majority strength there. Tory and Labour have remained far stronger than the Liberals, and recent gains by the Scottish and Welsh nationalists have further overshadowed them. Rather than being based in the 'Celtic Fringe', the Liberal Party's recent electoral revivals have occurred across the nation.[19]

An important element, broader in scope and implications than either centre-local or universality-selectivity choices, is related to the problem of administrative paradox or the vicious circle of bureaucracy; the ironic situation in which efforts at administrative rationality undermine themselves, and in consequence stimulate public discontent and lack of confidence. A less specific related incentive for voter rebellion is that the very sense of distance and insensitivity created by large bureaucratic organizations can foster public unhappiness and hostility to the way things work even when administrative routine remains 'rational' – i.e., not greatly afflicted by the sort of political independence which worried Weber or the more specific internal problems defined by Crozier.

Ultimately, each of the three problems of contemporary public policy outlined earlier is useful to an understanding of the Liberal Party's revival. Each helps explain the electoral advances of the party and the intellectual stimulus experienced by policy, though a complete discussion of recent party history requires consideration of other factors as well. All three issues – administrative paradox, central/

19 This lack of particularly strong sectional identification has been the normal position of the British Liberals, but puts them in contrast with other third parties in Commonwealth countries. See Leon Epstein, *Political Parties in Western Democracies*, p. 70.

local tension, and universal/selective tension, doubtless have played roles in drawing activists to the party. The Liberals, in both theory and practice resistant to central authority, are an obvious natural home for those antagonistic to modern collectivism. All three, and especially the second and third, have been important also as spurs to the generation and regeneration of Liberal policy during the Grimond years. The administrative paradox of collectivism encourages general interest in decentralization; the more explicit tensions associated with collectivism focus attention on policy alternatives involving devolution of political power and selectivity in public services. In fact, during the Grimond years a number of writers and scholars were drawn to the party as a vehicle for 'breaking out' of what were seen to be increasingly rigid, unimaginative trends in public policy-making.

The general public, and even some Liberals, may see the party as an odd, irrelevant, and even at times comical survivor of an age which ended long ago. It does not fit in with the spirit, the organization, the attitudes of modern collectivism. But it is this very quality which connects the Liberal Party to collectivist politics. In one aspect at least it is a peripheral party representing the interests of peripheral and neglected segments of the population. It has also served to define the problems which have accompanied collectivist politics, as well as reflecting some of the popular hostility which those problems have generated.

This implies the broadest reason for the continuing survival, and recent revival, of the Liberal Party. In the period after the Second World War, the consistent growth of prosperity in most Western nations, the apparent lack of energy in many formerly strong ideological political parties, and the refinement of management and administration as a specialized and arcane approach to decision-making encouraged a belief that severe domestic political conflicts and tensions were becoming a thing of the past. This was the position of those social scientists who predicted an 'end' to 'ideology'.[20] The recent experience of

20 See, *e.g.*, James Christoph, 'Consensus and Cleavage in British Political Ideology', *American Political Science Review*, September 1965, pp. 629-42.

the Liberal Party, and the somewhat comparable growth in importance of sectional issues and small protest parties and groups in other Western nations, is an argument for the proposition that politics remains something very much more than administration.[21] Politics interferes with bureaucratic procedures and charts of organization. The bureaucratic process itself tends to be self-defeating. Beyond this, the difference in values between various groups and sections in the population implies that the removal of some points of political conflict will only open the door to others.

The fact that politics is inevitable means that organizations to represent particular viewpoints on the political landscape are to be expected. The amalgamation of different political groups, the blurring of differences and the muting of quarrels between groups which were once clear enemies, the abolition of differences which were once a basis for division are all developments which indicate that a basis has been laid for new divisions between old foes or new combinations among political participants. If existing political parties are unable to represent the new calculus, then new parties or other popular formations should be expected to develop.

The limited electoral success which the Liberal Party, after almost total eclipse, has enjoyed under Grimond and, more recently, Jeremy Thorpe, at least suggests that the party has drawn to itself currents of changing political sentiment which the two major parties have been unable to accommodate. Yet, so far, the Liberals have themselves failed to capitalize on their new advances sufficiently to catapult into national political power. The party was not able even consistently to hold the gains, in image and votes, won under Grimond's leadership. Understanding the reasons for this requires a detailed examination of the various elements vying for political support in a nation undergoing important social changes. Additionally, closer attention should be paid to the incentives for discontent which can fuel a new party or other political group. As long

21 Prominent sectional problems: Brittany, Quebec, Flanders and the Walloons in Belgium.

as there is diversity within a population, there will be sectors which feel that the administration under which they live is more a curse than a blessing, more a pain than a pleasure. However, the problems of administrative paradox, central/local and universal/selective choice provide more specific foci for analysis.

Liberal Gains

The Liberal Party is an important indicator of discontent with the two-party *status quo*, but how significant has growth in support for the party been? Counting votes is one basic and preliminary index of progress and regress, but only partial. This is particularly so in the case of the Liberal Party, whose ethos in this respect was well represented by one activist who reflected during an interview: 'but what do votes mean anyway?'

Understanding the recent gains of the Liberals is an uncertain process, requiring examination of some vague evidence. Part of the explanation for the Liberal appeal can be found in the apparent fatigue of the major parties in the late 1950s and early 1960s. A symbolic representation of this comes from an odd source. *The Guardian Report* of the 1962 Liberal Assembly – the booklet which that newspaper used to publish after every conference of each of the three main parties – has, on its cover, a cartoon of the speakers' platform at the Liberal gathering. Naturally, Jo Grimond, the party leader, sits with the rest of the Liberal notables at a table on the stage. But Grimond's mind is clearly elsewhere. He isn't listening to the debate. Instead, he daydreams. In his dream, which is diagrammed over his head for the reader's benefit, he is skipping through a summer field with a young woman, who bears the significant label, 'Europe' (the Liberals were early advocates of British entry into the Common Market). Behind them is a fence, which has clearly been no barrier for Grimond and his companion. But a tired, dishevelled, very old-seeming Prime Minister, Harold Macmillan, has just barely managed to surmount that fence, and an exhausted Hugh Gaitskell, leader of the Labour Party at the time, still struggles to climb over it. It is obviously problematical whether or not he is going to make it.[22]

Silly, perhaps, but the drawing also seems to symbolize aptly, as much as anything might, the spirit of the Liberal Party's revival under Jo Grimond. It was not exactly a dream, for the party did enjoy in the 1960s a measurable increase in its appeal to the British electorate. But it was not entirely a concrete electoral reality, either, for the revival's most impressive aspects are found elsewhere – public visibility, policy definition, activist support. In hard electoral terms, the revival seemed always more a matter of mood and future promise than concrete success, and by the end of Grimond's term as leader the promise had definitely faded. Predictions about how well the party was going to do constantly outran actual election performance. If a case can be made for a significant Liberal Party revival during this period, it is in the area of ideas and policy. It was a real development, which can be measured and evaluated, but not with the concreteness of election returns. They only partially mirrored these more subtle and vague movements.

Aside from the problems of trying to come to grips with qualities as abstract as these, there is the fundamental logical problem that the Liberal Party revival – in decisive party realignment terms – was an event which did not occur under Grimond and remained highly problematical under Thorpe. The party had significantly increased its vote, and had seen its MPs grow somewhat in numbers, but has not yet replaced one of the major parties. It was not surprising that the Thorpe period ended in frustration for the party, as the Grimond decade did. In dealing with the political fate of the Liberals, there is the basic problem that it is quite impossible logically to prove why an event did *not* happen. Yet, with social issues and political history, it is possible to make informed inferences, intelligent inductions. The Liberal Party's revival has occurred to a measurable extent in general and other election returns, though it has failed to reach the peaks of success predicted by some, and hoped for by determined loyalists. Moreover, ideas may be nebulous,

22 *Liberal Assembly 1962, The* Guardian *Report,* front cover.

but policy-making is a fairly concrete activity – and one to which British political parties give some importance. Innovations from a party in the area of ideas would presumably provoke discussion groups, pamphlets and books, and academic interest. This kind of evidence would provide a base for examining the hypothesis of a large number of Liberals that the party served as a source of 'new ideas' during the Grimond period.

Table 2:1 Liberal Performance at General Elections, 1945-74

Year	Seats Won	No of Candidates	Popular Vote	% of Total Vote	Votes Per Candidate
1945	12	305	2,222,322	8·9	7,286·3
1950	9	475	2,621,489	9·1	5,518·9
1951	6	109	730,551	2·6	6,702·3
1955	6	110	722,395	2·7	6,567·2
1959	6	216	1,640,761	5·9	7,596·1
1964	9	365	3,092,878	11·2	8,473·6
1966	12	311	2,327,470	8·6	7,483·8
1970	6	332	2,117,638	7·5	6,378·4
1974 (Feb)	14	517	6,056,713	19·3	11,715·6
1974 (Oct)	13	619	5,321,477	18·3	8,919·9

Tables such as Table 2:1 are handy tools for rationalization and self-deception as well as prediction. Properly tinkered with and analysed, statistics have been used for years to make the case that the Liberal Party revival has been taking place with such force that it is about to bring about a basic realignment of the national political parties. For instance, it can be stressed that in 1964 the party was able to poll approximately 25 per cent of the vote given to each of the major parties, even though it offered candidates in only about one-half of the parliamentary constituencies. The two 1974 general elections were even more impressive. The party mustered far more candidates than for any other general election of the post-war period, and in February almost tripled its popular vote.

Nevertheless, the general election returns have been most impressive in a mathematical sense removed from politics. The electoral system has operated as a significant drag on the number of Liberal MPs actually elected. The momentum of 1964 did not continue. It is uncertain whether the party will be able to build upon and maintain the gains of 1974, but clearly the expectations raised in February were frustrated in October of that year. The party has not yet 'broken through' into the status of a major party, able to compete on consistently equal terms with the Tories and Labour.

What, therefore, led to those expectations of and speculation about a national party revival in the 1960s? Different, primarily abstract, factors contributed – Grimond's personality, the association of the party with 'new ideas', a detectable public malaise concerning politics in general. These important elements correlated with more concrete political progress in public opinion polls, local election returns, parliamentary by-election results. Compared with general elections, by-elections have been less constricted by habit and class patterns of voting, more open to innovative pressures. While the Liberal revival is most interesting and significant in areas where it had the least bearing on the concrete fortunes of the party, that changing party fate does provide a foundation and base for many of the other elements. Evidence which is more solid to the eye than the quality of leadership or new ideas is reassuring as well as reinforcing.

Throughout the slack 1950s, the occasional good showing in a by-election supplied party workers with some reason for keeping the faith. Since a Liberal almost never finished first, necessity dictated receiving solace from second place. A strong second place ahead of Labour at the Inverness by-election of 1954, for example, received considerable praise in the party press. Similar statistical progress was noted at Torquay in 1955; Hereford, Taunton and Gainsborough in 1956; and Rochdale in 1958, where a television personality, Ludovic Kennedy, was second. Also in 1958, the Liberals at last won the victory to which Inverness and Rochdale had been preludes. The month following Kennedy's excellent run. Mark Bonham Carter, a London publisher, brother-in-law of Grimond, grandson of Asquith, won the Torrington by-election, taking the seat away from the Tories by slightly over 200 votes of the 35,000 cast. The narrowness of the victory, which was in fact reversed in the general election of the following year, was overshadowed by the immense fact that the Liberals had won their first by-election since 1929. Alan Watkins notes in his narrative on the modern Liberal Party that 'it would be difficult to exaggerate the effect of the Torrington results on Liberal morale'.[23] Lady Asquith, Bonham Carter's mother, recalled later that her feelings at the time were profound: 'I had the strange sense of being a member of an army of liberation entering occupied territory which for years had been ruled by quislings and collaborators and that their day was over.'[24] Her melodramatic remarks capture the intensity and uncompromising zeal which are no doubt essential in remaining a small-party stalwart. Beyond this, her attitude was not entirely unreasonable. The 1959 general election witnessed notable Liberal popular advance. The electoral stage was set for the more noticed and noticeable Liberal upswing of the early 1960s, a surge which culminated in the 1964 general election.

Throughout this period, the Liberals did well in parliamentary by-elections, as Table 2:2 indicates. While Liberals between 1959 and 1963 placed in a profile which reflected returns of the 1955-1959 period, they fought over twice as many elections. Liberals, moreover, won two by-elections, Montgomery and Orpington. The more significant of the two was the latter, held in March 1962. Eric Lubbock, the Liberal victor, was a resident of the constituency and served on the local council. His victory, in which a Tory majority of over 14,000 was transformed into a Liberal majority of nearly 8,000, seemed to confirm the suggestion that the Liberal Party was emerging into a bright political future.

The nature of the Orpington constituency was especially

23 Alan Watkins, *The Liberal Dilemma*, p. 90.

24 Matthew Coody, 'Exit Jo, Enter Jeremy', *New Statesman*, 20 January 1967, p. 66.

Table 2:2 Liberals and By-election Results, 1951-70

	1951-5	1955-9	1959-63	1964-70	1971-4
Total by-elections	14	53	55	51	28
Percentage fought by Liberals	17	40	85	72	61
Percentage of Liberals losing deposits	88	5	4	29	28
Liberal order of finish (in percentages)					
1st	0	5	4	4	30
2nd	12	33	36	14	20
3rd	88	62	60	76	30
4th	0	0	0	6	20
	100	100	100	100	100

Source: Austin Ranney, *Pathways to Parliament*, for figures up to 1963; 1964-74 compiled from the 1966, 1970 and 1974 editions of *The Times Guide to the House of Commons*. The increase in fourth places is probably a reflection of the impact of the nationalist parties, and perhaps of a greater willingness of Liberals to fight hopeless seats.

important in creating optimism within the party. Since the Liberal Party's initial collapse as a major political force, pockets of remaining relative strength had been primarily within rural 'Celtic Fringe' areas of Scotland and Wales. Orpington, however, was a constituency very different from these largely agricultural areas of residual Liberal sentiment. It is a suburban area, part of the London commuter belt. As this implies, the district is largely white collar, middle-class, executive and professional in composition. In short, instead of winning only in declining, peripheral traditional sections of the country, the Liberals had won handily in a growth area. Given the concrete drama of Orpington, it was easy for party spirits to soar –

which they did, instantly. For the Liberals, as for the *Economist*, the question became: 'How many Orpingtons?'[25] 'Orpington Man' became the title for a new kind of voter, classless and untied from old voting habits, turning away from old-fashioned Tory and Labour conceptions and drawn to the Liberal Party.

In the Montgomery by-election during May of the same year, made necessary by the death of the former party leader, Clement Davies, the Liberal candidate made the issue of a growing Liberal Party revival the centrepiece of his campaign. He was warned not to do so, to rely instead on the continuity of the party's Celtic history and avoid the unsteady new patterns which the party's leadership was trying to create. He refused, and in consequence the Liberals' retention of the seat with an increased margin looked more like a *new* victory, reinforcing the high spirits created by Orpington.[26] If Orpington seemed to point to a profitable future, Montgomery implies the party was increasing its hold on its own past.

All this was prelude to the 1964 general election, the high point of the Liberal Party's electoral revival in that decade. A massive party effort was mounted, fuelled by new resources and manpower which the revival had supplied. The vote total of the party was increased impressively. The artificial declared party goal of 3 million votes was reached. But only a few more MPs were elected. In 1966, the further marginal increase in MPs was more than overshadowed by the decline in the party's total vote and the end of the razor-thin balance between the Labour majority and the Opposition parties in the House of Commons.[27] Additionally, the by-election story was very different after 1964, as Table 2:2 again indicates. During the last half of the 1960s, Liberal candidates won two by-elections – Roxburgh, Selkirk & Peebles in 1965; and Ladywood (Birmingham) in 1969. Neither, however, was part of a

25 The *Economist*, 24 March, 1962, p. 1090.

26 *Liberal News*, No 833, 26 May 1962, p. 2.

27 *Cf.* David Butler and Anthony King, *The British General Election of 1966*, especially p. 84.

national swelling of support for the party. Each, rather, was a fascinating, but unique, electoral experience.

During the early 1970s, with a Tory regime again in power, the Liberals showed signs of progress and scored notable parliamentary by-election victories – Rochdale, Sutton & Cheam, Ripon, Ely, Berwick-upon-Tweed.[28] The Liberal performance in the two 1974 general elections was in some ways extraordinarily good. Yet comparatively few MPs were elected, and the nationalists and some independents also did well; the Scottish Nationalists more than doubled their popular vote in February, and became the second party in Scotland in October with 30 per cent of the vote.

During the 1950s and 1960s, along with advances in parliamentary elections and public attention, the Liberal Party was also scoring successes in local government elections. A reversal in what had been a constant decline in Liberal Party representation on borough, urban district and county councils began at approximately the same time that parliamentary by-election improvement was noticeable at Inverness. The very first signs of new strength in local government, however, were visible as early as 1949 in Blackpool. Starting at that time with only two Liberal local councillors, the party gained steadily, if slowly, until reaching a total of 16 councillors in 1954.[29] One academic researcher, on the basis of a sample of local-election returns, has calculated that the Liberals reached a nadir in local support in 1952. From that low point, the party recovered at least marginally in 1953 and continued to build upward from there.[30]

Table 2:3 charts the limited, but detectable, Liberal advance, as well as the end of that advance in 1964. There was a comparatively great surge in Liberal councillors elected during the years 1958 to 1963, in rough correspondence with the period of very great speculation

28 See the *Economist*, 4 August 1973, pp. 19-20.

29 *Liberal News*, No 415, 21 May, 1954, pp. 1, 4.

30 William Wallace, *The Liberal Revival – The Liberal Party in Britain, 1955-1966*, unpublished Ph.D. thesis, p. 13.

Table 2:3 Net Gains and Losses in Borough, Urban District,
and County Council Elections

Year	Conservatives and Supporters	Labour	Independents	Liberals
1947	+787 (bors. only)	−661	−105	−9
1948	+320 (urb. dists. only)	−159	−148	−6
1949	+1,615	−1,172	−345	−59
1950	+258	+12	−238	−34
1951	+220	−37	−169	−14
1952	−1,058	+1,404	−320	−28
1953	−213	+319	−94	−12
1954	−442	+544	−95	−7
1955	+790	−830	+32	+7
1956	−260	+297	−48	+7
1957	−267	+260	−20	+27
1958	−690	+661	−48	+76
1959	+321	−379	+25	+33
1960	+554	−640	+4	+82
1961	+449	−643	0	+192
1962	−841	+391	−78	+527
1963	−807	+760	−117	+169
1964	−329	+567	−128	−112
1965	+901	−590	−43	−267
1966	+400	−287	−59	−54
1967	+1,373	−1,410	−41	+39
1968	+1,630	−1,602	−24	−20
1969	+955	−899	−63	+3
1970	−352	+645	−203	−70
1971	−2,349	+2,613	−199	−40
1972	−1,193	+1,390	−163	−27
1973	Total councillors elected under new local government system of counties, metropolitan districts, non-metropolitan districts.			
	7,781	8,442	3,940	1,377 (6%)
1972	Total councillors elected under former system.			
	1,575	2,607	916	266 (5%)

Source: Conservative Central Office. Figures exclude Scotland.
County elections were held 1949, 1952, 1958, 1961, 1964, 1967,
1970 and 1973.

about national Liberal Party revival, and in rough correlation with the party's peak in parliamentary by-election showings. In 1962, the year of Orpington, the Liberals ran 40 per cent more candidates than in 1961, and made spectacular gains. Significantly, many of the party's victories, both in the 1962 local elections and in preceding by-elections, came in suburban areas of the Orpington type. In Hendon South, the 1962 local election vote totals were as follows:

	%
Liberal	43
Conservative	36
Labour	21

In a by-election in February 1962 in one of the constituency's five wards, the Liberal vote increased from its May 1961 total of 26 per cent to 37 per cent. This ward voted 39 per cent Liberal in May 1962. Clearly, Liberal progress here, and presumably elsewhere, had been made before the Orpington by-election provided the party with even more momentum. Similar Liberal gains were registered in a number of the surburban areas around London, and in the southern suburb of greater Manchester.[31]

To keep the party totals in perspective, however, it should be borne in mind that at a peak of Liberal strength, just after the 1963 local elections, the party had a total number of councillors still considerably smaller than the totals of the major parties, or even of the unaffiliated independents. Table 2:4 shows this. Borough and urban district councillors – under the system predating the Maud Commission reforms – represented a minority of the total number elected to all the councils in Britain. Therefore, the Liberal strength was greater than indicated by this table, though boroughs and urban districts were among the more important types of councils.

Not all councillors have political affiliations, but many do. Moreover, small parish councils and rural district councils

31 *Liberal News Commentary*, 29 July, 1969, p. 4.

Table 2:4 Total Councillors Elected in 1963 Borough and Urban District Elections

Council Type	Cons. and Supporters	Lab.	Indep.	Liberal
Borough	973	1,733	524	255
Urban	653	992	704	174
Totals	1,626	2,725	1,228	429

Source: Conservative Central Office.

were – for paradoxical reasons of tradition and accessibility to small parties – probably more heavily endowed with Liberals than the borough and urban district councils. Sidney Hope, a long-time Liberal Party activist, has calculated that during the peak of the Liberal revival in local government, in early 1964, there were 1,885 Liberal councillors and aldermen on all councils in Britain, compared with an estimated 475 in 1959. Certainly, the party had made significant gains in relation to its own recent past. Moreover, the gains were largely maintained: the Liberal Local Government Office calculated that – before the recent Maud reforms – approximately 1,400 Liberal councillors remained in office. This Liberal Party accomplishment is especially impressive in view of the statement by Pratap Chitnis, soon after taking office in 1960 as the party's Local Government Officer, that generally Liberals are unwilling to run for local office under the party label, preferring to call themselves 'Independents' instead. But it must be kept in mind, when trying to see the Liberal Party's revival in its proper political context, that the party never approached, in any type of council, the massive totals of either of the two major parties.

During the second half of the 1960s, there was growth in Liberal Party strength in what are usually strong Labour areas. In the late 1950s and early 1960s, the Liberals had made their big gains primarily in Tory areas, most dramatically in commuter suburbs. With the election of a Labour majority to Parliament in 1964, however, Liberal appeal within the electorate detectably shifted its base. In 1965, the party newspaper reported that local elections in that year seemed to indicate a movement from Labour to Liberal in some industrial areas of the North.[32] The *Economist* detected a similar trend the following year in the wake of the local government elections, noting that Liberal strength was divided between 'Orpington-type votes which they have held on to (Cheadle, Eastbourne, and Sutton Coldfield) and one-time Labour strongholds where they have made recent progress'.[33] The Liberals made their most dramatic gains in the traditionally Labour cities of Birmingham, Liverpool and Leeds, and in Greenock in Scotland. In 1966 Liberals took control of the Greenock council, although there had been no seats there in the hands of the party as recently as 1960. Progress in the other cities was slower and more modest. The first Liberal councillor was elected in Birmingham in 1962; by 1973 there were 9 on the council. Leeds Liberals grew from 3 seats in 1968 to 14 in 1973. Developments in Liverpool were more dramatic. A Liberal was elected in 1962, but the party revival did not really get underway until 1968. In 1973 the Liberals, though falling short of an overall majority, did take a plurality of the seats on the Liverpool council.[34] In sum, these local election gains are impressive mainly when viewed of the context of what had gone before. The party's growth in each case has followed situations of literally no Liberal councillors, and little or no Liberal organization. While small in absolute numbers, the election of these Liberal councillors nevertheless moved Francis Boyd of the *Guardian* to declare: 'Those who know the party history of these cities understand the miracle of the Liberals' return.'[35]

32 *Liberal News*, No 989, 21 May, 1965, p. 1.

33 The *Economist*, 21 May, 1966, p. 834.

34 The *Economist*, 19 May, 1973, pp. 30-1.

35 William Shannon, 'A Letter From Brighton – Part One: The Liberal Party Conference', p. 7.

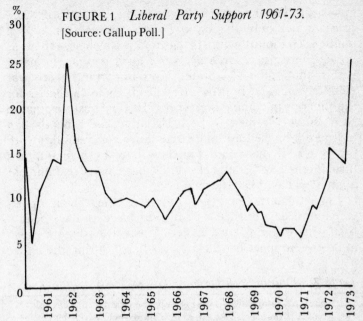

FIGURE 1 *Liberal Party Support 1961-73.*
[Source: Gallup Poll.]

There is a third measure of popular support for the Liberals, aside from the results of parliamentary and local elections – public opinion polls, the most abstract of the three measuring sticks, farthest from relationship to actual parliamentary power. This is where the Liberals have done their best during the peaks in the early 1960s and early 1970s. Neither the small increase in Liberal local councillors, nor the fractional increase in Liberal MPs, does justice to the extraordinary increase in support according to public opinion polls of 1962 and 1973. Figure 1 provides the Gallup Poll's registration of this trend. More dramatically, the National Opinion Poll discovered shortly after Orpington that a slight majority of the British electorate apparently favoured the Liberal Party as their choice if a general election were held 'tomorrow' (see Section I of Table 2:5). The most striking response of all was to a Gallup Poll of September 1962, which asked a question the organization had not put to voters since 1950: How would they vote if they thought the Liberals (1) would win a few seats, (2) would win a balance of power, (3) would win a majority? The responses (see Section II of Table 2:5) revealed not only the basic Liberal problem of lack of political credibility with the electorate which sees them as 'losers', but also a large degree of good will for the party within that same electorate. Most important, there was definitely marked improvement in all three categories for the Liberals in comparison with 1950. The post-Orpington NOP survey seemed to be a sign that the Liberals had indeed established an impressive degree of credibility with the voters. If this could somehow have been maintained through the next general election, a basic party realignment might well have been the outcome.

Unfortunately for the Liberals, the heady post-Orpington days turned out, in retrospect, to have been a brief peak in the party's career of revival. As Figure 1 also indicates, support for the Liberal Party during the entire

Table 2:5 Opinon Poll Data on Liberal Party Support

I	National Opinion Poll asking how the voter would cast his ballot if the election were held 'tomorrow', March 1962

Party	% supporting
Liberal	33·4
Labour	33·2
Conservative	32·4

II	Gallup Poll asking how the voter would cast his ballot if he thought the Liberals (1) would win a few seats, (2) would win a balance of power, (3) would win a majority.

Responses	% 'Yes' September 1962	% 'Yes' February 1950
Few seats	20	12
Balance held	37	28
Majority	41	31

III	Opinion Research Centre poll asking how the voter would vote at the next general election, October 1973.

Party	% supporting
Liberal	32
Labour	34
Conservative	31

period 1961-73 was considerably below the 1962 level,
hovering between approximately 5 per cent and 14 per cent.
This may have been well above the pit of decline of 1951
and 1955, when general election returns for the party
totalled only 2·6 per cent and 2·7 per cent of the popular
vote, but it was also a long distance from national power.
No general election was called in 1962, and this fragile,
dramatic moment of intense popular support for the
Liberals had been ended for some time when the governing
Conservative Party next went to the electorate in 1964.
Events of the immediate post-Orpington period reinforce
this sense that the escalation of popular support for the
Liberal Party was a sort of sudden, short-lived wave.
Perhaps the word 'fashion' describes most simply the
nature of a mood which resulted in the party being flooded
with volunteers to be candidates soon after Orpington. On
the day of the Orpington result, ten people, presumably on
impulse, asked to be Liberal candidates.[36] Spontaneously,
in an instant, the Liberal Party's revival was transformed
into a type of fad. A number of British celebrities
volunteered to be candidates for the party; many more
affiliated themselves, at least verbally, with the party. A
student of the phenomenon writes:[37]

> in a curious way Liberalism had become smart.
> Confessions like 'Oh, I'm a Liberal', delivered in a gay
> but defiant tone of voice, were to be heard at parties. And
> this increasing social (though not necessarily political)
> sophistication of the party was reflected in the choice of
> parliamentary candidates. Though there was nothing
> comparable to the pre-1959 influx of nationally-known
> 'personalities' – like Mr Ludovic Kennedy, Mr Robin
> Day and Miss Jacqueline Mackenzie, among others –
> there was a pronounced tendency for men and women in
> the more glamorous occupations to feel a sudden urge to
> stand as Liberal candidates.

This sort of image was hardly conducive to persuading
the electorate that the Liberal Party possessed substance

36 Watkins, *op. cit.*, p. 122.
37 *Ibid.*, p. 115.

and responsibility. Glamorous personalities newly recruited to the Liberal Party included Honor Blackman, the actress, who made some effective television appearances during the 1964 campaign. But generally the prominence of the party at parties contributed to the impression that the Liberal revival was a bubble, nothing more. Nevertheless, this particular phenomenon, while on balance not helpful, proved no more lasting than the earlier revival in votes and opinion poll support. The 1973-4 surge in opinion poll support, votes and general attention devoted to the party was not accompanied by the same sort of fashionable approval.

Victory and Defeat

What, finally, does this narrative of uncertain mixtures of success and failure outline in terms of causes and significance of the Liberal Party revival? When election returns, or even the more generous but nebulous public opinion polls, are examined, it is difficult to avoid the conclusion that the Liberal Party's revival may have taken place in quantitative terms, and may be leading to a party realignment; but that in the past it has been primarily – again by quantitative measures – a story of frustration, failure, defeat. The party has enjoyed impressive gains in public support; but it has been most dramatic in opinion polls, a clear step removed from the elections which bring political power. Overall, Liberals have done worst in general elections, when the largest portion of the electorate turns out to vote and the vast bulk of MPs for a particular Parliament are elected.

Yet analysis in the mass media did not see the Liberal Party's revival under Grimond as non-existent, but rather as a happening of some significance for British politics in the 1960s. Contrast, for example, the two following statements, the first from the *Economist* in 1946, the second from *The Times* in 1967:[38]

38 The *Economist*, 23 March, 1946, p. 447; *The Times*, 18 January, 1967, p. 12.

Plans for the reorganization of the Liberal Party, with an Appendix on Policy Making, look rather like the cart before the horse. The right way round would be first to discover whether there is a consistent body of thought that will be accepted by the public as a vital alternative to Socialism or Toryism ... Liberalism is more in need of a prophet than a director.

At one time it was possible to envisage a House of Commons without the Liberal Party, and to view the prospect without undue dismay. It is no longer so. By their independence of spirit, and their separation from 'the usual channels' which sometimes obscure the view, the Liberals perform a function which is quite indispensable.

Certainly, the statistical evidence of Liberal Party revival during the 1950s and 1960s is insufficient to support and justify this sort of development of sympathy within the press. The second statement, strangely, was written after Liberal hopes of that period for national party revival had been demolished, on the occasion in fact of Jo Grimond's resignation as leader of the party. He was effectively admitting that old hopes were dead. In the game of playing for actual political power, Grimond and his associates had clearly lost. Why did *The Times* write as if they had won?

An answer to this question requires examination of the other elements which contribute to the life of a political party. Public support is the most obvious aspect of political success in a democracy, the necessary condition to engaging in the competition for governmental power. However, a party is a complex collection of activists and leaders as well as voters, and of doctrine and policy positions which may have an impact of a sort which does not translate into votes. It is possible to create a generally positive image with the public at large which nevertheless does not bring electoral success. It is also possible to bring forward ideas and policies which have an impact on the sophisticated public, and even within the corridors of government, without generating the straightforward type of political support which wins parliamentary seats.

Unfortunately, this sort of success is nebulous and indirect at best. It is consequently very hard to verify with any sense of certainty. The two major parties would be unlikely to acknowledge any Liberal Party contributions to their own policy development. Nevertheless, it would be interesting as well as significant to trace the degree to which distinctively Liberal approaches to public policy became more characteristic of the two main parties during the period since the early 1950s. It would be sufficient for the purposes of this analysis to show that the two parties have responded to the same social changes which have spurred the Liberal advance.

Moreover, intellectual success is fully consistent with electoral frustration. Victory in the realm of ideas could easily be counter-productive for a party if it blurred an image of uniqueness and compromised a reputation for being different from other parties. The Tory and Labour parties, after all, are far more likely to hold governmental power and therefore have an opportunity directly to place their policies into practice. Electoral frustration for the Liberals, as a result, is entirely compatible with other sorts of success.

3

The New Liberalism

*'I have always felt that the Liberal Party's greatest
strength was that it was not involved in the crudities of
power and could, therefore, afford the luxury of
principles and new ideas.'*
A former Liberal Party official

The Social Context

Liberal activists stress with fair consistency that their party,
especially under Jo Grimond, has served as a source of fresh
ideas. Is this a valid point or a rationalization; is it a
realistic perception or based on old memories of people like
Beveridge, Keynes and the other thinkers and innovators
who once adhered to the Liberal Party? When coming to
grips with the intellectual life of the party, several elements
should be considered. First, there was Grimond himself,
with his particular talent for combining a spirit of activism
with an appreciation for reflection and thoughtfulness.
Second, aside from his own personality, but related to it,
there was his ability to draw intellectuals to the party.
Third, there is the more general political and emotional
mood and atmosphere of the time in which the Liberal
Party revival began and grew.

This last phenomenon, because it is both broad and
subtle, is the most difficult to capture and describe. Yet, it
forms an essential foundation for the Liberal impetus which
occurred, intellectually as well as electorally, from the mid-
1950s. The Liberal Party, unlike Labour and the
Conservatives, was not seen to be such a central or integral
part of the *status quo*. It profited from this position because,
during the late 1950s and early 1960s, the popular spirit in
many quarters of Britain was one of disillusion and despair
in the face of what was seen as general governmental and

societal incompetence, conservatism, and stagnation.

Extreme, emotional criticism of British social and political life was hardly an innovation of the 1950s. One might usefully recall V.O. Key's remark (which echoes many others) that alienation is an inevitable part of the human condition.[1] Popular cynics have been a staple of British literature and popular commentary. It was long before the Suez fiasco, before Butskellism, before the post-war balance of payments preoccupation that George Bernard Shaw directed scathing barbs at his countrymen with such comments as, 'Kings are not born; they are made by universal hallucination'.[2]

Yet, having considered this, it remains that favourable attention was devoted to Grimond and his party during a period of apparently great popular malaise. Economic problems were one specific source of unhappiness, decline from empire and world power was another. As Norman Birnbaum observes in his discussion of popular reactions to the Suez misadventure of 1956, the event was for many conservative Britishers a chance to 'show the wogs'.[3] Simultaneously, it was for others a shocking effort to return to an imperial past which they rejected, and their anger at the government's action drove many of them to demonstrate in Trafalgar Square. In the end, the way Suez worked out for Britain resulted in frustration for *both* the political right and the political left. For the left, it was not enough that it had failed. For the right, it was not enough that it had been tried.

Inevitably, national leadership was a focal point for critics of the era. From the time that Henry Fairlie revived the term 'Establishment' in 1955 to describe Britain's traditional – and traditionalist – ruling élite, the word became one of derision for many critics. Marjorie Bremner,

1 The reference to V.O. Key was passed on by Samuel H. Beer. There is, of course, a significant literature on alienation, reaching from the contemporary period far back into the past. One of the most intriguing recent discussions is in John H. Schaar, *Escape from Authority*, especially Chapter 3.

2 Drew Middleton, *These Are The British*, p. 13.

3 Norman Birnbaum, 'Great Britain: The Reactive Revolt', in Morton Kaplan, ed, *The Revolution in World Politics*, pp. 33-4.

writing in 1957, blamed Britain's leaders for lack of direction in national life, entitling her condemnation sarcastically, '*Noblesse Oblige*'.[4] Another observer, Brian Chapman, made a similar point in 1963: 'It is clear that over the last ten years British leaders and their assistants have consistently misread the European scene and have consistently underestimated France and the surge and dynamic building up inside the European movement.'[5] John Osborne, perhaps the leading member of the fashionable 1950s set of 'Angry Young Men,' singled out Establishment types in his play *The Entertainer*: 'There are plenty of these around – well dressed, assured, well educated, their emotional and imaginative capacity so limited it is practically negligible.'[6]

For a Kipling, both England and Empire were certain known elements in a universe, equally certain and known, of which they were the centre. For an Osborne, as for many other artists and intellectuals of the time, empire was not a source of pride, their universe was not clearly defined, and their major emotions were pessimism, uncertainty and negativism. This sense of negativism and malaise reached a peak of sorts in a special issue of *Encounter* magazine in 1963, at approximately the same time that the Liberal Party was enjoying one of its peaks of public support. Particular authors stressed different specific points, but their general tone and mood remains uniform:[7]

> When Parliament is fit to investigate thoroughly the work of the Executive, and when the public is free to watch, day by day, the work of Parliament, we shall have come nearer to reconciling our ancient aristocratic machinery of government with the spirit of modern democracy. [Lord Altrincham.]

> What ails Britain is not loss of Empire but the loss of incentive ...

4 Marjorie Bremner, 'Noblesse Oblige', *Twentieth Century*, October 1957, pp. 391-400.

5 Brian Chapman, *British Government Observed*, p. 14.

6 John Osborne, *The Entertainer*, p. 83.

7 All quotes are from *Encounter*, July 1963, pp. 89, 8, 115, 94, 14, 39.

It all hangs together by invisible threads: loss of imagination, intellectual affectations, the cult of ineffectuality, economic stagnation, waste of talent, waste of energy, fear of change. There are the foxes that spoil our vines. [Arthur Koestler.]

... we have the worst taste in the world, the ugliest streets, the gloomiest interiors, the most desecrated countryside. [Cyril Connolly.]

Each time I return to England from abroad the country seems a little more run down than when I went away. [Malcolm Muggeridge.]

The real reason why the grimy windows had suddenly produced such intense feeling in me was that they were an integral part of a definite and well-understood attitude – an uncreative attitude towards simple amenities. [Andrew Shonfield.]

This theme, stressing at once society as a whole and mundane specific indications of deterioration, ran through such books of the early 1960s as *The Outriders* (1963) by James Morris, *Ramshackledom* (1962) by L.G. Pine, and parts of *Anatomy of Britain* (1962) by Anthony Sampson. This last author begins his book: 'A loss of dynamic and purpose, and a general bewilderment, are felt by many people, both at the top and the bottom in Britain today, including many of the 200 I talked to, and I see no point in disguising it.'[8]

No intelligent person would suggest that the mood of intellectuals, which tends to be visionary and therefore also sometimes disenchanted and unhappy, necessarily echoes a broad, popular sentiment. Yet, there is the subjective impression that the self-critical mood was very wide and deep in Britain at this time. Just as the fashion for being a Liberal after Orpington was a reflection of what public

8 Anthony Sampson, *The Anatomy of Britain*, p. xiii.

opinion polls showed to be a broad – if brief – growth in popular support for the party, so the intense unease and frustration of many writers in this period may well have been a reflection of a similar spirit among the less articulate general public. Certainly Suez had been a trauma; certainly the Liberals were collecting new support.

Grimond and Policy

If Liberals prospered amidst malaise, the sense of unhappiness with the *status quo* qualifies only as a necessary condition for the party's revival. A sufficient condition for at least the partial success which the Liberals enjoyed was the creation of a new degree of Liberal Party credibility and acceptability to the electorate. It is difficult to move far from Jo Grimond's leadership when trying to understand how the Liberals were able to find this increased respectability. His complete style and role will be examined more broadly later; for now, in terms of this aspect of his contribution to the party, his performance can be separated into direct and indirect elements. Directly, he wrote two books and several pamphlets, and was constantly visible to the public promoting innovative aspects of party policy. The title of one of his essays, 'The New Liberalism', became a slogan for change which was supposedly altering party philosophy to make it appealing to a contemporary, modern electorate.[9]

In contrast to the sense of lethargy typifying the malaise of the time, a spirit of change and reform, and of the urgency of reform, animated Grimond's writings. Usually, his essays were written in general and highly speculative terms. He stated his basic attitudes categorically, in his brief, exhortatory pamphlets: 'It is notorious that we lack dynamism'; 'Neither 1913 nor 1938 will ever return. We must disentangle ourselves. Cut the past, assess the present, prepare for the future'.[10] The same tone runs through his books. From *The Liberal Future*: 'the existing situation needs

9 Several articles in the party newspaper tried to flesh out policy details of the New Liberalism after the essay was published.

10 Jo Grimond, *Let's Get On With It*, p. 25; *The New Liberalism*, p. 2.

drastic change. Change which is so drastic that doctoring here and there is not sufficient'.[11] From his more considered and elaborated *The Liberal Challenge*: 'The conditions in which freedom can flourish need to be constantly examined. Change and reform are essential to a free society.'[12]

Indirectly, Grimond was instrumental in the creation of new party policy panels and the attraction of people to the party who were capable of skillfully defining new reports. Again, while disenchantment with the two major parties may have been a necessary condition to the movement of academics and other writers to the Liberals, the efforts of Grimond and his coterie provided the sufficient incentive to draw them. Most of the academic immigrants who were most active in the Liberal Party at this time testify to the importance of Grimond in creating an atmosphere which interested them. One academic, for instance, reported:[13]

> I would say that there was a great deal of academic interest in the Liberal Party in the Grimond period, but my own feeling – and this is both impressionistic and biased – is that relatively few of the people affected were attracted by the actual policies promulgated, and many more by the 'image' Grimond *et. al.* produced. I think that the academic connections of the Grimond hierarchy had a good deal to do with the claim which some Liberals make that the party was a source of new ideas.

Another don: 'I think it was partly that Grimond was an intellectual. I was myself brought back into political activity through Mark Bonham Carter who was part of that circle.'[14] Another Liberal scholar, who in recent years has become increasingly removed from party affairs, testified that he and other scholars were charmed by Grimond's careful attention to them when they were presenting their ideas (an ability to listen, he added, which he found very rare among politicians). Additionally, he noted that

11 Jo Grimond, *The Liberal Future*, p. 33.
12 Jo Grimond, *The Liberal Challenge*, p. 32.
13 Correspondence, Spring 1970.
14 Correspondence, Spring 1970.

Grimond had an ability to pick up ideas, to become excited by them, to carry on an academic discussion when meeting with his advisers and policy committees.[15] A very close associate all through his leadership period, a big businessman who is distinctly non-intellectual, stressed that one of Grimond's several virtues was his ability to draw academics to the party: 'he knew how to talk to dons ... and was smarter than some of them.'[16]

There were no doubt other more secondary reasons for the Liberal Party's sympathetic acceptance by many academics during the revival period. As a small, weak party, it lacked the power and funds to draw full-time professional advisers. Hence, an academic who wanted to feel that he had some impact on practical politics had more ready access to the top than was likely to be the case in one of the major parties, where talent was plentiful and competition for the ear of party leadership consequently intense.

But the Liberal Party was always available for this purpose. What created the migration during the revival period was the very fact that the party seemed on the move, combined with the impression that the two major parties were frozen into an unchanging *status quo*. It was not just a matter of competition for the ear of the élite in the Conservative or Labour Party; it was the sense that these ears were deaf to change. Grimond and his very few closest advisers were alive to this sentiment, and did their utmost to encourage thinkers to work for the Liberal Party. An American is more likely than a European to pass over the importance of this element in the party's projections for revival. American parties, with their informal, lax and often cynically drafted convention platforms, lack the formal doctrinal base which conference resolutions, general election manifestoes, and other party publications provide the more policy-conscious British parties. If the Liberals were to compete with the major parties, they had to have competence in drafting policy. On the other hand, an

15 Interview, Spring 1970.
16 Interview, Spring 1970.

impressive policy-drafting experience could have a doubly dramatic positive impact on the electorate, since the annual Liberal Party assemblies from the end of the Second World War had been noted mainly as centres of confusion and eccentricity. Evidence of policy competence could serve as a reply to the kind of criticism voiced in 1960 by Michael Young, a Labour Party reformer who was unhappy with the stagnation he sensed in the major parties but could not support the Liberals:[17]

> the Liberals have not had a distinctive constructive programme of their own since they last enjoyed power, or at least since the *Yellow Book*. They have teetered between the other two parties like a drunken referee who despite his size is constantly trying to separate the heavyweights and fell each of them with a blow which is neither a left nor a right.

Clearly, by the late 1950s and early 1960s the party was developing the resources for the policy-drafting job. It was during this period that the New Orbits Group, a discussion club of younger Liberal Party activists, began publishing periodic essays in order to promote thought and controversy. The Unservile State Group, an Oxford-based study group formed in 1953 by Liberals and others, began publishing a large bulk of its Liberal-oriented essays during this time. In 1959, this group was joined by another, the Oxford Liberal Group. In time, each produced a book of party theory and suggested policy – the former's was entitled *The Unservile State*, the latter's *Radical Alternative*.[18]

On a more formal level, Grimond and Mark Bonham Carter, in conjunction with a few other close associates, began the production of two series of pamphlets which were to draw together a number of strands of party philosophy into a coherent, policy-oriented whole. The first series was entitled New Directions, the first pamphlets of which were issued in 1960. According to one of Grimond's closest party

17 Michael Young, *The Chipped White Cups of Dover*, p. 2.

18 Interviews, 1969-70, plus examination of literature of these groups on file at the Liberal Party Organization (LPO) and the library of the National Liberal Club in London.

associates of the time: 'New Directions pamphlets grew out of discussions among several of us ... [who] felt there were a number of issues being missed by the major parties'[19] Confusion was prevented, both in issuing pamphlets and in deciding on their topics, by the fact that Grimond himself chaired the small, changing discussion group, while Bonham Carter, who was chairman of the Publications Committee at party headquarters, exercised a co-ordinator's function.[20]

The second, more important series of pamphlets was issued by a group of formal policy panels, created by the party hierarchy in order to take advantage of, and reinforce, the new support the party was drawing in the early 1960s – to use intellectual talent which was being acquired in order to try and increase Liberal momentum within the electorate. To some extent, the topics chosen duplicated themes discussed in New Directions essays; but the policy reports were geared to becoming adopted as party policy, as a result of which they were more formal in style and more concrete in content. At a meeting of the party Executive Committee on 11 March 1961, policy committees were set up to deal with the following topics: (1) consumer protection, (2) local government reform, (3) transport policy, (4) land, rents and housing. At this same meeting, the party's Standing Committee on Education, as well as the Standing Committee on Foreign and Commonwealth Affairs, were reappointed.[21] In the same year, the party Council passed a resolution 'to create an Industrial Committee representative of the consumer as well as of managerial experience and trade union experience', in order to propose policy on industrial and trade questions. During 1962, the Education Committee was reconstituted, and a Taxation Committee created.[22]

The new committees were recognized as very important from the start. At the 1961 Executive meeting where the

19 Interview, Autumn 1969.

20 Interview, Autumn 1969.

21 'Minutes of the Meeting of the LPO Executive', 11 March 1961, p. 4.

22 *LPO Report 1961*, p. 4; *LPO Report 1962*, pp. 7-8.

first of them were created, some members present felt 'anxiety that the Policy Committees of the Party would be duplicated by unofficial groups'. In reply, it 'was pointed out that nothing could be done to inhibit the first stage in the preparation of policy by informal groups such as the Grimond groups'.[23]

Table 3:1, which shows the years of publication of both the policy panel reports and the New Directions essays, indicates clearly that the early 1960s were the peak period for the Liberals in terms of their capacity to put ideas and policy into print. All of the policy panel reports, in fact, appeared in 1962. The late 1960s witnessed the presentation of several pamphlets by the party. Two, on devolution and industrial affairs, were important in dealing with themes traditionally of interest to Liberals. This production, however, did not equal that of the earlier years.

Table 3:1 Party Pamphlets and Reports, (By year of publication)

Year	Policy Committees	New Directions	Totals
1960	0	2	2
1961	0	2	2
1962	7	3	10
1963	0	1	1
1964	0	1	1
1965	0	2	2
1966	0	3	3
1967	0	0	0
Totals	7	14	21

Industrial Affairs

The Liberal Party report on industrial affairs contained a detailed discussion of joint consultation through works councils, and suggested amendments to the Companies Act to enable employees to be more fully represented in public companies and their wholly-owned subsidiaries. The representation was to occur through the replacement of

23 'Minutes of the Meeting of the LPO Executive', 11 March 1961, p. 3.

annual general meetings of stockholders with annual *representative* meetings, at which half of the representatives were to be elected by stockholders and half by employees who had attained a certain degree of seniority. The report suggested three years as an average apprenticeship before employees became 'established' and entitled to vote at company elections of representatives.[24] Two members of the Industrial Affairs Committee dissented from this recommendation, and it was not until 1968 that the party's assembly was willing to accept this proposal, which seemed quite radical to many Liberals. The 1962 Liberal Assembly resolution on the issue limited itself to declaring that the Company Law be amended to recognize 'established employees in public limited companies as members of their company', and that both shareholders and employees be given 'more effective participation' in the determination of companies' policies. It was advocated that employees be given their proper representation through membership on 'a joint management council' or 'the right to elect directors to the Board'. Aside from this, Liberals at this point limited themselves to support for employee shareholding and profit-sharing.[25]

Though Liberals in the 1960's were reluctant to accept truly radical conceptions of industrial co-ownership, general interest in joining management and labour in the context of the individual firm had been a constant of the party through most of this century. A major incentive for party work in this policy area came as early as 1916, when Prime Minister Asquith appointed a Committee on Industrial Relations under a Liberal Member of the House of Commons, J.M. Whitley. This commission was given the task of recommending methods for conciliating industrial disputes, and for creating employee participation in decision-making. Specifically, it was charged with developing 'means for securing that industrial conditions ... shall be *systematically reviewed by those concerned*'. The Whitley

24 *Industrial Affairs* (panel report), p. 31.
25 *Liberal Assembly 1962 – Resolutions Adopted at Llandudno 19th-22nd September, 1962*, p. 4; see also *Liberal Assembly 1962. The* Guardian *Report*, pp. 1-2.

Report proposed the creation of Joint Industrial Councils, composed of equal numbers of representatives from management and labour, to meet periodically for consultation on the members' management policies.[26] During a 1920 by-election campaign, Asquith touched on the theme of industrial partnership, stating: 'Let us associate labour with the management of industry so as to secure for it a living voice in the conduct of the adventure to which it is committed and a fair apportionment of the fruits.' In contrast to the Socialist solution of nationalization, he placed the Liberal approach: 'I would set up in different areas ... a joint board or council, of employers, managers and the workmen and entrust to it ... a general supervision, control and conduct of the industry.'[27]

The most well-known Liberal statement on this issue is contained in the party's *Yellow Book* of 1928. There, the Liberals advocated the creation of a small national Council of Industry, to contain nine representatives of employers, nine of organized labour, and six other members directly appointed by a proposed Minister of Industry. The functions of the Council would be, first, to work with the proposed Ministry of Industry to review the machinery of industrial relations; second, to make reports to the Ministry on the creation and reform of trade boards, on applications for compulsory powers from joint industrial councils and other negotiating bodies, and on proposals for avoiding interruptions of essential public services; third, to maintain a surveillance of wage levels and conditions of work, as well as the activities of trade associations; fourth, to give attention to measures introduced into Parliament which affected industrial relations. Additionally, concerning local joint industrial councils, the *Yellow Book* proposed that they be given compulsory powers of enforcement of their decisions, combined with certain safeguards to protect the rights of both employers and workers.[28] The Association of

26 *Britain's Industrial Future*, pp. 173-5.
27 Quoted in *Liberal News*, No 849, 15 September, 1962, p. 4.
28 *Britain's Industrial Future*, pp. 222-4.

Joint Industrial Councils had long demanded such a grant of powers. In 1924 a Liberal MP, Frank Murrell, proposed a bill requiring just this, and received a Second Reading on it.[29]

The detail of the *Yellow Book*'s proposals indicates the importance of the industrial relations topic for Liberals. While this statement remains the party's most impressive on the subject, the basic Liberal approach has remained the same through time in virtually all party pronouncements on industrial affairs. Towards the end of the 1930s, the party created the first of several 'Ownership For All' committees. This first one, in its 1938 report, praised the *Yellow Book*'s support for co-ownership, but also warned against any idea of making it compulsory in industry. After the Second World War, another Liberal co-ownership study group produced a 1948 report which seemed to reverse ground again on the issue of compulsion. This Liberal Party statement affirmed the proposition that employees had a right not only to a share of profits, but also to a share of decision-making, and that compulsion should be used when companies refused to grant either of these to workers.[30]

The fact that party controversies have been raised, by the issues of compulsion and the proportion of boards of directors to be composed of workers' representatives, should not detract from the fact that the Liberal Party has shown general acceptance of the ideal of co-partnership to be one of its most consistent twentieth-century themes. By so acting, the party has doubly reaffirmed its traditional commitment to individualism. First, despite the national committee proposed in the *Yellow Book*, the basic scheme for achieving industrial concord has been designed to operate on the level of the individual firm. The Liberal perspective is eminently local, not national. Second, the willingness to accept workers as equals of managers reflects the party's traditional hostility – at least in theory – to the class system which has been as dominant in British industrial life as it has in British society generally.

29 *Ibid.*, pp. 211-12.
30 *Liberal News*, No 849, 15 September, 1962, p. 4.

The distinctiveness of this Liberal Party position on industrial affairs may be shown by contrasting it with Tory and Labour perspectives on the same subject, which have been largely both nationalist in mechanism and class-conscious in outlook. While both the Labour and Conservative parties in recent years committed themselves to trade-union reform in the wake of public hostility to unions and strikes, neither major party has adopted the Liberal Party's option of working for industrial peace through vertical integration on the level of the individual firm. Both, instead, have sought reform through legislated rules to be applied on the national level.[31]

There have been brief movements toward a sort of neo-Liberalism in each of the major parties, but it has triumphed in neither. Briefly, in its 1955 election manifesto, the Conservative Party did specifically advocate co-partnership schemes in industry: 'We wish to see proper rewards for extra skill, effort and responsibility. Where they are suitable and desired, co-partnership and profit-sharing schemes should be encouraged.'[32] In the Labour Party, there were 'sparks' of syndicalism in the early years of the Labour Movement, which had nevertheless died out by the time the post-Second World War Labour Government took office and turned to the actual logistics of the nationalization of industry.[33] The Fabians were major opponents of anything resembling co-partnership in the policy statements of the Labour Party. To them, such conceptions were subversive of working-class solidarity. Ideas of workers' 'control', they felt, effectively 'placed the demands of the workers in a particular industry above those of the community as a whole'.[34]

In each of the major parties, its own variety of class consciousness has militated against accepting co-partnership ideas. For a good Tory, there is an integration

31 Cf. the Labour Party's *In Place of Strife*, 1969; the Conservative Party's *Putting Britain Right Ahead*, 1965; and *Fair Deal at Work*, 1968.

32 The Times *Guide to the House of Commons 1955*, p. 258.

33 Harry Eckstein, 'The British Political System', in Samuel Beer and Adam Ulam, eds, *Patterns of Government*, p. 212.

34 Robert Dahl, 'Workers Control of Industry and the British Labour Party', *American Political Science Review*, October 1947, p. 877.

of classes, but in a differentiated sense. It is based upon concrete differences in natural abilities and roles. To urge a practical integration, which mixes the role of worker with that of manager, is unnatural, for the irony of historic Toryism is that abstract integration is based on practical separation. Class consciousness, for such Toryism, cannot be removed. Nor can it be removed for the good Socialist, whose sense of cohesion of class and party is bred by a very conscious, explicit vision of a horizontal division separating the working class from others.

The Liberal vision is entirely different. On a spectrum of doctrinal class-consciousness, in fact, the good Liberal should be put at one (Individualist) pole, the Tory and Labourite at the other (Collectivist) pole. Just as neither major party has really embraced the Liberal theme of co-partnership, so Liberals have been unwilling to part with their traditional belief in the validity of individual plant bargaining. Harold Wilson's 1969 trade-union reform proposals, *In Place of Strife*, based upon the idea of nationally-negotiated industrial agreements, were opposed by Liberals in Parliament.[35] During that same year, there was an instructive exchange in the House of Commons on the topic of industrial organization. Eric Heffer, Labour MP, conceded that 'plant bargaining' might be preferable to some extent to national agreements. 'But,' he added, 'if this were applied as a blanket across industry, the situation would be chaotic.' Replying for the Liberals, Richard Wainwright declared, 'I believe, as a Liberal, that there is practically no limit to the possibility of plant bargaining.[36]

Devolution

This faith in diffusion and dispersion for the largely private world of industrial relations is present also in the Liberal Party's approach to government reform. The local government report of the Grimond period is a strong statement – and a detailed one – in favour of devolution of particular functions to the lowest possible level of

35 *Liberal News Commentary*, 13 May, 1969, p. 3.
36 777 *House of Commons Debates* 1654-1655 (13 February, 1969).

government. The Liberals did grant that 'most cases' of recent transfers of power to larger units of authority were justified 'for reasons of economy and efficiency. Given the present structure of local government they were, in fact, inevitable'.[37] But they proposed a complex structural alteration, specifically involving reorganization: (1) to produce 'a more rational set' of upper-tier local authorities and (2) 'to provide a structural framework which will permit more powers to be given to the lower-tier authorities'.[38] This rationalization of upper-tier structure was to occur mainly through giving it overall planning authority, but with this authority limited to lower-tier review. County (i.e., upper-tier) status was to be reserved for 'fully viable' units of government. Concerning lower-tier authorities, new 'urban counties' created in the large conurbation areas of the country would be subdivided into most-purpose city boroughs. Outside of these urban counties, other counties were to be divided simply into boroughs and districts, with the larger boroughs to become most-purpose municipal boroughs. Parishes were to be preserved through the creation of 'urban parishes' either when all or part of a parish was brought into a borough, or when there was a 'recognizable sub-community' inside the boundary of an urban area. To further preserve localism, it was suggested that Wales be separately governed by a Council of Wales, which would be directly elected and receive functions then being handled by county councils and the central London government. London itself was to be governed by a Greater London Council, but with main authority resting beneath it in London boroughs.[39]

The local lower-tier units were to be given considerable power to veto county-wide planning authorities because Liberals, while recognizing a need to plan for each county as a whole, also argued that 'Local amenity is still an important element in town and country planning and the vast majority of planning applications raise no other question'.[40] Not only

37 *Local Government* (panel report), p. 23.
38 *Ibid.*, p. 26.
39 *Ibid.*, pp. 28, 42 ff., 49-51, 111.
40 *Ibid.*, p. 56.

would the upper-tier authorities be required to consult with boroughs and districts in the creation of plans, but the smaller units would have a right of appeal to the Minister. The Liberals noted a number of functions which they felt should rest as much as possible with lower-tier authorities: roads (with the exception of main and trunk roads); housing; primary and secondary education; personal health, welfare and children's services. In regard to the last service mentioned, the Liberal Party report argued that they 'should be organized on as local a basis as possible. They are the most personal of all local government functions.'[41]

The local government report went on to list several specific advantages to the Liberal emphasis on localism in the provision of health, welfare and child aid. Generally, it was seen as a way to restore morale in local government. Additionally, these services were connected with housing and environmental health. The report also argued that 'a more local form of administration concentrated on the Town Hall gives the best chance of achieving the fuller co-operation of general practitioners and local voluntary bodies engaged in social welfare work'.[42] Hence, with the exception of overall county control of the training of specialist personnel, and county construction of some therapeutic centres, Liberals stressed the need to keep social-welfare functions as local as possible. In the words of the report, 'They are all services in which councillors show great interest and to which they can contribute a great deal.'[43]

The local government and industrial relations reports both address important problems of collectivist policy, though the former does so more explicitly than the latter. Each relates to the central/local and universal/selective tensions discussed earlier. Liberal reforms would balance central and national perspectives with diverse local ones. Shop floors and local governments would be given greater influence in the definition of public and private economic

41 *Ibid.*, p. 62.
42 *Ibid.*, p. 63.
43 *Ibid.*, pp. 62-3.

plans and social welfare policies.

As with industrial relations, the preoccupations reflected in the local government report are very consistent with the party's heritage. Liberal emphasis on an important role for local government may be traced well back into the nineteenth century. H.J. Hanham has observed, for instance: 'The virtues of local self-government had become part of the orthodox Liberal creed by the 1850s.' It was a theme fed from a variety of currents, most notably perhaps by John Stuart Mill in *The Principles of Political Economy, On Liberty*, and *Representative Government*. When the party enjoyed power, Liberal Ministers did their utmost to prevent their offices from interfering in local affairs.[44]

Historically, the Liberal Party's advocacy of devolution was most dramatically represented by the political conflict over 'Home Rule' for Ireland, a battle which lingered and grew until it became a political disaster for the Liberal Party. Gladstone's first Bill on the subject, in 1886, suggested that Ireland be given partial independence, with its own parliament and ministry, and some limited control over the collection and dispersal of revenue. His second Bill, presented in 1893, was similar, though this time marginally less independence was proposed. The first Bill aroused such strong opposition that it was not only defeated, but literally split the Liberal Party. In 1886, as a direct result of Gladstone's advocacy of Home Rule, the Liberal Unionists under Chamberlain seceded from the party, eventually joining the Conservatives. The second Bill led to a physical brawl on the floor of the House of Commons. It passed here, but only with the support of the Irish Members, and met defeat in the Lords. In the general elections of 1886 and 1895, each the most recent after the failure of a Home Rule Bill, the Liberals suffered defeat.[45]

The advocacy of Home Rule not only split the party and contributed to electoral defeat, it also served as a constant potential menace to Liberal Governments. In 1882, the double assassination of two English officials in Dublin

44 H.J. Hanham, *The Nineteenth-Century Constitution*, p. 372.
45 Charles Andrews, *A History of England*, pp. 533-6.

almost brought down the Liberal Government. Informed opinion during the crisis held that it was saved only because the Tory leader was an ineffective speaker, while at the same time the Tories' fiery Randolph Churchill was absent from the Chamber.[46] These were the risks which Gladstone and his supporters were willing to run for the principle of a measure of Irish independence. The depth of the Liberals' philosophical commitment to the principle may be seen in part by the political price they paid for it.

The issue of Irish Home Rule is also useful for indicating contrasting Conservative Party attitudes toward devolution. Not only did the Tories generally oppose Home Rule; but, on the rare occasions when they did accept the principle and reason upon it, available evidence reveals a clear bias toward collectivism even during the Liberal Age. In October 1885, as an example, Lord Salisbury made a speech in which he seemed to accept the principle of devolution, at least in some form, for he advocated the transfer of British institutions to Ireland. But he added an explicit defence of centralism in which he argued that smaller units of government were much more likely than larger ones to be unjust to minority groups. The diversity of larger areas tended to cancel out particular abuses, for 'the wisdom of several parts of the country will correct the folly and mistakes of one'. Hence, 'it would be impossible to leave that out of sight in any extension of any such local authority to Ireland'.[47]

The Liberal Party's stance on Irish Home Rule illustrates broader historical party interest in the issue of regional devolution generally throughout the UK. Gladstone, in opening his Midlothian campaign of 1879, addressed himself to this. He stated that if Ireland, Scotland, Wales and parts of England could be given independent authority to deal with questions of particular regional interest, 'that would be the attainment of a great national good'.[48] Later, during Asquith's Government, the

46 Robert Rhodes James, *Lord Randolph Churchill*, p. 110.
47 John Morley, *The Life of William Ewart Gladstone*, vol. III, p. 242.
48 Quoted during Parliamentary debate, 759 *House of Common Debates* (21 February, 1968).

party continued to be concerned with devolution and to press for reform along lines consistent with its past. A Liberal Bill for Scottish Home Rule reached and passed a second reading in 1913. The *Liberal Magazine* observed in that year that Scotland's representation in the Commons would remain unchanged until similar plans for devolution could be made for England and Wales, at which time the nature of representation of 'the component parts of Great Britain in the Parliament of the United Kingdom will fall to be considered and adjusted'.[49] Before any of these plans could materialize, however, the First World War intervened, ending not only the Scottish Bill's chances of passage but also Liberal plans for more general devolution.

Party interest in devolution not only dates back a long time, but has been consistent – and consistent in advocacy – through time. Periodically since the turn of the century, the Liberal Party has reaffirmed its commitment to devolution, its sincerity highlighted by the political unpopularity of its stand through most of this time. During the revival under Jo Grimond, the party not only produced its detailed report on local government; Liberals in Parliament were active in defending the principle of greater sensitivity for the peripheral regions which most Liberal MPs represented. In a revealing House of Commons exchange in 1962, for instance, Grimond noted that remote areas – such as his own Scottish constituency – suffered from such special problems as high proportions of old people, travel which was not only especially expensive but also especially necessary, and comparatively little local taxable value. He felt that these were problems which might not be addressed in use of the General Grant for Scotland. In his words, 'we believe that it is time that many of the special considerations of these counties should be taken more into account'. Pointedly, he asked specifically how the equalization grant for Scotland was applied. This led to the following exchange:[50]

MR MACLAY (Secretary of State for Scotland): It was

49 *Scottish Self-Government*, Scottish Liberal Party, pp. 7-8.
50 658 *House of Commons Debates* 169 (16 April, 1962).

once said that there were only three people in Europe who knew about the Schleswig-Holstein problem, and one of them was mad.

MR GRIMOND: I recognize that reference. One was dead, one was mad, and one had forgotten. I am very much afraid that the Secretary of State has been so long at the Scottish Office that he has forgotten. We cannot think that he is dead, and we are reluctant to think that he is mad. I hope that, by the end of the debate, his memory will have been refreshed.

Liberal policy history toward local government has reflected this same interest in functional devolution, and in addition has included advocacy of reform of procedural methods. There have been three foci to Liberal Party efforts in these areas. First, and most important, they have believed in greater independence for local units of government. This goal, which Hanham describes as firmly rooted in the approach of nineteenth-century Liberals, carried on into the later Liberal Party. The last Liberal Government passed the Housing, Town Planning, etc. Act of 1909. Only limited powers were provided to councils under this act, since it gave them the right to plan only for 'land in the course of development or likely to be used for building purposes', not for completely developed or open undeveloped areas. But it did give councils direct authority over town and city expansion actually in progress.[51] Second, Liberals have been concerned with creating more openness in local council affairs. In an effort to bring about this reform, the Liberals in 1908 passed a Bill admitting journalists to council meetings, though over the years after its passage the Bill's intent was circumvented by councils which conducted more and more of their business in private committee sessions.[52] Third, Liberals have worked against party politics in local government, although, where party politics has seemed inevitable, they have reasoned that it is prudent to accept it while simultaneously working against

51 *Local Government Handbook*, p. 54.
52 'Public Relations and Local Authorities', *Local Government Newsletter*, March 1963, p. 1.

the whip system. Ironically, one of the first and most successful impositions of party politics in a local council was conducted by the well-organized Liberal machine, the Liberal '600', in Birmingham in 1870.[53] Despite this departure, the broad thrust of Liberal Party policy and sentiment was strong hostility to the organization of local party caucuses in councils.

However, by the 1930s the trend towards councillors adopting party identifications had gone so far that the Liberals felt it necessary to compromise. The 1937 Liberal Assembly therefore declared that the 'monopoly hitherto enjoyed by the Socialists and Conservatives in local affairs' should be met by candidates running with the Liberal label.[54] Nevertheless, the party continued its strong resistance to the introduction of a whip system in local government, advocating a party council 'group' meeting rather than a caucus. More generally, Liberals agreed that as an overall policy they should not be the first to introduce a party label within a council whose members otherwise sat as Independents. Acceptance of the use of party labels for local elections, where the major parties were already doing the same, was reaffirmed by the party Executive in 1947, and by the party Council in 1950.[55]

In recent years, Liberals have done their best to stress the contrast between themselves and the two main parties on the general subject of devolution. They have been anxious to make their party appear more sensitive and responsive to particular local and sectional needs.[56] There is persuasive evidence to support the Liberal argument of contrast with the major parties here. In 1959, Hugh Gaitskell felt it necessary to address himself to the 'unpopularity of certain Labour councils', noting that 'criticisms are too widespread to be ignored' concerning such issues as 'excessively rigid standing orders, or more generally ... apparently arbitrary

53 *Local Government Handbook*, pp. 11-12.
54 *Liberal Party Resolutions – Adopted by the Assembly of the Liberal Party at Brighton*, 27-9 May, 1937, p. 6.
55 'Policy Resolutions of the Council', *Twelfth Report to the Assembly Meeting at Scarborough*, September 1950, p. 42.
56 See, *e.g.*, *Local Government Newsletter*, March 1963, p. 6.

and intolerant behaviour'.[57] While the Conservative Party has been perhaps less obvious in its efforts at discipline, such activity has not been absent. A recent study of party politics in local government relates: 'The main Conservative Party pamphlet on the subject ... espouses the principles of local autonomy and freedom from party discipline; in practice it contains several suggestions ... which would, if adopted, divert a local party from such principles.'[58]

This philosophical dichotomy between the Liberals and the two major parties on the devolution issue, however, is not quite so clear and clean as Liberals might imply. It is present, but in less pristine form. Each of the major parties has shown some tendency in the past to entertain notions of devolution. In the 1920s, the Labour Party introduced into Parliament a series of Bills to broaden the powers of local authorities, to alter the rule of *ultra vires*, but Labour interest in this does not appear to have survived that decade. At about the same time, there was Labour interest as well in more general types of regional devolution. Both in 1918 and 1929, Labour conferences passed resolutions favouring a federal reform of British government and administration, designed to hand functions downward to Scotland and other regions within the nation.[59]

In the Conservative Party, the 1950s witnessed a neo-Liberal revival which not only led to advocacy of industrial co-partnership, but to an awakening of interest in local government. The 1955 Conservative Party manifesto declared that upon 'first seeking to establish the widest measure of common ground between local authorities of all kinds, the Conservative Government will introduce effective machinery for adapting local government to modern needs. In so doing we shall give full weight to valuable local

57 *Partners for Progress* (1964 Liberal Candidates' and Speakers' Handbook), p. 210.

58 J.G. Bulpitt, *Party Politics in English Local Government*, p. 106. The same author notes elsewhere in the book that the Labour Party has been considerably more aggressive than either Liberals or Tories in establishing local councils as partisan bases for party growth.

59 Neil MacCormick, ed., *The Scottish Debate*, pp. 12-15.

traditions.'[60] After the Tory victory in that year, the new Government indicated continuing interest in local government, notably in its 1956 White Paper on Areas and Status. In 1958, the Conservatives passed a Local Government Act, which was aimed partly at giving more independence to local authorities through increased and more flexible financial resources, combined with delegation of authority to the lower-tier councils in districts and boroughs. Among other administrative changes, from 1 April 1959, General Grants replaced a previous system under which grants were given to local authorities only when specifically earmarked for particular purposes.[61] Aside from the increased flexibility offered to local authorities through the new General Grants, however, there was no significant tendency to move toward the drastically increased local independence and initiative advocated in Liberal policy. In addition, critics later charged that only one of the two original purposes of the General Grant system was achieved. Spending was reduced, as planned, but a high level of checking by central government apparently still continued under the new system.[62]

In the Labour Party, the period of power after the Second World War found party tendencies very much out of tune with the earlier sympathy for devolution. The post-war Labour Government abolished the Boundary Commission for England and Wales, and the special committee on London government, bodies which had been created in 1945 by the Coalition Government to examine the needs and shortcomings of the local government structure.[63] The party's long period out of power after the defeat of 1951 revealed no Labour inclination to take up old themes of devolution. The significant Labour Party document, *Signposts for the Sixties*, which contained domestic policy adopted at the 1961 party conference, omitted the topic of

60 *The Campaign Guide 1959*, p. 321.

61 *Ibid.*, pp. 320-1.

62 *Twelve Wasted Years*, pp. 251-3; see also (1959 Liberal Candidates' and Speakers' Handbook), pp. 155-6.

63 *Partners for Progress*, p. 207.

local government entirely. *Twelve Wasted Years*, published by the Labour Party Research Department in 1963, dealt with only narrow specifics of local government – criticism of the regressive nature of rates, and of the General Grant system of the Tory Government.[64] The 1960s witnessed movement in local and regional reform on the part of both Tories and Labour, a phenomenon which will be elaborated and discussed later. Each, however, took only a few steps in the direction of the Liberal conception, neither moved all the way to the Liberal side.

In summary, Liberals have generally proposed spreading power outward and downward in advocating reform in these policy areas. In industrial relations, the Liberals hope to bring the representatives of the shop floor *up* into boardroom deliberations; in local and regional relations of government, the Liberals hope to move decision-making *down* to lower-level units. Liberal fear of concentrations of power removed from responsible supervision is present in each.

A third party report, on transport, was very much in tune with this basic theme. This time, the Liberal goal of diffusion of power was to be found through a maximum emphasis on competition, with the role of government limited to preventing restrictive practices, guaranteeing safety and prohibiting public nuisances, and subsidizing those 'unremunerative services which are continued for social reasons'. The report did mention that railways and canals might have their uneconomic lines subsidized when justified by social purposes.[65]

This position argues doubly against the sort of rigid central outlook which produced the Beeching Report, noted earlier as an ideal example of the problems connected with uncompromising central criteria in planning. First, if free market conditions were to be encouraged, the resulting economic environment could make some transport lines, which were unprofitable from the point of view of national planners in London, nevertheless profitable for local independent carriers. Second, even if this transformation

64 *Twelve Wasted Years, passim.* and especially pp. 250-63.
65 *Transport* (panel report), p. 75.

did not occur, Liberals urged the maintenance of such lines anyway if they were crucial to the economy or the social life of particular localities. Greater dispersion of control over transport would provide the flexibility necessary to meet particular needs, whether of an economic or welfare nature. As a later Liberal Party pamphlet argued, reinforcing the position of the party report on transport:[66]

> The principal Liberal objection to the Beeching Plan is that, while a reorganization of outdated railway systems is needed, it cannot be carried out solely on the basis of profitability without reference to the future needs of the country as revealed by regional planning.

Liberal Diversity

In the foregoing reports, the Liberals consistently focus on the promotion of diversity, the maintenance and creation of independent free units – units of government, units of enterprise. In industrial relations, the blanket, class-conscious reform of nationalization is rejected; the particularistic Liberal idea of co-partnership within individual firms is promoted.

The Liberal approach to social-welfare and social-service policies is more complex than this, however, in keeping with the difficulty of consistently providing aid to the very poorest elements in society. It has already been noted that there is the double dilemma in considering how to alleviate poverty: that neither universality nor selectivity is free from tendencies which undermine the goal of helping those who most need assistance. The obvious antidote to the rigidities of centralism in planning is more local influence. The solution to excessive universality in welfare planning is more selectivity, but more localism in welfare control is unlikely to achieve this. Neither central nor local government can be relied upon to promote selectivity in welfare, for it is usually politically unpopular. Moreover,

66 Desmond Banks, *Liberals and Economic Planning* (Unservile State Paper No 8), p. 19.

while central institutions tend to be especially rigid in
structure, local government is often especially parochial in
outlook.

The Liberal approach to social welfare seems to be a
policy portrait which includes a mix of central and local
efforts to attack the pockets of poverty. The thrust of reports
discussed so far is towards decentralization and increased
importance for local government. Simultaneously, however,
other party reports – in line with other party themes –
urged changes at the central level, both towards more
inclusive universality and more intensive selectivity,
depending upon the policy area involved. In both their
education and taxation reports, the Liberals sought to
promote greater equality between rich and poor; in the
former through increasing equal opportunity for access, in
the latter through the equability of simpler tax rules and
fewer loopholes. In education, Liberal thinking is well-
reflected in a statement by Grimond: 'I am not convinced
that there should be this separation of the sheep and the
goats at eleven-plus.'[67] Thanks to the efforts of their policy
panel, Liberals were provided with several concrete
educational recommendations. They advocated giving
education the highest national priority through a Ten Year
Development Programme; by significantly expanding
facilities and the number of teachers available, not only to
increase enrolment but also to reduce class size; and finally,
most dramatically in the context of British society, by
abolishing the eleven-plus examination and encouraging
local authorities to develop types of non-selective secondary
education.[68] In justice to the Labour Party, it must be noted
that the Liberals were not alone in calling for educational
reform of a drastic nature. While the Conservative Party
remained committed to early selection, determined to
defend it 'against doctrinaire Socialist attack', the Labour
Party was strongly committed to 'comprehensive
education' before the Liberal Party report appeared.[69]

Liberal tax proposals were more distinctive, in their

67 Jo Grimond, *The Liberal Future*, p. 117.
68 Quoted in *Current Topics*, May 1963, p. 3.
69 Interviews; *Partners for Progress*, p. 35.

expertise the most creative and complex of the policy suggestions of the party at this time. The main recommendations dealt with the formulation of taxes on incomes, profits and inheritances, with a view to trying to make them more simple and equitable. The complicated allowances and exemptions of the British tax system would be removed, and the five schedules of income and surtax would be replaced with an income tax collected under various categories: (1) personal employment tax, (2) personal business tax, (3) personal property tax, (4) company tax. This proposed simplification was seen as a method for removing the protection enjoyed by persons and firms capable of hiring specialist tax experts, and of reducing the administrative costs of collecting and evaluating tax receipts. The proposals were rounded out with specific recommendations for ending tax avoidance, including arguments that deeds of covenant and other intra-family methods of tax evasion be abolished. It is worth special note that the report included specific proposals for tax alterations to encourage forms of industrial co-partnership.[70]

As with other areas of public policy, the Conservative Government had made some examination of tax reform. Under pressure because of the extreme complexity of British tax law, the Government appointed several commissions to study the problem – the Tucker Committee, the Royal Commission, the Richardson Committee – but little in the direction of real change occurred. While there was some tax relief created for people with special needs, the structure under which taxes were collected remained basically the same during the period of Tory rule.[71] The Labour Party put forward nothing in the way of detailed tax reform proposals during its years of Opposition. Harold Wilson promised to discriminate between distributed and undistributed profits, with the aim of taxing the former far more heavily than the latter. There was some resurrection too of the notion of a wealth tax.

70 *Taxation* (panel report), pp. 5, 17.
71 *Partners for Progress*, p. 146; *The Campaign Guide 1970*, pp. 120-1.

Liberals opposed the heavy taxation of distributed profits because they believed it would injure the small investor 'many more people than those normally conjured up by "capitalist" '. They viewed the term 'wealth tax' as an ideological slogan, conducive to uneconomic consumption, easy to avoid, expensive to collect.[72]

The party's report on consumer protection proposed other reforms at the central level of government, specifically the establishment of a National Consumers' Council which would 'be a representative body, not a Government controlled one or financed by Parliament ... Administratively its model should be the Arts Council'.[73] In discussing, labelling and standards, the Liberals recommended 'the creation of an Institute of Informative Labelling under the National Consumers' Council. The existing organization of the Consumers' Advisory Council might well undertake this work ...'[74] The report implied a lack of faith that traditional competitive forces, in the context of contemporary Collectivist Britain, would function to maximize efficiency and minimize collusion without public regulation. Regarding the Consumer's Council, the party report specifically dismissed forms of functional representation characteristic of other bodies: 'we reject the representation on the Council of, for instance, manufacturing, advertising and distributive interests and all the arguments (mostly based on claims of special knowledge and expertise) usually put forward in support of such representation'.[75]

Tories stress the removal of wartime controls during their 1951-1964 rule as an important mark in their favour. The elimination of such controls did certainly open up a freer market to the consumer. In addition, the Conservatives passed the Food and Drugs Act during 1954-5 to modernize and reform older procedures for regulating these industries in the interest of public health. At the same time, Britain was hardly based on a model of a truly free economy, nor

72 *Partners for Progress*, pp. 150-1.
73 *Consumer Protection* (panel report), p. 3.
74 *Ibid.*, p. 11.
75 *Ibid.*, p. 4.

was the Government particularly consumer-oriented. The Tories, for instance, were instrumental in retaining Resale Price Maintenance through the years, a practice whereby a manufacturer or group of manufacturers could specify a minimum price below which their products could not be resold.[76]

While it would be politically damaging for a Government to press home a decision which aroused vast, strong public hostility, such practices as Resale Price Maintenance indicate the extent to which functional representation implies the influence of producer groups on institutions of government. One critic of British sluggishness in moving toward drastic reforms in the interest of the consumer has suggested that the delay in 1951 in dealing with the Hodgson Report, with its recommendation to end the practice of selling consumers 'short weight, measure and number', indicates that 'we are a country of producer-dominated politics'.[77] This issue was taken up by the Liberals in party literature. They specifically condemned the fifteen-year differential between the time the committee was appointed, in 1948, and the passage of the new Weights and Measures Bill of 1963.[78] On the floor of the House of Commons, Liberal MP Arthur Holt criticized the bill for not going far enough. He complained about the fact that it was often hard to tell which product on a shelf was less expensive without doing complicated arithmetic: 'The modern techniques of packing do not allow weight by net weight to be known. I understand that most other countries enforce sale by net weight.'[79]

Liberals were also notably critical of the 1955 Food and Drugs Act. Despite the fact that the Conservatives cited it as proof of their commitment to consumer protection, Liberals argued that not one prosecution for misleading patent-medicine labelling had been taken up by the Tory regime between 1955 and 1964. Liberals similarly attacked the Labour Party for ambivalence on the Resale Prices

76 *The Campaign Guide 1970*, p. 249; *Partners for Progress*, pp. 92-3.
77 Young, *op. cit.*, p. 12.
78 *Partners for Progress*, p. 134.
79 667 *House of Commons Debates* 77-78 (12 November, 1962).

Bill.[80] This theme was echoed by the young Labour rebel Michael Young, whose well-publicized pamphlet, *The Chipped White Cups of Dover*, urged the Labour Party to throw off its collectivist inhibitions and reform itself into a radical consumers' party.[81]

In contrast to the image of a rigorous universalist enforcement of equality of opportunity present in the Liberal Party's education, taxation, and consumer reports, the party's housing report shows a marked selective orientation. This position stood in direct contrast with the reality of Britain's council housing programme under both Tory and Labour rule, described earlier as an excellent example of the way the universalist bias of the British welfare state has tended to exclude the minority of the most needy. To the Liberals, the basic problem was the need to replace the very poorest housing with something approximating the national average. The party advocated a housing survey to determine the national requirements (which, had it been implemented when proposed, would have been the first such survey since the last Liberal Government had conducted one). The report urged that efforts be made, once the extent of the problem had been determined, to use the Land Development Corporation's powers to finance the purchase of slum housing, and to concentrate available resources in the clearing of the *worst* housing.[82]

The selective approach visible in the housing report is reflected in the statements of Liberals when they discuss other issues as well. In the chapter of *The Unservile State* which deals with social welfare, for instance, the means test is defended, as long as its use is discreet and considerate: 'There is no reason why enquiry into means cannot be conducted with sympathy and tact as it is done today by the National Assistance Board. Anyone who objects to a means test on principle must ask himself whether he objects to claiming allowances under income-tax.'[83] A Liberal party

80 *Partners for Progress*, p. 134.
81 Young, *op. cit.*, *passim*. and especially p. 20.
82 *Liberal Assembly 1962, The* Guardian *Report*, pp. 28-9.
83 George Watson, ed., *The Unservile State*, p. 123.

official, writing in a 1968 issue of a party journal, stressed
that the party had never favoured the sort of punitive,
excessively exclusionary selectivity toward which he
accused the Tories of moving. But he chose to note as well
that, aside from favouring a universal floor for the social
insurance of the entire population, 'we have always realised
that this system must be supported by a supplementary
scheme based on a means test to meet particular cases of
need.'[84]

The Liberal approach of selectivity in welfare is
combined with a constant stress on the importance of
voluntary societies in efforts to alleviate poverty. It has been
noted that the local government report specifically
described local voluntary associations as a most important
ally of local public agencies. Liberals regard professional,
reform and service organizations as useful tools for
providing flexibility to pension and health schemes. Their
adaptability and variety imply that they can fill in the
chinks of special, atypical need which universal
programmes tend to skip. The party's 1964 candidates' and
speakers' handbook, *Partners for Progress*, stressed this point
by arguing that improved social security will only come by
'operating through independent as well as state agencies,
with many openings for initiative and progress'. It also
notes that this 'is one of the most important differences
between the Liberal and Labour Party social security
provision schemes'.[85] The Liberals mentioned a number of
proposals to assist in using voluntary and private agencies,
including government provision of information and
guidance, publicly-defined minimum requirements,
penalties for employers who did not meet minimum
standards, use of funds collected from these to support a
Central Fund for employees inadequately protected, and
improvement in the performance of occupational schemes
for public employees. More specifically dealing with
housing, the Liberals at their 1962 Assembly advocated

84 Desmond Banks, 'Social Services – Selectivity or Not', p. 3, a
reprint from *Current Topics*, January/February 1968.
85 *Partners for Progress*, p. 52.

more assistance for non-profit housing associations, as well as for local authorities, in order to help fill needs for rented housing. In 1967, the Liberal Assembly urged an end to tax discrimination against such non-profit associations.[86]

Almost all of these policy panel reports were quickly passed by the Liberal Assembly of 1962. Taken together, they represent a compact statement of the themes of the modern Liberal Party's revival. Significantly, these themes are in general, and sometimes very intimately, connected with the party's philosophical history.

Race Relations, Europe

The early policy reports were intended to be inclusive in their coverage of party positions. However, at least two important subjects of significance to Liberals were left out, although they have been discussed at length in other party and party-related literature. The first is race relations. Here the Liberals, in a variety of public statements and stands since the Second World War, have defended the ideal of racial integration and equal opportunity in seeming correlation with the growth of racial tensions in Britain. Liberal tolerance is eminently in line with Liberal philosophy, which rejects collective groupings of people, be they according to economic class, social class, or racial caste. One very dramatic example of this conviction in operation occurred in early 1950, when the Labour Government refused to allow Chief Seretse Khama of the Bamangwato tribe in Bechuanaland to return to his tribe after marrying an English girl. This led to considerable heated public discussion, in which the Liberals were especially vocal in criticizing the Government. In 1952, the party went on record in opposition to any scheme for Central African Federation which was not backed by 'the freely expressed consent of the African people concerned'. Racial disturbances in Nottingham and Notting Hill during the late 1950s brought forth declarations from the

86 *Loc. cit.*; 'Liberal Housing Policy', *Liberal Information Department Brief*, May 1968, p. 3.

party Executive and assembly which condemned racial discrimination. The party did come out in 1965 in favour of immigration regulated according to work voucher or possession of particular skills needed by the country. At the same time, Liberals have consistently resisted discrimination on the basis of race, and opposed the Commonwealth Immigrants Acts of 1962 and 1968 partly on these grounds.[87] It was during the debate over the latter Bill that Liberal sentiment perhaps came through best in all its intensity and spirit. Witness the following exchange between Jo Grimond and David Ennals, Minister of State, Department of Health and Social Security:[88]

> MR ENNALS: Is the right hon. Gentleman really suggesting that as a result of this Bill any who wish entry and whose entry is not controlled ought to be turned away if the colour of their skin is not white? Because I must point out to the right hon. Gentleman what, if he was in the House yesterday, he would have known, that there are many people who will be entitled under this Bill to admission and who are not white faced. Therefore it is quite incorrect to say that this is a racial bill.

> MR GRIMOND: No. This is humbug. Anybody who believes that this Bill has been brought in for any other reason than to check coloured people coming to this country is really beneath contempt, if I may say so. What would the Minister himself say if it had been brought in by the Tory Party? We should never hear the end of it.

The second policy area of importance to Liberals, but excluded from the first formal panel reports, is the question of British entry into the Common Market. As with race relations, the Liberal position was unlikely to increase support within the electorate. As with race relations, the party's interest and position were consistent during the

87 D.E. Butler, *The British General Election of 1951*, p. 18; *Liberal Policy 1952 – Being the Party Resolutions Adopted by the Assembly of the Liberal Party at Hastings on May 15-17, 1952*, p. 7; *The Way Ahead* (1970 Liberal Candidates' and Speakers' Handbook), pp. 197 ff., 205.

88   759 *House of Commons Debates* 1450 (28 February, 1968).

post-war period. As early as 1945, the party went on record in favour of a European community which would include Britain. In 1956, before the Treaty of Rome was signed, a Liberal assembly came out in favour of economic integration in Western Europe, specifically through the means of a common market, with Britain assuming a leading role in this process. In contrast, though Winston Churchill did speak in general terms about European unity after the Second World War, the Conservative Party was opposed to British entry into the Common Market until its policy transition of 1960-1. As for the Labour Party, it did not shift position to support British entry until 1966, later returned to a stance of opposition, and still later pursued an ambiguous course of renegotiating entry terms and putting the whole question before a public referendum.[89] The long separation between Liberal and major-party acceptance of British entry led to special identification of the Liberal Party with the Common Market. Doubtless because of the deep-rooted popular ambiguity in Britain concerning entry into the Community (resolved ultimately by referendum), Tory and Labour representatives were quite willing to give the Liberals credit for being ahead of them on this particular point. In late 1966, in answering a question put by Grimond in the Commons, Harold Wilson noted: 'The right hon. Gentleman will have great justification in claiming that his party was in favour of this long before any other.'[90] This may or may not have been a subtle dig at the Liberals. Not subtle at all was the unidentified MP who replied to a rhetorical question put by Grimond to Prime Minisater Macmillan in 1961 concerning the Common Market:[91]

> MR GRIMOND: ... Can the right hon. Gentleman also tell us who suggested that we could walk into the matter without negotiation?
>
> AN HON. MEMBER: The Liberals.

89 *The Way Ahead*, p. 173; *Partners for Progress*, p. 227; Brian Lapping, *The Labour Government 1964-1970*, p. 97.
90 *The Way Ahead*, p. 173.
91 640 *House of Commons Debates* 1113 (16 May, 1961).

Despite the exclusion of race relations and the European Community, the early policy reports cover a broad range of topics, with both examination of important issues and suggestions for reform. Because they were impressive, they performed several functions for the Liberal Party. First, within the context of the national electorate, the policy reports provided the party with an unaccustomed credibility and prominence. Commentary, by generalists and specialists, was favourable to both the research and the creativity reflected in Liberal efforts. Very positive testimony for the Liberal tax proposals came, oddly, from the Labour Parliamentary Party Front Bench spokesman on taxation, Douglas Houghton. In an article published in *Taxes*, the journal of the Inland Revenue Staff Federation, he noted that the Liberal Party's tax report 'is a work of great importance'.[92] The journalistic evaluation of the 1962 Liberal Assembly, at which the policy proposals were debated and – for the most part – passed as policy, was laudatory. Observers of the new Liberal Party seemed very strongly impressed by the concreteness of the party's policy proposals, as well as by the energy of the Liberals' reformist ethic. Here are some samples of remarks in the press:[93]

> They have practical social policies on housing, town planning, health and old people ... The Liberals have successfully projected an image of a party led by hundreds of intelligent young professional men, technologists and executives. They are real radicals who want a new society ... watch out, George Brown and Iain Macleod. These Liberals are more dangerous than you think. [*Daily Mirror.*]

> the Liberal Party Assembly, once it got under way, revealed that it is becoming mature and thoughtful of the burden of responsibility. [*Daily Express.*]

> It can no longer be said that the party has no policy. On

92 Cited in *Current Topics*, December 1962, pp. 11-14 and back cover.
93 Quoted in *Current Topics*, October 1962, pp. 1-2; *Current Topics*, December 1962, p. 5.

the contrary, it is bubbling over with ideas and proposals which ... seem practical and relevant to the 1960s. [*Observer*.]

The virtues of modern Liberalism – freshness of appeal, open-mindedness, a knack of pointing an accusing finger – in the right direction, were all on parade at Llandudno. [*The Times*.]

What Liberals project for Britain is a dynamic and therefore much less class-stratified society, in which ownership of shares and real property will be widely distributed. [*Economist*.]

the Liberals ... are now speaking with more attractive economic expertise than either of the other two parties. [*Economist*.]

The Liberals' relatively impressive showing in the 1964 general election was doubtless due in part to the public impact of the effort at policy definition. In that election, sales of the Liberal manifesto were triple those of the Labour or Tory platform, even though it was three times more expensive.[94]

The reports were significant for other reasons as well. They were a direct reflection of Grimond's ability to draw talented people to the party, and to stimulate them to work on policy production. Of the reports, the one on local government was the longest and most detailed, the one on taxation the most well-received. The Local Government Committee was headed by Professor Bryan Keith-Lucas, a politically active Liberal academic specializing in local government affairs. The tax report was prepared by a panel headed by Professor G.S.A. Wheatcroft, who was drawn into the party during the Grimond period and, later, after Grimond's resignation as leader, was a chief tax adviser to the Conservative Party. In addition, a number of the New Directions pamphlets were written by academics. Of those

94 *Sunday Times*, 27 September 1964.

which were signed by specific authors, two were co-authored by Christopher Layton, who served for a time as Grimond's personal aide, worked for the *Economist* – where he specialized in European affairs – directed a university European studies centre, and went on to become an official on the European Economic Community Commission.[95]

Additionally, the new policy declarations were important to the Liberals as a source of internal cohesion. They enabled the party to draw together around a few specific, fairly concise themes which were largely not among those which set left against right. Industrial relations reform to some extent contains the potential for controversy over the particulars of implementation, but more generally co-partnership is an idea broadly accepted among Liberals. Tax reform is an especially esoteric matter, likely to discourage ideological clash even while impressing specialists. Richard Lamb, a publisher and Liberal Party activist, noted this general role of policy work in 1963: 'During the last two years the speeches of Liberal Peers, MPs and Candidates have become far more uniform in their policy content. At the same time the Party exponents have become better briefed.'[96]

Finally, the policy proposals, though drawing on very old Liberal philosophy, were timely in speaking to the centralist and universalist dilemmas of collectivism discussed earlier. Liberal localism and selectivity, simply because their perspectives are so different from that of collectivism, addressed the kinds of problems inherent in collectivist structures and policies, with the *caveat* that the Liberals proposed some different forms of centralism as well.

Intellectually, the Liberals were providing basically individualist solutions to the problems of collectivism. Their improved poll showings and election returns imply that this policy effort was helping to increase respect for them amongst the electorate, at least to some extent. The selectivity and localism of specific Liberal proposals no

95 Interviews, 1969-70.

96 Richard Lamb, 'What Makes a Liberal Tick', *The Liberal Way Forward*, November 1963, p. 1.

doubt drew some voters. The generalized, simpler, more emotional Grimond attacks on the *status quo* of alleged inertia, lack of creativity and governmental remoteness were probably responsible for garnering much more support for the party. Beyond this, the willingness of voters to reject traditional class-bound habits of voting for Tory or Labour, in favour of a blatantly anti-class Liberal Party, implies a growing individualism within the British electorate. If this is true, and given the extent of the praise of the Liberals as a party of ideas, why was electoral revival under Grimond not more dramatic? It was well after the termination of this period of intellectual liveliness that the party began to make more significant electoral gains under Thorpe. Thorpe himself has noted that the party was not nearly as active under his leadership in policy definition as it was under his predecessor. He stated in an interview in late 1973, 'Grimond's great achievement was to give the Liberal Party *intellectual* credibility. I think my task has been to try to give it *political* credibility ... to prove that it can succeed, that it can win seats.'[97]

In effect, the discussion is moving beyond the policies and publications of the Liberal Party to elements of party structure and social change. Consideration of the party's life of ideas, in the context of an era of self-questioning and malaise, helps to explain one aspect of revival and the sentiment that the Liberals were a source of new ideas. It does not explain why the party did not do better under Grimond, or why it drew a much larger share of the electorate under Thorpe.

97 *The Observer*, 16 September 1973, p. 29.

I don't particularly care for party politics.
A Liberal MP

The Role of Party

The elements of the Liberal revival which have been analysed in detail so far – the party's energy in definition of policy during the 1960s, the national malaise in which this activity occurred – have been highly abstract and tentative. These may be the most significant aspect of the party's revival, but complete analysis also requires consideration of concrete factors. Unfortunately, because of the small size of the modern Liberal Party, and because of the limited nature of its actual electoral gains, the conceptual tools normally used by political scientists are especially difficult to apply. Students of political parties generally try to enumerate the connecting and integrating functions those parties perform within the broader society. Democratic parties are seen, to borrow Bagehot's term for a different relationship, as 'a *hyphen* which joins, a *buckle* which fastens' institutions of government to the electorate.[1] Sigmund Neumann has enumerated four general functions which modern democratic parties perform, all of them directly or indirectly concerned with the process of legitimately integrating publics with the state or with each other: (1) forming compromises between various competing viewpoints, (2) general socialization of the citizen into the political culture, (3) intercommunication between government and population, and (4) leadership selection.[2]

1 Bagehot, *The English Constitution*, p. 60.
2 Sigmund Neumann, 'Toward a Comparative Study of Political Parties', in Harry Eckstein and David Apter, eds., *Comparative Politics – A Reader*, pp. 252-3.

In the case of a party such as the Liberals, however, it is difficult to see a simple or direct application of such rubrics as these. The Liberal party's supporters, defined in terms of members or voters, are small and it entirely lacks association with organized interest-groups. The party's communication with institutions of government is direct on the national level only through the handful of Liberal Lords and MPs. The Liberal Party has not been represented in a Government since its inclusion in the wartime Coalition of 1940-5.

The fact that the party's importance is not established within the context of schemes such as Neumann's would be less significant if it could be determined that the party represents, is an interest-group for, some particular social minority in Britain. But the Liberals do not appear to have such a role, at least in the economic and sociological terms which define the constituencies of similar parties in other Commonwealth nations. It was noted at the very start of this study that the Liberal Party has no clear-cut constituency. This contrasts with most established third parties in English-speaking parliamentary countries, which normally have quite distinct class or sectional ties.[3]

This quantitative weakness and unspecific composition make a conventional analysis of the role of the British Liberal Party, along the lines of Neumann's scheme, both especially difficult and likely to be unrewarding. These very qualities of the Liberal Party, however, conform with a major hypothesis of this study. That is. that the diversity of the party is a function of its role as a haven for those antagonized by collectivism. Earlier argument has held that the individuals and groups disturbed by collectivist bureaucracy are varied. Central planning tends to short-change the Celtic areas; the modern welfare state tends to exclude certain sociological minorities. But the basic administrative paradox of bureaucracy would presumably create a diverse constituency of hostility. Antagonism to remote central bureaucracy need not necessarily be based upon concrete economic grievances.

3 Leon Epstein, *Political Parties in Western Democracies*, p. 64.

The very general quality of the Liberal Party's constituency, which makes it atypical, would be in line with this sort of anti-collectivist reaction. Similarly, Liberal distance from big business and big labour would make it appealing to the refugees of collectivism. In this manner, the Liberals do not stand where analysts so often put them – between the parties of business and labour – but instead at one end of a spectrum separating them from the Conservative and Labour parties, which are at the opposite, collectivist pole. Needless to say, the Liberals also suffer in practical political terms from their lack of clear-cut constituency. It means absence of money for campaigns and publicity, absence of class identification in a nation which has been noted for class voting, absence of the sort of sectional dominance which can be a secure anchor for a small party at a large disadvantage in tests of national competition with the major parties. Therefore, in these broad terms, there have been concrete political forces dragging down the party's efforts at revival, forces ineluctably tied to the very factors would have encouraged the Liberal Party revival.

While the discussion so far has had a clear structural bent, arguably the Liberal Party's recent political history also has been composed of even more concrete components: party leadership, activists and a noticeable fraction of the electorate which has given its vote to the party although its cause has seemed lost since Lloyd George fought Asquith in the early years of the Collectivist Age. A description of the revival has been presented, and analysis begun through argument that the party experienced an important intellectual revival as well as the electoral one. More specific party elements remain to be examined, especially in the light of the argument that Liberalism contains potential for both revival of the party and failure to establish a base comparable to those of the modern Tory and Labour parties.

Leadership

The term Liberal revival grew and became dramatic under

Jo Grimond, and his leadership of the party is therefore an appropriate place to begin this discussion. It was his personality and style which were crucial in drawing thinkers and writers to the party. More, he was vital, especially in his effectiveness in communication via the mass media, in establishing the Liberal Party as a force which seemed once again to be a contender for power in British politics. The party has never been able to catch up, in terms of organization or votes, with the promise which Grimond represented. His personal appeal made him, therefore, a source of escape from political reality as well as hope for the political future. *The Times* observed when he resigned from his post as party leader:[4]

> So long as Mr Grimond was leader, his personality hid from his party the true frustrations of its position. Because he looked the equal of the other party leaders, it was possible to believe that the party itself might one day win the same equality.

Yet his promotion to party leadership corresponded with the early years of improvement in Liberal Party showings at the polls, and for some time he was justifiably more the representative of hope, less the representative of escapism, than he became for party activists in the later years of his tenure. His role was significant both in terms of his positive impact on the electorate at large, and in holding the Liberal Party together. Despite the fact that the revival has failed to materialize on a large scale, Grimond remains an excellent rebuttal to those who would undervalue the potential influence of personality in politics.

Grimond's predecessor, Clement Davies, was liked and admired within the party, but in the context of the revival he seemed both too old and too traditional to serve appropriately as leader in the new, potentially very profitable, situation. The Radical Reform Group, composed of younger, progressive party activists, was an important faction urging that Davies be eased out of his post. Not insignificantly, in 1958 Grimond was to become

4 *The Times*, 18 January, 1967, p. 12.

president of the Group.[5] Correspondence from one member
of the RRG to another during the period just before Davies
was replaced indicates the mood of many members of the
Liberal Party, not just young activists on the left:[6]

> Clem Davies, of course, has always been a staunch free
> trader (although he voted for the introduction of the
> tariffs we have today!) and a strong radical (although he
> supported the Tories for eight years!) ... I don't mean
> this unkindly. He, himself, has always been most kind to
> me and I have quite an affection for him but we have to
> face facts! Grimond is interested and not unsympathetic.
> Personally, I think he will make a very satisfactory leader
> for the Party. I think there is a certain amount of fear
> among the hierarchy about what the RRG may do. And
> so long as what we do, when·we do it, is effective I think
> this is a good thing.

The actual retirement of Davies came at the 1956 Liberal
assembly. To ease the old man's retirement, the
directorship of a television company had been arranged for
him. As it turned out, the directorship did not materialize,
but by that time he had already given up his post.
Normally, the Liberal Party leader has been elected by the
parliamentary party. This was true in Grimond's case, too,
but he was also accepted prior to this through the general
acclamation of the 1956 Liberal assembly. His acceptance
by popular emotion as well as formal parliamentary vote
reinforced his authority, undercut a sometime Liberal
Party issue of whether or not the leader of the party in the
Commons is also the leader in the country as well, and
simultaneously symbolized the personal emotional hold he
had on the party. From that point, the Liberal revival
effectively became the Grimond revival. The party was his
from the moment of the assembly demonstration, the later
vote by the Liberals in Parliament only a formality.

Grimond was an ambitious man, who probably would
not have consented to become party leader had he felt he

5 'Annual General Meeting', *Radical Reform News-Letter*, March 1958,
p. 2.d
  6 Correspondence file of a Liberal activist.

could not lead the Liberals on to a revival which was already stirring. But it seems to have been a hesitant ambition. Elected politicians characteristically deny their appetite for power in favour of stressing a concern for public service and a desire to please their supporters. With Grimond, the traditional charade of electoral politics seems to have been less charade and more reality than is normally the case. He had a kind of automatic, affectionate support in the party which made it unnecessary for him to have to campaign for the leadership. None of the other MPs in the Liberal Party seemed to be potential national party leaders; Grimond clearly did. More concretely, he was the only Liberal MP to win re-election in 1955 in a three-way race which included a Conservative challenger. He was, in sum, the obvious choice to be party leader, popular in the party, solid in his constituency, with no challengers on the horizon. Had the field been less empty, he might conceivably not have done the things necessary to win the leadership; his wife has remarked: 'I don't think he so wanted power.'

He seems to lack the ruthlessness which is essential for national political success. One fairly constant observation by Liberals interviewed concerning Grimond was that he was too 'nice', too 'liberal' in the sense of being tolerant and humane, to pursue political success with the requisite avidity. His failure to secure a political realignment of the parties, to secure his own entry into No 10 Downing Street, can only have been a profound personal disappointment. Grimond drove himself to exhaustion campaigning for the party. Yet, there is the uniform sense in the remarks of Liberals that Grimond was not single-mindedly devoted to achieving power. There are many reasons why the Liberal Party revival under Grimond failed electorally, but his own personality cannot be neglected when trying to understand the Liberals' intellectual success but political failure. More, in his openness to new ideas and unwillingness to play rough politics, Grimond may have served as double personification of the strengths and weaknesses of his party. There is at least some inferential support for this proposition in the research of H.J. Eysenck, who attempted to scale electors according to their degree of 'tough-mindedness' or 'tender-mindedness'. A reporter of his findings among British voters relates: 'Communists were found to be more "tough-minded" than Conservatives and Socialists, Liberals being the most "tender-minded" of all.'[7]

Yet Grimond, like his party, was able to enjoy some political success – although, as with the party, it was mainly of an abstract sort. First, he made an extraordinary personal impact on the British public, considering the small base from which he operated. With a leader such as Grimond, there was the risk that the Liberals might appear to be top-heavy in having a prominent man leading them but an unimpressive organization beneath. Grimond, however, seems to have been able to overcome this handicap, at least to some extent. He was never able to carry the party forward to decisive electoral success, but neither did the party's heritage of failure entirely defeat his efforts. Grimond apparently overcame many public relations handicaps through sheer force of personality. One former party leader, now pursuing a career in business, recalled that it was fascinating to watch Grimond, in the fashion of a juggler, keeping the idea credible that the Liberal Party was either dramatically reviving or just about to do so. Party activists were well aware of Grimond's ability to impress and interest the public at large, as the following excerpt from the minutes of a 1961 party Executive meeting clearly shows:[8]

> Mr George Patterson told the Executive that last July the London Liberal Party had secured Mr Byers's agreement for a large rally with Mr Grimond as Speaker in March. Since then different officers of the London Liberal Party had had talks at LPO. [Liberal Party Organization] but for one reason or another had not been able to commit Mr Grimond. The Rally which had been intended to provide publicity for the LCC elections

7 Jean Blondel, *Voters, Parties and Leaders*, p. 86.
8 'Minutes of the Meeting of the LPO Executive', 14 January, 1961, p. 1.

was now off as it would be impossible to fill the Central Hall without Mr Grimond's presence.

Mr Patterson was told that if the London Liberal Party could postpone their decision ... Mr Grimond would be contacted concerning all the rallies and the London Liberal Party would be given priority ... Mr Grimond was already in demand for Television, the writing of articles, appearances at By-Elections, and before audiences of opinion formers – apart from his obligation to his constituency.

In an era of self-criticism, pessimism, and malaise, Grimond was especially effective in striking a dramatic posture of energy and activism, optimism and reform. It was an image which shrewd Liberal spokesmen tried to promote. In 1962, Eric Lubbock, the new Liberal MP for Orpington (now Lord Avebury), addressed the Oxford University Liberal Club, telling the members in the course of his speech that the 'mutton-chop whiskers' image of the Liberal Party had been abolished. Instead, he went on, the party under Grimond's leadership was 'dynamic, forward-looking, young, zestful, and up-to-date'. He argued that Prime Minister Macmillan, in contrast, was at a disadvantage when compared with the young American President, John Kennedy. After all, Macmillan's was a 'drooping, bloodhound' type of personality. The Labour Party, similarly, was composed of old men at the top. Obviously, the Grimond Liberal Party was the party of Britain's future.[9] The party newspaper played up the general resemblance between President Kennedy and party leader Grimond. The US Chamber of Commerce, convening in London in 1962, was addressed by Grimond, who was described in the Chamber president's introduction as a 'frontiersman'. In January 1963, Grimond went to the USA as a Yale Chubb Fellow, and met with Kennedy while he was there. The *Liberal News* gave considerable coverage to both events, as might be expected, and headlined the latter by noting that Kennedy and Grimond were of 'The

9 *Liberal News*, No 831, 12 May, 1962, p. 8.

Same Generation'. The personal resemblance between the two seemed to catch on. One Sunday newspaper described the Orpington victory as 'Britain's New Frontier'. George Lichtheim, in surveying British politics, wrote that the Grimond Liberal Party was 'clearly modelled upon the "New Frontier"'.[10]

Aside from the obvious stylistic similarities in terms of youthful appearance and personal charm, there were two rather more specific and important resemblances between the two leaders. First, Grimond, like Kennedy, had a talent for attracting intellectuals to his service. As the leader of what remained a small party, Grimond could hardly expect to have the same drawing-power for dons that the American President had had for noted professors. Yet, as has already been pointed out, there was a significant attraction of intellectual talent to the Liberal Party during this period. Second, again on the Kennedy model, Grimond worked hard to project himself by means of the mass media, especially television, and was very successful at it. While he was party leader, Grimond appeared effectively on television, campaigned tirelessly for Liberal candidates, and wrote a long series of articles for a variety of newspapers. These varied widely in content, depending on the publication. *Times* and *Guardian* pieces tended to be thoughtful – as they still are. Simultaneously, and illustrating his media sense, he also wrote a number of flip, gimmicky articles for the tabloids. An example of this genre was an effort by Grimond to describe briefly the desirable things that would be done if he were Chancellor of the Exchequer. This appeared in the *Daily Sketch* of 1 April 1960, under the appropriate headline, 'My Budget'.[11]

The 1964 general election campaign amounted to a finale of this sort of effort by Grimond. He exhausted himself in a tremendous exertion of campaigning. His personal impact appears to have been significant. Jay Blumler and Denis McQuail, in their study of the impact of television in two

10 *Liberal News*, No 822, 10 March, 1962, p. 1; no 837, 23 June, 1962, p. 1; No 867, 19 January, 1963, p. 1; George Lichtheim, *The New Europe*, p. 104.

11 *Daily Sketch*, 1 April, 1960, p. 1.

constituencies during the campaign, discovered that Grimond made a considerably greater positive personal impact than either Douglas-Home or Wilson. These authors also argue that television exposure was an important element in the Liberals' comparatively strong showing at the polls.[12] It is unlikely that the extra visibility which television provided the party would have been as useful without the presence of Grimond.

Aside from making an impression upon the electorate, Grimond had a second personal achievement to his credit as leader of the party – his capacity to maintain party unity. This was generally a function of the same sort of personal qualities which impressed the electorate. Grimond is a man of diverse political appeal. He combines a personal aura of conservatism with a radical message, and thus has something for both wings of the party. The key to his success as leader is very personal indeed, for it was not a matter of his reconciliation of large policy and temperamental differences within the party. Rather, through the force of his personality and the breadth of his appeal, he simply transcended particular disputes and basic philosophical differences. The antagonisms remained unresolved, but lived on in muted form, and the party retained its unity.

Members of the Parliamentary Liberal Party interviewed for this study included people on both the right and the left of the party's political spectrum, yet they were all unanimous in their affection and admiration for Grimond. In a party such as the Liberal Party, which lacks the ideological community provided for the Labour Party by Socialism, and lacks too the automatic deference which is an important part of Toryism, such personal charisma as Grimond possesses is perhaps the only way of maintaining effective unity.

Grimond's very personal leadership was aided by his lack of concern with party administration. Though he apparently had an important role in the decision to set up a

12 Jay Blumler and Denis McQuail, *Television in Politics: Its Uses and Influence*, pp. 206-7, Chapter 13 *passim*.

party research department in the late 1950s, Grimond generally stayed absent from party meetings and appeared at party headquarters only rarely and only when it was absolutely necessary. One activist of the period has used the term 'oracle' to describe his behaviour in descending upon the toilers at party headquarters, making the required decision, and departing again. By avoiding the internal disputes which are rampant in the party, he did not make enemies and left his prestige undiluted. By relying heavily on the force of his personality, he was able to transcend particular disputes. Grimond summed up his attitude toward the party's administrative structure in an interview with the *Daily Mail* in 1959: 'I like politics. It's a crude thing, but I love it. I'm a political animal. I am permanently interested in the machinery of politics, the growth of society. I am bored by administration.'[13]

Disdain for party administration may not conform to collectivist styles, but it is strongly in tune with significant currents of the Liberal tradition. Structure for the old Liberal Party became a necessity but remained ambiguous, despite the fact that the National Liberal Federation was the first of the modern mass-party organizations. With his personal, above-the-battle approach, and his haughty lack of concern with the daily details of party administration, Grimond seems distinctly reminiscent of a nineteenth-century style of political leadership. With his aversion to the administrative trappings of the modern party, he recalls the great age of parliamentarism, when the MP was not tied to party discipline, when party had not yet begun to assume its paramount collectivist importance.

The political importance of a leader's personality is hardly a phenomenon unique to the Liberal Party. Personality factors, in the sense of the importance of the personal impression made by national political figures on the public at large, have not been absent from collectivist politics. Macmillan, Eden and Wilson are all good examples of post-war leaders who have profited from particular favourable personal factors. Churchill as

13 *Liberal News*, No 699, 29 October, 1959, p. 4.

courageous, unyielding wartime leader is probably the best example – though he is a very special case. Nevertheless, in terms of internal party affairs and external electoral victory, the party leader in the major parties has been a figure whose personal importance has been considerably diluted by two characteristics of collectivist politics. First, party structure has developed into a feature of importance and prominence. Second, the strength of class-based habit in voting has led to an electorate which, except for a rather small floating vote, has consistently voted for one *party* or the other, with the particular identity of the national party leader relegated to a much less significant role.

These elements in combination dictate a system in which the leader is considerably less important than he is in American politics, with its less predictable electorate, its national election of a President, its more open party structures and more frequent turnover in party hierarchies. The opportunity for a winning personality to sway the American voter, and the lack of party traditions and bureaucracy to prevent takeover bids, leads to considerably greater electoral fluidity and much more attention devoted to party leaders. Recent Tory and Labour history contains no Kennedys plunging upward through the party to the top, nor any Eisenhowers or Willkies suddenly moving to take over from a non-political occupation. Rather, the large parties – and, to some extent, even the Liberal Party – are fraternities in which power is bestowed as well as won, achieved usually through long service rather than political daring alone or personal capacity to draw the electorate.

If the modern Liberal Party does qualify as a type of fraternity, . it is one prone to considerable internal disharmony and civil war. Nothing better highlights the importance of Grimond in preventing internal feuding than the bitter quarrels and party fractures which occurred after he resigned as leader in early 1967. Liberals clearly realized their dependence upon him as a source of inspiration and internal peace, for great shock-waves travelled through party circles earlier, during late 1965 and early 1966, when rumours floated that he might soon resign. The reaction compelled Grimond to yield a denial. This impression of party dependence on the leader is dramatized by the fact that the original furor was raised not by a specific statement by Grimond that he would soon resign, but rather by a remark at a meeting with the party hierarchy that 'he had no wish to remain as leader in perpetuity, and that the party would be wise to consider the question in due course'.[14]

When he did finally resign, press commentary upon the occasion lauded him highly. *The Times* praised him as a positive, impressive voice – witty, intelligent, forceful.[15] It is indicative of Grimond's stature and the impact he made that even the *New York Times* chose to discuss his departure at comparative length, editorially crediting the work the Liberals had done under his leadership.[16]

Mr Grimond set out to make the Liberals a radical, reform party that might eventually displace Labour or coalesce with centre and right-wing forces in Labour's ranks. Labour's decisive victory in 1966 destroyed this hope.

The Liberals under Grimond have served, instead, as 'a small, first-rate, irrepressible minority – a leavening in Parliament, a yeast.' And that is surely accomplishment enough for Jo Grimond's decade.

Jeremy Thorpe was Grimond's personal choice to succeed him. Moreover, a number of Liberal activists believed that he was unquestionably the most broadly acceptable of the available candidates. Nevertheless, the manner of Thorpe's selection not only created considerable bitterness within the party generally, it also detonated a long war between the Liberal Party Executive and Liberal MPs. The Liberal magazine, *New Outlook*, was filled with the complaints of Liberals who resented what was considered blatant élitism in the party, as a result of the fact that party MPs had selected Thorpe without consulting anyone else. In reaction, the party Executive in late 1967 passed a resolution of concern which was interpreted by

14 The *Guardian*, 31 January, 1966, pp. 1, 16.
15 The *Times*, 18 January, 1967, p. 12.
16 The *New York Times*, 18 January, 1967, p. 42.

some as a censure of Thorpe. The statement which was
passed unanimously, noted 'with serious concern the failure
of the Liberal Party to make an impact on the electorate as
an alternative to the two discredited main parties'.[17] This
declaration became the opening round of a bitter and
protracted intra-party war. Members of the national
headquarters at Smith Square passed out press releases
attacking other party leaders. The party Executive felt it was
being ignored especially by Thorpe and Chief Whip, Eric
Lubbock, party MPs felt they were being harassed by
amateurs. One Liberal MP remarked angrily to the press:
'Why is it that some Liberals, who do very little work
themselves, are always readier to undermine the leadership
of our own party than to attack the Tories and the
Socialists?'[18] Richard Lamb, with a tone of despair for the
future of his party, noted concerning the 'war of the press
handouts' that party officials were forced to distribute them
even though they contained no 'constructive Liberal policy
at all'. He reflected: 'This was the sort of internecine warfare
which so nearly killed the Liberal cause during the
Asquith/Lloyd George split.'[19]

During 1968, there was a general calminy of the serious
intra-party crisis. In June, the Executive on decisive terms
gave a vote of confidence to Thorpe. By then, however,
serious damage had been done; the party battle had received
maximum publicity. One unhappy party leader wrote to the
party newspaper: 'Some of the "leaks" from private
meetings and some of the public comments by some of our
supporters, gleefully recounted in a hostile press, must
inevitably convince, even Liberals, that maturity and
responsibility are in short supply in the Liberal Party
today.'[20]

The resignation of Grimond symbolized and brought

17 The *Guardian*, 27 November, 1967, p. 16.

18 The *Guardian*, 28 November, 1967, p. 4.

19 Richard Lamb, 'Liberal Sickness Diagnosed', *New Outlook*,
July/August 1968, p. 5.

20 Alan Butt Philip, 'Where Richard Lamb is Wrong', *New Outlook*,
September 1968, pp. 4-8; *Liberal News Commentary*, No 90, 18 June, 1968,
p. 1.

home the end of the Liberal Party's earlier and more colourful political revival. It resulted in turmoil within the party which was not just a matter of Liberals reasserting their typical individualism; the internal quarrels which followed his departure seem, rather, a cathartic exercise, with party people turning their disappointment inward upon one another.

Thorpe's problems as party leader did not end with the removal of the censure motion. Rather, into the early 1970s he led the party in the shadow of Grimond's more magnetic personality and the faded hopes of significant national revival. Liberals characteristically note that Thorpe was probably the only MP among the party's handful with the talent and skill to handle the leadership of the party. Nevertheless, he did not carry Grimond's weight within the party. For years he had been a general assistant to Grimond, working on normally mundane and thankless details of party planning and administration. This reinforced the impression among some Liberals that he was a junior man, who could only fill his predecessor's shoes with difficulty if at all. Moreover, where Grimond avoided or brushed over interpersonal and other rivalries within the party, Thorpe became a target for controversy. The internal strife which greeted his accession to the leadership continued in more muted form after the censure motion was rescinded. The fact that the criticism was generally quite vague did not make it ineffective.

In large measure, the more difficult and unhappy atmosphere within the party during much of Thorpe's tenure as leader has reflected the reaction to the declining fortunes of the party. In 1966, the Liberals won 12 House of Commons seats. They added another in the 1969 Ladywood by-election, but then were reduced to 6 in the slicing defeat of the 1970 general election. Liberal by-election returns lost momentum (see Table 2:2). The party revival in local government clearly had passed its peak (see Table 2:3). Thorpe lacked Grimond's interest in and capacity for drawing writers and intellectuals to the party, with the result that the party lost the policy-drafting dimension which was so prominent in the earlier revival.

The Liberal Party also entered a severe and continuing financial crisis soon after Thorpe assumed command. The party characteristically has been pressed for funds ever since the collapse from national political power. However, the Grimond revival had brought an improvement in the financial picture. Contributions increased significantly. Liberals responded to the more promising situation by expanding party staff and organization, and moving to new headquarters in Smith Square where the two major parties were also located. This meant that the party found itself seriously over-extended when the Grimond revival tide receded. In 1968 it proved necessary to leave Smith Square for more modest and inexpensive quarters in Exchange Court, off the Strand. Headquarters' staff was reduced. Various fund-raising efforts were launched, most notably the 'Liberal Million Fund' campaign of 1967, which had the impractical goal of gathering £1 million in time for the next general election. Nevertheless, party finances continued to deteriorate. Pratap Chitnis, one of the party's chief administrators and generally highly regarded, resigned in protest because he felt budget cuts were not severe enough. Only a sudden last-minute large contribution to the party in the 1970 campaign put the books temporarily back in the black and prevented what would probably have been an even worse electoral result.[21]

As a consequence of these deteriorating conditions, Thorpe was forced to spend a great deal of time working on organizational and administrative problems, and trying to maintain lagging Liberal Political credibility. Where Grimond had the asset of an atmosphere of Liberal progress during most of his tenure, Thorpe had to deal with an aura of defeat and decline during most (though not all) of his. It was therefore difficult for Thorpe to attempt to project his personality on the national stage with Grimond's consistency. Additionally, Thorpe's parliamentary constituency, Devon North, was at times held by him with a very narrow margin. As a result, he was more restricted than

21 *Liberal News*, No 1063, 14 October, 1969, p. 1; No 1070, 9 December, 1969, p. 8; David Butler and Michael Pinto-Duschinsky, *The British General Election of 1970*, p. 115.

Grimond in campaigning around the country during general elections. It was only with the recent improvement in the party's electoral position that Thorpe was free to devote comparatively large amounts of attention to playing a prominent public-political role from a reasonably secure electoral base.

Grimond and Thorpe therefore faced very different situations during their tenures as leader. Nevertheless, in some respects their experiences were comparable. One constant between the two periods, which relates directly to the character of the historic Liberal Party, has been the difficulty of imposing and maintaining any consistent discipline within the party, even among its presumably more sophisticated representatives in Parliament. There has been continuing tension between a party élite which has been willing to entertain coalition government in order to achieve tangible political power, and a significant section of the party membership which has strongly opposed any such arrangement. This has severely restricted the efforts by Liberal leaders to take advantage of the potential coalition opportunities which have appeared. During the period 1964-6, for example, when there was great speculation about a Lib-Lab deal in the House of Commons to firm up the Labour Government's fragile majority, Grimond was doubly hurt in his position – first, by a tactical inability to withhold Liberal support from the Government; second, by a converse strategic inability to guarantee Liberal support to the Government in the event an accord was reached. The death of the Speaker during this period raised the possibility of a Government majority of only one. At this crucial moment, however, one Liberal MP defected from his party to accept the most junior of three non-voting offices in the House of Commons. More broadly, a significant section of the Liberal MPs opposed any sort of agreement with the Labour Government.

A generally comparable situation developed in 1974 between the two general elections, although this time neither of the major parties had a clear majority of seats in the House of Commons. After Labour secured a plurality in the February election, the Conservatives made an approach to the Liberals for a coalition. This was rejected, partly no doubt because of the clumsy manner in which the offer was made, but also because Thorpe and the Liberal Whip, then David Steel, faced considerable resistance within the party to any arrangement. Throughout that summer, Thorpe and his immediate associates hinted at the possibility of a coalition following the next general election if no party had a majority in the Commons. At the same time, they tried to mute Liberal complaints concerning any deal. After considerable manoeuvering, Thorpe was able to secure a resolution at the autumn Liberal assembly which kept the door open to the possibility of coalition, but only if the nation faced 'catastrophe'.[22] The Labour victory in the October election discouraged such speculation.

Liberal Strategy and the Party Elite

This diffuse and undisciplined quality of the Liberal Party highlights the need for central direction of some sort to avoid confusion and make the best of limited resources. The party under Thorpe generally lacked the capacity for maintaining a significant central party structure. As the 1970 Nuffield general election study observed, in a statement which is apt for most of the Thorpe period, 'In its unpromising situation, the party became more inward-looking ... some of those who felt dissatisfied with the conduct of the party's affairs lapsed into inactivity ... little that was new or challenging seemed to emerge.'[23]

On the other hand, a great deal of planning and structural alteration had accompanied the Grimond revival. Growing resources, plus the leader's unconcern with administration, required that the burden of planning the tactics and projecting the strategy of revival be carried by others. Of those at the top of the party, two names aside from Thorpe's stand out because of their closeness to Grimond and involvement in planning – Mark Bonham Carter and Frank Byers. Their capabilities are reflected in

22 *The Economist*, 29 June, 1974, p. 17; *The Times*, 12 September, 1974, p. 1.

23 Butler and Pinto-Duschinsky, *op. cit.*, p. 116.

the positions they attained outside the Liberal Party, Bonham Carter as head of the Race Relations Board and the Community Relations Commission; Lord Byers as chief executive officer of Rio Tinto Finance and Exploration Ltd, a large mining firm.

Bonham Carter came to the Liberal Party's élite with impeccable Liberal credentials: a grandson of Asquith, son of the notable party stalwart Lady Violet Bonham Carter, brother-in-law of Grimond, hero of Torrington. During his tenure with the party, he planned tactics and strategy, and was active with Grimond in directing the effort to redefine Liberal policy. Byers has been primarily involved in handling the party's administrative affairs. The Liberals' debt to him, in fact, is immense. At the end of the Second World War, Byers was elected to the House of Commons, and almost immediately became the Liberal Whip. In this position, he not only worked to maintain some semblance of unity among Liberals in the Commons, but also gradually managed to get Clement Davies (who was elected to leadership by the Parliamentary party in 1945) accepted by the rest of the party as well. Simultaneously, during the late 1940s and early 1950s, Byers worked mornings at the party's London headquarters, doing the paperwork and decision-making necessary to keep the party functioning at the national level. Since then, Byers has served as chairman of the Executive, run every Liberal general election campaign between 1959 and 1970, and held a number of other prominent and important positions in the party, including that of leader of the Liberals in the House of Lords. One Liberal Party worker testifies that Byers was especially important to the party because planning and administration seem to be things which are almost congenitally foreign to so many Liberals. In his words, Byers was most crucial because 'most [Liberals] ... don't live in the real world' when it comes to political decision-making.

Grimond, these two lieutenants, and others at the top of the party appear to have decided on a revival strategy of at least five prongs. First, there was the effort to project Grimond on the national stage. Second, the Liberals tried to establish their intellectual credibility through drawing thinkers to the party in order to produce both policy and prestige. Third, there was the more concrete effort to turn party organization and structure from a formality into a useful tool for imposing discipline, control, political planning. Effective organization could lay the groundwork for Liberal Party advance; specifically, there was a keen effort to use the national headquarters of the party to plan for local election campaigns. Fourth, Liberal strategists hoped that by concentrating on by-elections, where they were more likely to win, they might create a snowball effect in which momentum from these victories would carry the party into the realm of political credibility and, eventually, political power. Fifth, the most important and sophisticated planners in the Liberal Party clearly believed from the start that some sort of arrangement would have to be made with elements of the Labour Party if the revival was to succeed. It was a strategy which not only hoped for party realignment, but assumed a form of party reconstruction. When Grimond spoke of 'a realignment in British politics', he referred to a merging of the Liberals with the right-wing of the Labour Party, not simply a constant growth of the Liberal Party's vote and membership.

The first two goals were reached. In addition to the intellectual revival, which resulted in the production of the new policy reports and a number of other essays and papers, there were efforts to set up a Liberal Writers' Association. The activities of this group, which held its first meeting in December 1958, were directed to the organization of publicity for Grimond and the party's policies. One notion was to sponsor letter-writing campaigns to the press, another to try to improve the standards of the party newspaper, and still another to improve the quantity and quality of party election-campaign publicity. A somewhat similar body, the Campaign Planning Group, was set up in 1966. It was led by advertising executives, notably one by the name of Richard Holme, and was geared toward trying to 'sell' the Liberal Party to the electorate through the use of advertising techniques similar to those employed to try to revive the flagging markets of well-known but under-purchased products.

The fourth and fifth goals, which were concrete in nature and more difficult to achieve, were never realized. Liberal votes in by-elections continued to increase through the 1950s and into the 1960s, but the surge was only partially translated into improved Liberal performance at the general elections of 1959 and 1964. The concept of Lib-Lab is fascinating as a possibility which failed to materialize, but which might have occurred had Labour lost the 1964 elections. Labour's own internal party battles were increasingly ferocious in the early 1960s, and the party, had it lost in 1964, would have lost four general elections in succession. The pressures bred by this sort of frustration might have caused more moderate Labour Party activists to separate themselves from their party's increasingly militant and extreme left wing and make an alliance with Grimond's Liberals. There actually were contacts and feelers, of the most private and unofficial kind, between some Labour Party moderates and associates of Grimond during 1962-3. Liberals who know the names of those involved are not telling who they were. However, it is a fact that Mark Bonham Carter and Roy Jenkins are very close personal friends. Jenkins is a leading member of the moderate wing of the Labour Party. Bonham Carter has published Jenkins' books, among which is *Asquith*, a biography of Bonham Carter's grandfather. It is very possible, therefore, though not established, that what contacts there were occurred through them. While this interpretation is plausible, it is nevertheless not an established fact, and the success of the Labour Party in maintaining its internal cohesion condemned the Liberals to failure and rendered the whole issue moot.

Even if the opportunity for such a realignment had been presented, the question remains as to whether the Grimond hierarchy could have persuaded the Liberal rank-and-file to accept it. The hostility of some Liberal MPs to the notion of any accord with the Labour Government implies that there might have been more general hostility to an alliance with even a moderate breakaway wing of the Labour Party. It is equally doubtful that the party membership would have accepted such a merger. For the party élite, it can be said in their favour that they had the element of Grimond's personal prestige and popularity for any manoeuvre they might plan. In addition, in order to surround the Grimond mystique with something more concrete and specific, an effort was made to improve party administration at the centre. By implication at least, improved central party organization might encourage greater party discipline and solidarity. At the very least, such a change would enable growing party resources to be used more efficiently.

Several reforms were made toward this end. First, in early 1959 a committee, the Pre-Election Campaign Committee, was appointed to handle day-to-day party business. This group later became the General Election Campaign Committee. It did its job so well during the 1959 general election campaign that it was decided to continue its existence under the title Standing Committee. It took over the duties of the former chief national executive officer of the party, the General Director, whose position was abolished. The terms of reference of this small, central body – whose name was changed again, to the Organizing Committee, in 1961 – illustrate its importance in the eyes of the planners of the revival: 'To improve as rapidly as possible the national, regional and constituency organization of the Party; to strengthen the impact of Liberalism on the electorate; and to inform the Executive of progress made.'[24]

This transition was not without unhappiness. The General Director at the time was not included in the new committee when his duties were removed. In good Liberal fashion, he called a press conference to express his sense of outrage towards the party hierarchy. The creation of the new body also distressed at least one of the party's three treasurers. One of his colleagues was included in the new directorate; but he, excluded, resigned with a condemnation of the new developments, which he termed

24 'Minutes of the Meeting of the LPO Executive', 14 January, 1961, p. 10; 10 February, 1961, p. 2.

undemocratic (and therefore, by implication, un-Liberal). Again, his complaint was vented in public. None of this internal unhappiness appears to have damaged the party decisively, however, for there were soon clear indications that the efforts to make administration more efficient were having some effect. An official of the party, who also served as treasurer, notes that despite the stress connected with putting the party's fund-raising work into different hands, the new methods resulted in increased contributions. Beyond fund-raising, the Organizing Committee served to make explicit the existence of a small, coherent directorate at the very top of the party. What had been until then *de facto* became a more obvious *de jure* arrangement as well. The new powers which were given to what was in fact an old directorate made it even more central and crucial to the party's affairs. As might be expected in Liberal circles, this created a gradually growing resentment, which led to the abolition of the group in 1966. While it lasted, however, the Organizing Committee proved a flexible tool for making the most of what resources the growing party could acquire.

A second thrust by the party élite was the decision to emphasize local government elections as a party target, an effort given far more central direction, with noticeable central planning tools created, than the more informal similar effort to win parliamentary by-elections. When the Standing Committee was formed in 1959, Byers was quoted to the effect that local campaigns would occupy much of its attention: 'I think we shall place emphasis on fighting local government elections and training people as candidates and workers in them. Richard Wainwright has already done some work in this direction.' The underlying tactical theory argued that since Liberals seemed to gain entry into local government more easily than they won seats in the House of Commons, the party should concentrate where access was easier, using success here as a base for building upward into more substantial power. Bonham Carter wrote along these lines in 1962:[25]

25 *Liberal News*, No 823, 17 March, 1962, p. 4; also No 723, 14 April, 1960, p. 1, 3; No 706, 17 December, 1959, p. 1; and interviews with activists of the period.

we are extending our front in the local government elections ... They accustom people to voting Liberal; they reactivate derelict areas; they provide a training ground for candidates; they bring Liberalism into the everyday life of the community; they show what Liberals can achieve in practice.

With several other Liberals, Jeremy Thorpe conducted a party broadcast in 1959 which centred on the theme that Liberals were working in local government to solve 'the sort of problems that interest and worry ordinary people like us'. He spoke in detail about how Liberals on the Blackpool Council, since gaining control in the previous year, had managed to increase efficiency in transport, had spent more on education, and simultaneously had been able to cut the rates.[26]

This Liberal interest in local government flowed naturally from the party's historic emphasis on its importance. It also corresponded with more recent party activity. In 1946, for example, the party Executive set up an advisory committee to provide advice to Liberal local government candidates.[27] The creation of the Standing Committee, however, was parallel 'with the first really concentrated national Liberal Party effort to use local opportunities, an effort which contrasted somewhat with the party's traditional opposition to party politics on local councils. Beginning in October 1960, the party issued a *Local Government Newsletter* every second or third month until January 1968, when it was replaced by a periodical issued by the Association of Liberal Councillors. One of the brightest and most capable of the younger workers at party headquarters, Pratap Chitnis, was appointed to the new post of Local Government Officer. In September 1960, he completed a party *Local Government Handbook*, describing the history and problems of local government in England and Wales, and providing advice on organizing to contest local elections.

26 *Liberal News*, No 674, 7 May, 1959, p. 4.
27 *Eighth Report to the Assembly*, 1946, p. 16.

A new party constitution amounted to a third effort to modernize and centralize administration. It was completed and adopted in this period. Under its rules, greater central control was established over the selection of parliamentary candidates by means of a national selection committee. Additionally, the national organization was given explicit power to disaffiliate constituencies which were not conforming to what was deemed to be appropriate conduct in the view of the national leadership. While the new controls have not been much used, and could not be expected to be used extensively in the Liberal Party, they have been employed to a degree. Candidates have occasionally been rejected by the national party because they have been considered unfit, even though the Liberal Party is candidate-poor. Also, one party official recalls at least one constituency which was briefly disaffiliated because of rebellious lack of conformity to party policy.

Fourth, the party leaders attempted to establish some political control over the policy statements and general tone of party assemblies. For some years, Liberal Party gatherings had suffered from a reputation for being chaotic affairs. In 1958, the party reached a point of seeming total disarray at its Torquay Assembly. In an atmosphere which the *Economist* later described as dominated by a combination of 'vacuous youth' and 'blithering old age', the party faithful lurched about with neither discipline nor leadership.[28] The party president, who was at that time automatically chairman of the proceedings, was quite aged and unable to exercise competent authority. After this awful experience, Grimond and his planners determined that the embarrassment would not be repeated, with all its encouragement of journalistic amusement and public scorn. The Executive turned the party Steering Committee into an Assembly Procedure Reform Committee and asked it to suggest changes. Also, a number of *ad hoc* committees were set up by the Executive at this time in order to improve party administration. The Assembly Procedure Reform Committee recommended fewer resolutions, fewer

28 The *Economist*, 27 September, 1958, p. 1005.

amendments, fewer procedural gambits, and more effective
control by the Agenda Committee (later renamed the
Assembly Committee). These changes would be within the
terms laid down by the new Assembly Standing Orders.
Both the party Executive and the party Council accepted
resolutions delegating to the Assembly Committee the main
duty for controlling the content and order of presentation of
Assembly business. Among other powers given the
committee was supervision of the final wording of
resolutions and amendments selected for assembly debate.
The chairmanship was turned into a rotating honour under
the control of the party hierarchy, rather than having the
party president automatically chair the assembly. In
discussing this new control from the top, the *Economist*
remarked in 1962: 'The Liberal executive keeps a watch
over this agenda by compositing into multi-point motions
the ideas it wants approved, and by inserting into other
people's motions amendments to points with which it
disagrees.'[29] In addition, control over the writing of election
manifestoes was given to a small, unofficial group of the
same informal leaders who had key influence in the party
on other matters.

The effort to impose centrally directed coherence and
control appears therefore to have enjoyed at least some
success. Candidate selection, constituency affiliation with
the national party, assembly agendas and policy
propagation were all brought under more central influence.
The significance of these alterations, however, should not
be exaggerated. One of the party leaders, when questioned
about what innovations he and his colleagues had brought
to the top of the party's administration during the 1960s
revival, replied that the word 'innovations' incorrectly
implies that they had discovered a party administrative
structure worthy of the title when they began their
planning. On the contrary, he stressed, the Grimond élite
found nothing that elaborate either at the London party
headquarters or in the party regional organizations around
the nation. They started from scratch and, beginning from

29 *Liberal News*, No 961, 5 November, 1964, p. 4; The *Economist*, 8
September, 1962, p. 873.

this lack of base, almost any change would have been impressive. As long as there were people to man offices and money to pay them, the improvement in administration was inevitable.

It should also be stressed that the control which was established was largely of a formal and technical, rather than a fundamentally political, kind. Candidate selection, constituency affiliation, policy formation could all be handled in a formal and central manner; but administrative tinkering was not the same as a change in the psychology of the party. Liberal guiding themes, basic to the general atmosphere within the party, remained highly individualistic. Therefore, the possibility of undisciplined revolt was always present, albeit muted by Grimond's presence and the newly-energetic party élite. An extreme and uncompromising faction of the left in the Young Liberals, dubbed the 'Red Guards', created considerable disarray at Liberal assemblies for several years, beginning in 1966; and, while their dress and style were hardly in tune with the rest of the party, their willingness to express lack of respect for the leadership corresponded well with the general lack of discipline within the party.

More significant examples of the absence of political control of the rank-and-file by the top of the party are provided by the two recent periods of Lib-Lab speculation, which have already been mentioned – 1964-6, and 1974. The earlier is more instructive because a longer period of time, and more complex political manoeuvres, are involved. Labour, in office with only the slimmest of margins, might at any moment have become dependent upon Liberal support. If Grimond was to make the most of this opportunity and approach something at least vaguely resembling the Liberal-Labour co-operation which had always been at the centre of the grand strategy of Liberal Party revival, internal party unity would seem essential. It was precisely at this time, however, that party discipline and order disintegrated, not just within the Liberal Parliamentary Party but among party activists generally. Grimond's magnetism could easily hold the party together when the vote was rising and the issue of tactics remained ambiguous. But when party prospects began to slip, as they did after the 1964 general election, and when Grimond began to hint at co-operation with the Wilson Government, party unity crumbled.

Grimond had always been cautious on the issue of Lib-Lab, sensing strong hostility to the idea from less political, more uncompromising Liberals. In 1961, the party newspaper quoted him: 'Why should Liberals, whose vote is rising, who are attracting the young and the radical, tie ourselves up with a Labour machine which is bureaucratic and quite out-of-date, quite apart from being riddled with dissension?'[30] In 1962 Woodrow Wyatt, Labour MP, had urged a selective abstention by Labour and Liberal candidates in order to try to combine their support against the Conservatives. Grimond had retorted that Wyatt's suggestion was 'both naive and cynical'.[31] In part, Grimond and his associates were forced to disguise their true strategic intentions because many Liberals were not really very interested in political power, at least if it required compromise with a major party – an alternative they rigidly and emotionally opposed. Other Liberals, who might possibly have been more interested in power and were more flexible in their attitudes concerning how to get it, were unsophisticated about what had to be done. One analytic study of the politics of this period contains the comment: 'Mr Grimond himself and others close to him were continually frustrated by what they considered to be the naivety of most Liberals confronted with a sophisticated political situation.'[32]

During these two years of Labour's razor-thin majority, the Prime Minister was careful and made no overtures for Liberal support. In 1964, Wyatt returned to his old proposal for Lib-Lab accord, this time in the pages of one of his local newspapers, the *Birmingham Planet*. He suggested specifically that Labour drop its plans for the renationalization of steel and give Grimond a Cabinet post

30 *Liberal News*, No 807, 23 November, 1961, p. 1.
31 'Instant Politics', *New Outlook*, February 1962, pp. 19-20.
32 David Butler and Anthony King, *The British General Election of 1966*, p. 84.

in return for Liberal Party support. Wilson replied through making the point that he felt the Wyatt idea might be of concern to the Labour Chief Whip, but hardly to the Prime Minister.[33]

Grimond, still cautious, nevertheless had to drop old poses in favour of discreet feelers aimed at the Government. In an interview published in the *Guardian* on 24 June 1965, he seemed to be hinting at a deal with Labour. He told the newspaper that, while there was 'no basis for a coalition with the Conservatives' except possibly for short, emergency periods, the Liberals would consider joining with Labour in a Coalition Government in return for 'a serious agreement on long-term policies'. Even this statement apparently was too daring, for the next issue of the newspaper carried a letter from Grimond stating that he did not mean to imply that he was making an offer to Labour.[34] The internal party damage had already been done, however, both by the *Guardian* piece and by an article by Grimond in the *Sun*, which had suggested that a deal with the Liberal Party would be a useful way for Labour to secure its majority. The *Guardian* and the *Liberal News* were swamped with letters from irate Liberals. In justice, it should be noted that some of the letters were favourable to an arrangement with Labour. By far the more numerous and deeply felt letters, however, were uncompromisingly against any sort of accord with the Labour Party. Several examples follow:[35]

It is time someone spoke up from the ranks of the thousands of Liberal workers in the country and expressed the deep concern felt by many of us at the suicidal policy of fraternization with Labour being advocated by Mr Grimond.

It is rather surprising that Mr Grimond is so out of touch with the ordinary membership on this issue, still more surprising that no one of position in the party has

---

33 *The Times*, 22 October, 1964, p. 8.

34 The *Guardian*, 24 June, 1965, pp. 1, 20; and letter to the editor from Jo Grimond, The *Guardian*, 25 June, 1965, p. 12.

35 *Liberal News*, No 996, 9 July, 1965, p. 7; No 997, 16 July, 1965, p. 7.

bothered to acquaint him with the facts.

I would like to add my voice to what I hope must be an
intensive barrage of protest over Jo Grimond's proposals
for a coalition with Labour. Whether or not these have
been wildly misrepresented as is claimed, the impression
they have given is clear and insufficient has yet been said
or done to dispel it.

We think it would be unfortunate if the impression were
to grow that the Liberal Party is angling for a pact with
Labour. There must be no truck with Socialism any
more than with Toryism.

An unsolicited article, appearing in the party newspaper in
February 1966, argued that Liberals had attacked the
Labour Government to some extent, but that these Liberals
had been 'smothered by a suffocating blanket of sweet
reason, sympathetic understanding, a desperate desire to
see all sides of every question, to give these political
charlatans who run the Labour Party "a sporting
chance" '. In an accompanying statement, the publisher of
the newspaper remarked that he would not have published
the vitriolic article had it not represented 'vividly a mood
expressed in a series of articles and letters offered to us for
publication since the last Liberal Assembly'.[36]
The sense of the Liberal Party diffusing beneath
Grimond's feet, with the clear and public hostility of both
MPs and activists to any sort of arrangement with Labour,
recalls earlier events in the history of the party – the refusal
of Liberals to accept constant central direction from the
party élite or the mass organization during the late
nineteenth and early twentieth centuries, and the
consequent ambiguous nature of authority relationships
within the party; the speed with which the party collapsed
after the First World War, caught up in the personal clash
between Asquith and Lloyd George, lacking a disciplined,
coherent electorate. The same individualism which in

36 *Liberal News*, No 1027, 11 February, 1966, pp. 1, 4.

recent years has provided the party with a distinctive political appeal and innovative policies has also frustrated efforts at internal discipline on the part of the élite. Liberal philosophy not only lacks the communality present in Tory and Socialist creeds, it positively if implicitly encourages dispersion.

The issue then arises of how the Liberal Party has been able to survive at all, far from power, far from wealth, far from great public support. If its modern behaviour has been so atomistic, how was it able to maintain any cohesion during the bleak decades before Grimond and his associates took charge? The answer seems to be that the party has had, through time, an informal broader élite – a party Establishment – which has kept the candle of Liberalism burning even during the party's darkest days. It held the party together in the years before Grimond took over, and has performed the same function as well. A disgruntled Liberal once complained in the party newspaper that the Liberal Party was really a 'club'. A good Liberal, her anti-élitist instincts rebelled against this.[37] It is unlikely that the entire party is aptly described by her choice of terms. Rather, it would seem more that the Liberal Party's activists are a diffuse collection of clubs, defined by social and geographic lines. The most significant of these is the particularly influential club, centred in London, which has relatively great national influence and maintains what general party unity there is to be had. The Establishment, this most important club, is also so defined in the sense that its cohesion and membership are not tied strictly to formal offices, but rather to links of friendship and long party service. A Liberal activist, who is also an academic political scientist, describes this phenomenon as one which involves not explicit election or appointment to positions, but initial acceptance by insiders through personal rapport, and loyalty to and experience in the party. The criterion for selection, according to this analyst, is being accepted by the leader and his very closest advisers. These managers are the party 'Establishment'.[38]

37 *Liberal News*, No 1044, 10 June, 1966, p. 2.

38 William Wallace, 'Liberal Party Managers', *New Outlook*, November 1966, p. 30.

Though required by the diffuse nature of the party, neither the subtle party Establishment, nor the few highly influential individuals around the leader, have imposed consistent discipline on the Liberal Party. These bodies were nevertheless essential to party survival and more recent efforts to increase support and make the most of the revival opportunities. The party Establishment has provided a core of activist loyalists to maintain some semblance of national organization and co-ordination even in the bleakest periods. The Grimond élite managed at least some central tactical direction and strategic planning as party resources grew. Because the spirit and ethos of the Liberal Party reject such groups with particular force, their presence is especially necessary.

Party Administration

Presenting these problems of leadership in the party tends inevitably to portray structure as non-existent, beyond the formal committees near the top, and activists as a barrier to the discipline which is essential to making the most of tactical opportunities. There is considerable truth to both of these observations. However, in the analysis of revival both structure and activists deserve more detailed examination. There are two things which make party structure important. First, and less significantly, information about growth of structure serves as a concrete measuring-stick of party revival, in the same manner as election returns. Second, more subtly, the Liberal approach to party structure, not only in the general lack of concern but also in specific efforts to strengthen it, reinforces earlier conclusions about the psychology of Liberalism itself.

The elementary building blocks of the Liberal Party's structure are the constituency associations. These affiliate, through the payment of an annual fee, with the national party headquarters. As Table 4:1 shows, constituency affiliations in the early 1960s tended to reflect the growing strength of the party, reaching a peak during 1963-4. After this time, they just as accurately reflect the declining fortunes of the party. There is less obvious correlation

Table 4:1 Affiliated Liberal Constituencies (Excluding Scottish Constituencies)

Year	Number Affiliated
1973	287 (as of 15 June 1973)
1972	300 (as of 1 August 1972)
1971	Not available
1970	295 (as of 1 August 1970)
1969	315 (as of 1 August 1969)
1968	362 (as of 1 August 1968)
1967	355 (as of 1 August 1967)
1966	376 (as of 1 August 1966)
1965	402 (as of 1 August 1965)
1964	Not available
1963	436 (as of 26 July 1963)
1962	418 (as of 31 July 1962)
1961	369 (as of 31 July 1961)
1960	320 (as of 31 July 1960)
1959	320 (as of 31 July 1959)
1958	231 (as of 30 June 1958)
1957	290 (as of 30 June 1957)
1956	288 (as of 30 June 1956)
1955	320 (as of 31 December 1955)
1954	332 (as of 31 December 1954)
1953	Not available
1952	351 (as of 31 December 1952)
1951	367 (as of 31 December 1951)
1950	248 (as of 6 July 1950)
1949	381 (as of 31 December 1949)
1948	351 (as of 31 December 1948)
1947	355 (as of 31 December 1947)
1946	290 (as of 31 December 1946)
1945	235 (as of 31 December 1945)

Source: L.P.O. annual reports. The slump in registered constituencies between 1955 and 1956, when the electoral revival of the party was already beginning, may be due to the fact that the date of tabulating the numbers affiliated was changed from December to June. Constituencies have an incentive to affiliate in the summer and early autumn in order to attend the annual party assembly. Recording affiliations in June would miss those who pay their fees later in order to attend the conference.

between affiliations and electoral strength in the early 1970s, reinforcing the point that the revival under Thorpe has not been as significant to the party itself.

Above the constituency level, there are 'area groups,' which are nothing more than a few neighbouring constituencies co-operating for their mutual benefit. Beyond this, but below the national level, are Liberal regional federations. Mainly paper organizations before the Grimond years, they nevertheless were in existence and ready to be built up when the party's fortunes improved.

While not impressive in comparison with the size and scope of organization within the Labour Party or, more especially, the Conservative Party, the Liberal Party's national structure, a relic of tradition which was given a boost by the modern revival, remains a framework of loose but real substance. Moreover, it is the only one, aside from those of the major parties, worthy of the name. The British Communist Party has pretensions to national status, but has been able to muster only a fraction of the candidates available to the Liberal Party (except in 1950, when 100 Communist Party candidates were offered). The nationalist parties have surged in recent years, indeed have to some extent overshadowed the Liberal Party, but they are strong *only* in their regions. Many Liberals seem to consider this national structure a valuable commodity in itself, justification for fighting on and a source of hope for the future.[39]

At the national level, the party gathers annually for its assembly. Theoretically, the will of the assembly travels upward to set guidelines for the party Council, which meets quarterly to redefine party policy in the interests of clarity and timeliness. The Executive, again theoretically, handles day-to-day affairs and is responsible to both the Council and the assembly. In reality, the situation has been shown to be much less clear, with the hierarchy trying to control and dominate party policy and decision-making to the extent that such things can be controlled in the Liberal Party. At the national level, administration is filled out by the Liberal Party Organization (LPO) – which is the mass

39 Interviews, most notably with Lord Byers, brought out this point.

membership's national headquarters – and the Liberal Central Association (LCA). The latter agency staffs the Liberal Parliamentary Whip's office, maintains a pension fund for party employees, and – most important of all – symbolizes the independence of the parliamentary party from the mass party.

The really interesting facet of the relationship between the Liberals and their party structure is that they appear to use and attend to it mainly as a vehicle for alleviating the frustrations of political defeat at the polls. Each period of recent party disaster seems to have been followed by an internal re-examination of party structure, leading to a tinkering with the works in order to try to improve performance in elections. After the very limited party revival of 1929, for instance, the Liberals experienced an ambiguous performance in 1931 thanks to the presence of the National Government Coalition, then suffered an obvious sharp reverse in the general election of 1935.[40] In the face of this demoralizing reaffirmation of decline, the party set about changing and reforming structure. The Meston Commission was set up to propose changes, and its terms of reference were defined as broadly as possible. If salvation was available through re-juggling party structure, the Liberals clearly did not want to miss the possibility. Specific proposals of the Meston Commission included changing the name of the National Liberal Federation to the Liberal Party Organization, as well as putting the general organization 'on the broadest possible democratic basis, compatible with the existence of a strong unifying force at the centre'. Constituency associations were to be retained as the basic units of the party, but the concept of area federations was proposed. The constitution drafted by the commission was adopted at the 1936 Liberal assembly, and remained in force until it was replaced in 1960s.[41]

40 Trevor Wilson, *The Downfall of the Liberal Party 1914-1935*, pp. 398-421.

41 'Report of the Liberal Reorganization Commission', in Annual Reports 1936-1950, LPO, vol. I, pp. 3, 8; William Wallace makes a similar point in *The Liberal Revival – The Labour Party in Britain, 1955-1966*, unpublished Ph.D. thesis, pp. 212-13.

A similar party reaction followed the electoral disaster of 1945. This time, the revising body was entitled the Liberal Reconstruction Committee. Its report, not unlike that of the Meston Commission, both expressed general faith in party philosophy and advocated a number of specific structural alterations. The Radical tradition in the party was reaffirmed in the exaltation of the party assembly in the committee's document, *Coats Off for the Future*!: 'The position of the Assembly in the Party is of paramount importance'.[42] In specific organizational terms, the committee recommended the selection of an 'Officer for Headquarters comparable with the Managing Director of a commercial concern'.[43]

This idea eventually was realized in the office of General Director, but another election defeat would have to come first. After the 1951 general election, the party Establishment held a private meeting. Since confronting the philosophical implications of basic lack of electoral appeal of the Liberal message would have been too traumatic, the meeting centred instead on the usual organizational reforms to try to improve the political position of the party. Byers, who was at that time chairman of the Executive, introduced a number of proposals, among them the creation of the post of General Director. All were accepted.

The second half of the 1950s and the early 1960s saw a change in the role of this structural fetish, in correlation with the improving position of the party. The changes of the Grimond group, already described, reflected improved resources and the consequently enhanced capacity of the party élite for efforts at policy creation and internal discipline, not the escapism of reshuffling resources which were either constant or declining in the aftermath of defeat. With the dissipation of the Grimond revival, however, Liberals returned to their old form and concerned themselves with restructuring party mechanisms. At the start of 1965, the party announced a complete review of its

42 *Costs Off for the Future*!, p. 14.

43 *The Campaign Guide 1955*, p. 547. Liberals generally respect the research competence of the Conservative Central Office.

constitution. In April of that year, Byers was appointed
chairman of the party, to co-ordinate various activities. He
had already held the post for some months in an informal
capacity. At the same time, Lord Beaumont was made
administrative head of the Liberal Party Organization.[44]
The resignation of the previous chief administrator at LPO
necessitated some changes, but clearly the party was again
in one of its unhappy tinkering moods. In the autumn of
1966 the Political Directorate was created to replace the
Organizing Committee.

In the face of all this administrative instability, the role of
the party Establishment as a continuing anchor becomes
very clear and important. While it could provide some
consistency to party statements and administration,
however, this group was too small to do the entire job of
spurring the revival at the grass roots, let alone trying to
maintain that momentum through time. For this, a large
body of fairly independent activists was required for
manning local headquarters, assisting candidates,
canvassing, and doing the variety of other tasks which a
political party must accomplish to stay alive and prosper.

The Young Liberals

Because the Liberals keep no detailed national membership
records, trying to analyse the movement of volunteers into
the party is a difficult task. It involves assembling the pieces
of a jigsaw puzzle, not the copying of LPO files. Despite this
handicap, it does seem clear upon investigation that there
was a notable increase in the number of serious party
activists before the post-war revival period. Beyond the
hard data of increasing constituency affiliations with the
national party, presented in Table 4:1, evidence tends to be
partly impressionistic — but nevertheless persuasive. One
activist, who joined the party after the Second World War,
recalls that most Liberals he met in party circles seemed to
be in their fifties or older. At the same time, with him and
following him, there was a growing stream of younger

44 Butler and King, *op. cit.*, pp. 81-2.

people into the party. Because one could stay in the Young Liberals up to the age of thirty-five until the 1960s, when the limit was reduced to thirty, the youth arm became a focal point for a rather large portion of the party's membership. Because the Young Liberals had a relatively high upper age limit, they carried a fair amount of weight with the rest of the party. Because they were relatively young, they lacked the memory of Liberal collapse from greatness which would have been the experience of people coming to political maturity and receiving the vote after 1918 – the very age group which the activist witness (just cited) could not find in the party.

Whatever the specific reasons, the early 1950s saw what was clearly the start of a growing migration of young people, especially university students, into Liberal Party ranks. The private correspondence of a Young Liberal leader, who did a great deal of travelling in the 1950s as part of the organizational efforts at the universities, reflects their enthusiasm for the Liberals. Some samples:[45]

> The numbers at Cambridge Liberal Club are very encouraging and of course give excellent publicity in the national press. [Letter from officer of the Nottingham Liberal Club, 1 November, 1955.]

> Further to my suggestion and plea that you might come and speak to my newly-founded Liberal Society at this College I can now offer you the following dates ... The subject of the talk should be entitled, in my submission, something such as 'The Liberal Revival in the Universities' or the 'New Awakening' or something equally strong. [Letter from faculty member of University College, London, 14 January, 1956.]

> We have been a very active Society this last year and the impression we have created in the University over this period necessitates our obtaining interesting and notable speakers who will be able to nourish the idea of the resurgence of Liberalism in this country. [Letter from the

45 Correspondence file of Liberal activist.

Honorary President of the Leeds University Union Liberal Society, 22 June, 1958.]

Since you came to the University last, with Mr Ludovic Kennedy, the Liberal Society has gone from strength to strength and is in the position of the largest political society in the Guild. [Letter from the Honorary Secretary of Birmingham University Liberal Society, 11 November, 1958.]

Quantitative evidence tends to reinforce this impression. During 1957, the Young Liberals were forming branches at a rate of one per week. A special article in the party journal *New Outlook*, in November 1963, described Young Liberal history from the formation of the youth arm in 1903, and stressed its more recent growth by noting that the organization had doubled the number of branches in the 1950s. As their numbers increased, so did their tactical shrewdness: 'They ... showed the Party the use that could be made of really good literature, showering the country with posters, leaflets and booklets and issuing, for the first time, a printed *Young Liberal Handbook.*' The Manchester Regional Young Liberal Organization emerged especially strongly after the 1950 elections, increasing the number of active branches from 6 to over 40. In the two years before the 1959 general election, the National League of Young Liberals' membership doubled, to nearly 10,000. After Orpington, it shot up to 15,000. The New Orbits Group, the intellectual hub of many Young Liberals, was formed in 1959.[46]

The money granted to the Young Liberals by the national party was yet another measure of the growing strength of this group. Contributions to the National League of Young Liberals and the Union of Liberal Students, grew from £115 in 1955 and £65 in 1956 to £720 in 1960 and £2,438 in 1961, when aid to the Young Liberals was combined with other subsidies.[47]

46 *Liberal News*, No 596, 8 November, 1957, p. 1; Adele Bagnall, 'The Young Ones', *New Outlook*, November 1963, pp. 20-2.
47 LPO annual reports.

As the 1960s wore on, the Young Liberals continued to grow in numbers. Far more political than the Young Conservatives, who had the public image of a fun-loving social group, far more free than the well-controlled Young Socialists, they were an ideal home for the politically serious, activist youth of the period. For the party, the Young Liberals provided the infantry of revival, volunteers to do essential organizing and campaigning on the grass-roots level. In this, they were invaluable – and still are. But the 1960s also witnessed the growth of more extreme forms of political and social protest. This aspect of popular activism also became characteristic of a number of Young Liberals from the middle of the decade to its conclusion, especially among the visible national leadership of the organization. Young Liberals had always been an object of attention – and some criticism – from more conservative elements in the party and press. In 1963, for example, there were complaints, some YLs had gone to the rude length of silencing Lady Violet Bonham Carter with slow handclaps while she tried to speak at the party assembly.[48] In the mid-1960s, the more militant, younger activists had been dubbed "Red Guards" by the press. They were accused of concerted and organized efforts to enforce their policy will on the party assembly. The ethos of the new style of activism was clearly stress on far-reaching change in social and political institutions. George Kiloh, a leader of the group, declared at the 1966 Young Liberal Conference: 'Long-term plans have been drawn up for a concerted attack on the inadequacies of parts of the Liberal Party, and a militant attitude towards problems that all young people find important.'[49] From 1966 onward, this faction was prominent at Liberal assemblies, pressing to have its policy views adopted by the party. At first they were comparitively successful; and this is no doubt testament to the lack of strong organization, and discipline which have been continuing characteristics of the Liberal Party. The *Economist* complained of their easy impact in gaining an anti-Vietnam War resolution accepted at the

---

48 Alan Watkins, *The Liberal Dilemma*, p. 131.
49 *Liberal News*, No 1045, 17 June, 1966, p. 1.

1967 Liberal Assembly, despite efforts to defeat the motion. A more ambiguous resolution was proposed, but due 'largely to as inept a display of chairmanship as even a Liberal Assembly has ever seen, this was brushed aside without a vote. And the young ones had their anti-American spleen adopted as party policy'.[50]

In 1966 and 1967, the party Establishment tried to bend with the challenge, hoping that co-operation with the most radical elements in the party would dilute their fervour while avoiding an open split with Young Liberals. One younger compromiser wrote a *New Outlook* essay which attempted to find common ground between older Liberals and the militant younger wing by noting that emphasis on the importance of the individual and hostility to concentrations of power were common to Liberals of every type.[51]

In reality, the effort at subtlety on the part of the party leadership made things doubly bad from a practical political viewpoint. First, the militants were encouraged by success to press on with their causes. This in turn served further to alienate older, more traditional Liberals, who proceeded to write angrily in party organs about 'Mr Kiloh and his cronies ...' policy statements which were 'clearly immature politically and generally inconsistent' and a party hierarchy which seemed to tolerate and tried to work with the radicals.[52] Second, the whole phenomenon was seriously damaging to the party's reputation with an electorate for whom its credibility was always fragile at best. The Liberals have been required to mix caution with hard work as part of the effort to be taken seriously as a political force in the nation. There is, to be sure, that small residual Liberal vote which is consistently loyal. But to go beyond this, it is necessary to overcome the general tendency, visible in the press, and among many Liberals themselves ('we're all mad you know'), not to take the party seriously. The lack of discipline, the confusion at party assemblies, the party's old

50 The *Economist*, 23 September, 1967, p. 1072.

51 William Wallace, 'After Blackpool', *New Outlook*, October 1967, p. 8.

52 John Derry, 'Liberal Row', *New Outlook*, April 1968, p. 33; Richard Lamb, 'Liberal Sickness Diagnosed', *op. cit.*, p. 4.

reputation as a haven for various sorts of political extremists – all of this is far more likely to promote popular amusement than popular support.

A great quality of the Grimond period was the credibility the party seemed to be developing. In providing workers, and psychologically paving the way, for the Grimond era the Young Liberals of the 1950s and early 1960s were vital to this party success of the mind and spirit, as well as of the ballot box. But the Young Liberals of the late 1960s and their press image were just as instrumental in weakening the whole edifice. Grimond resigned in early 1967, the party was beset with internal strife in the wake of his departure, the Liberal vote was declining, the money was evaporating – and on top of all this the new internal strains emerged. In 1968, the party élite began vigorously to oppose the militants' tactics. This served to prevent the youthful activists from passing their policy motions with ease, but did not remove their presence from the assembly floor or meeting hall. Moreover, some Liberal activists, though not specifically sympathetic with the militant faction, were put off by what they perceived to be il-Liberal efforts to control it.[53] Under this challenge, it was impossible for the party to avoid suffering politically. But there were other things which were endangering the revival. Other forces, outside the Liberal Party's own internal problems and tensions, were moving to close off potential avenues of growth and advance.

53 See e.g., article by David Steel, *Liberal News Commentary*, No 48, 22 August, 1967, p. 1.

> *At the time I became involved in politics, the Labour Party was rather a shambles and consisted of right-wing trade union elements and a left-wing section which was authoritarian to the point of being Stalinist ... Things are rather different now.*
> A Liberal MP

Aside from the internal weaknesses of the Liberal Party, three major outside factors have worked against its efforts to revive. Each of them bears upon more general changes in British politics. First, both the Conservative and Labour Parties have responded to the changing social and political environment through a combination of policy reform and tactical political moves. Second, the nationalist parties in Scotland and Wales have flanked the Liberal Party from another direction. Third, while the electorate has moved noticeably toward the Liberal Party under Grimond and Thorpe, it is also clear that the party has never carved out a specific, distinct sector of the electorate which can be relied upon with assurance.

Tory and Labour

As the decade of the 1960s progressed, the two major parties moved to adopt a neo-Liberalism of their own. In the realm of industrial relations, both major parties committed themselves to reform. Neither was willing to adopt the anti-class co-partnership perspective which plays such a strong part in Liberal thought, but each concentrated more and more on the need for change. Labour's *In Place of Strife* (1969) and the Tories' *Putting Britain Right Ahead* (1965) responded to a public mood first sensed by the Liberals in their advocacy of trade-union reform. In the 1964 Tory campaign guide, mention of unions was limited to a factual description of the history of the trade-union movement and its ties to the Labour Party.[1] The very next year, however, the party struck a different theme, one very similar to that of the 1964 Liberal candidates' and speakers' handbook, *Partners for Progress*:[2]

> Liberals would encourage the trade-union movement in the review of its organization and aims. Unions should reform abuses in election and the use of rule books themselves, but if they fail to do so the State should step in through the Registrar of Friendly Societies. [*Partners for Progress*.]

> Our suggestion is to establish a new and powerful Registrar of Trade Unions and Employers' Associations. He would see that the rules of both conformed to certain basic principles. [*Putting Britain Right Ahead*.]

In consumer affairs, the Labour Party established a council for the protection of consumers after taking office in 1964. Previously, however, Labour Party neglect of this topic had led Michael Young to write his *The Chipped White Cups of Dover* in criticism of both main parties on the consumer issue. The Tories, in the 1964 campaign guide, had mentioned the need to strengthen competition in industry for the benefit of the consumer, but the thrust of Tory remarks there stressed the importance of economies of scale:[3]

> In comparatively small countries such as the UK it is necessary to weigh the benefits of competition against the benefits of large-scale production. Under modern technological conditions large industrial groups may be essential in some industries if we are to compete effectively with the USA or the Common Market.

1 *The Campaign Guide 1964*, pp. 588-95.
2 *Partners for Progress*, p. 172; cited in 'Liberal Left-overs', typed manuscript in the Research Department at LPO.
3 *The Campaign Guide 1964*, pp. 588-95.

Later, however, Tory statements on the issue of competition, which relates directly to that of consumer protection, followed earlier Liberal emphasis:[4]

> Liberals will check the rise in prices by action against monopolies and price rings; tariff cuts and tax policy ... In particular we will outlaw certain restrictive practices and make take-over bids and mergers subject to public scrutiny. [1964 Liberal manifesto.]

> We would close the loopholes in the present legislation dealing with restrictive trading agreements which harm the interests of the public. A Registrar of Monopolies needs to be appointed to speed up and give more punch to the work of the Monopolies Commission. [*Putting Britain Right Ahead.*]

In the area of devolution to local and regional levels of government, and the opening up of local government both to publicity and from party discipline, Liberal approaches have had no exact reflection in the policies of either of the two major parties. As in industrial affairs, however, the years of Liberal Party revival brought increased Tory and Labour attention to these general areas of policy. Clearly, the two main parties were responding to the same popular sentiments which traditionally have moved the Liberals, and whose resurgence was essential in carrying along the Liberal revival.

This trend was especially apparent soon after Labour took power in 1964. An analyst of this period of Labour Party rule has observed that, ' "Regionalism" was the great rage of the early years of the Labour government'. The Government appointed a Secretary of State for Wales, a Cabinet member who gave that region the same high-level representation which Scotland had enjoyed since 1885.[5] The Department of Economic Affairs, created by Prime Minister Harold Wilson in 1964, was the new regime's first truly broad and comprehensive effort at concentrated regional development. Within two months of the 1964

4 The Times *Guide to the House of Commons 1964*, p. 284.
5 Brian Lapping, *The Labour Government 1964-1970*, pp. 198-200.

elections, the new Secretary of State for Economic Affairs, George Brown (now Lord Brown), announced to the House of Commons the creation of the first six planning regions. Each region was provided with an economic planning council and an economic planning board. The former was concerned with broad issues of regional development and resource use. The latter co-ordinated the work of different government departments concerned with regional affairs.[6] It is not difficult to infer the effect of these types of reform in diluting Liberal momentum. In 1964, the Liberals won 4 of the 6 Scottish Highland parliamentary seats on a platform which included a proposed Highland development board and other regional programmes. In 1965, the Labour Government created an appointed development board and made plans for installing a new atomic reactor in the Caithness constituency. The Liberals lost that very seat to Labour in 1966.

While in power, Labour also created the Maud Commission which resulted in far-reaching recommendations for the reform of local government. As for the Tories, during the early 1960s they established the North-East as a special development area, created a specific Minister for Wales, and located several offices of government departments in Wales (this was termed 'devolution' in 1964 Tory campaign statements).[7] The 1958 Local Government Act, described earlier, was an effort to increase the financial flexibility of local authorities and the powers of some lower-tier councils.[8] As in other areas of policy, however, the Tories moved farther toward the Liberal position with the publication of *Putting Britain Right Ahead*. The argument was made there that 'tasks which are best tackled over a larger area are growing in number all the time'. In consequence, there had developed a need for expanding the size of local units of government. However, it was also seen as essential to ensure 'that they are subject to proper democratic control'. Not only was there sensitivity to the need for local representation, there was also attention to the special

6 703 *House of Commons Debates* 1829, (10 December, 1964).

7 *The Campaign Guide 1964*, pp. 240 ff.

8 *The Campaign Guide 1970*, p. 526.

problems of deprived localities. The report stressed the requirement of encouraging new industry 'near districts of high unemployment'.[9]

Crucially, however, neither Tory nor Labour policies of government (as opposed to the implications of party statements and literature) carried provisions for actual delegation of political control to new, popularly elected bodies. Additionally, few if any substantial administrative powers were delegated to lower levels of government. To Liberals, historically and currently, administrative discretion is essential to real delegation of power, and the democratic election of regional bodies is equally vital. As Clement Davies put it to the House of Commons: 'Then there is the Council for Wales. I have never regarded this as being truly representative of Wales. It is a nominated body, and I do not like nominated bodies – I like to have elected bodies in control.'[10]

The party whips remain in local councils. The Labour Government specifically rejected the Maud Commission recommendations that most of the members of eight proposed provincial councils be elected by local councils. The Commission itself had advocated that only advisory functions be involved. Both Maud, and the earlier Conservative reform of London local government in 1963, eliminated small units of local government in the interest of creating larger entities which would – hopefully – enjoy greater administrative uniformity and competence.[11] As we have seen, the General Grant system of the 1958 Local Government Act, potentially a dramatic change, remained subject to continued checking by central ministries. The Heath Government set in motion planning for a form of devolution to Scotland, and the Labour Governments since have pursued the most dramatic regional delegation of power so far undertaken. Nevertheless, the proposed

9 'Liberal Left-overs', p. 3.

10 631 *House of Commons Debates* 227-228 (29 November, 1960).

11 *The Way Ahead*, p. 89. Many Liberals speak bitterly of the reorganization of London local government, which had the immediate effect of making it much more difficult to elect Liberal councillors in the metropolitan area.

Scottish and Welsh assemblies are to have only very limited policy control, in such fields as education, health and housing. No independent authority is to be exercised over industrial, employment or other economic policies. Liberal trends may be detectable in policy movements within the major parties, but clearly the reflections have so far been only partial.[12]

Other Liberal policies have been reflected in varying ways in the two major parties. In education, Liberal initiative for reform was matched, rather than really copied, by the Labour Party. The specifics of Liberal recommendations on transport do not seem to have become adopted by the main parties, except indirectly and implicitly in the general increase in Tory emphasis on the virtues and values of competition. Taxation, however, is a different matter, where concrete Liberal suggestions can be traced through time into the policy development of the Conservative Party. The only taxes abolished by the Tories during their long rule from 1951 to 1964 were the Entertainments Tax and the Schedule A Tax on owner-occupiers. In view of previous Tory Government inaction, the abolition of Schedule A seems to have been a direct result of the Liberal Party's Orpington victory in 1962. Liberals had pressed for the end of Schedule A for some time, arguing that it was a poorly conceived form of taxation. In 1957 and 1959, no Tory MP voted for a Liberal proposal for tax relief for owner-occupiers. In 1960 and 1961, proposals by Tory MPs to enact tax relief for owner-occupiers were voted down in the Commons, despite the fact that Tory Party conferences in these years had recommended abolition of Schedule A for owner-occupiers. During the same period, Liberal amendments to end Schedule A were not even called in the Commons.[13] In these circumstances, Jo Grimond tried to publicize Tory inconsistency, declaring at one point that, 'We who have fought the Conservatives know that year after year, and at election after election, they denounce this tax but when the

12 See, *e.g.*, the *Economist*, 8 June, 1974, p. 15, 29 November, 1975, pp. 13-15.

13 *Partners for Progress*, pp. 148-9.

opportunity arises to get rid of it by voting against it they do not do so.'[14] Lubbock's victory, in a suburban seat filled with owner-occupiers, was followed by quick repeal.

There were additional indications that Liberal tax proposals were making their impact on Conservative policy. An official Conservative Party publication, in the course of discussing a 1962 tax on speculative gains which was designed to make quick financial killings less profitable, mentioned that 'The new tax is similar to proposals that have been put forward by the Liberal Party. It is, however, very different from a full capital gains tax advocated by the Labour Party'.[15] In discussing the need to reduce surtax to encourage initiative, the Tories in 1964 went so far as to quote as evidence statements made by Grimond in his 1961 pamphlet, *Growth Not Grandeur*.[16] The changes in Conservative Party attitudes toward a payroll tax were also in a Liberal direction, at least to an extent. In 1961, the Macmillan Government had obtained the power to impose a payroll tax as a regulator for that year, but the authority was never used and eventually lapsed.[17] In 1964, the Liberal Party manifesto declared that 'Social Security should be financed by a social-security tax levied in proportion to their pay roll, on employers two-thirds and employees one-third'.[18] The Tory publication, *Putting Britain Right Ahead*, returned to much the same idea: 'More of the cost of the social services should be transferred from the Exchequer to the employer.'[19] In advocating a tax which would relieve the individual taxpayer, and progressively increase the tax commitments of larger employers, the Conservative Party was returning to a position toward which it had edged in 1961, and which the Liberals had publicized in the interim. During the same period, the Labour Party did little in the way of adopting new tax proposals. Labour Party conferences urged tax

14 642 *House of Commons Debates* 1,393 (20 June, 1961).
15 *The Campaign Guide 1964*, p. 30.
16 *Ibid.*, p. 29.
17 *Ibid.*, p. 34.
18 The Times, *Guide to the House of Commons 1964*, p. 286.
19 'Liberal Left-overs', *op. cit.*, p. 1.

relief for workers, but specifically rejected surtax relief.[20]

On housing, the policy area used earlier to contrast the outlooks of Liberalism and collectivism, there was also some detectable movement toward the Liberal Party position on the part of others. Labour remained effectively bound to the council housing *status quo*. The Tories, in contrast, became more Liberal. In the past, the Conservatives had encouraged the sale of council houses.[21] With the appearance of *Putting Britain Right Ahead*, however, there was distinct sensitivity shown to the issue of poverty beneath the safety net of the welfare state: 'We would place an obligation on all local authorities to introduce rent schemes to ensure that the housing subsidies go to those who really need them.' In the same essay, the Tories seem to move more toward selectivity in their general approach to social welfare: 'We would help the local authority social services – health, welfare, child care and others – to be more effective by reforming their structure.'[22]

After taking power in 1970, the Heath Government took steps to relate benefits more closely to need. Charges for medical prescriptions were increased, but at the same time the exemption from this payment which was provided to poor families was extended. The government began a new family income subsidy which allowed benefits to families containing members working full-time but who were still below the poverty line. In the specific area of housing the sale to tenants of council houses was encouraged, public sector rents were increased for those who could afford it, but in addition rent rebates for the poor were broadened and – for the first time – extended to include private-housing tenants.[23]

More generally and vaguely, the Liberals saw their political style and campaign tones mimicked by the major parties. A party's political personality consists not only of specific positions on particular issues, but of a less concrete

20 *E.G.*, *Report of the 60th Annual Conference of the Labour Party*, p. 149.

21 Lapping, *op. cit.*, p. 170.

22 'Liberal Left-overs', *op. cit.* pp. 2, 3.

23 Samuel Beer, 'The British Political System', in Samuel Beer and Ulam eds., *Patterns of Government*, 3rd ed. p. 294.

atmosphere too. The Grimond Liberal Party developed distinctive themes of activism, energy, change, reform which contrasted dramatically with the mood of the times in which they appeared. As Tory and Labour strove to shake off their respective damaging associations with uncreative fatigue and ideological civil war, they moved toward the Grimond image. The more dramatic capture of the abstract was accomplished by Harold Wilson, with his 1964 rhetoric about employing the tool of 'technology' to solve problems which were unsolvable by the traditionalist and stuffy Tories. Similarly, if less clearly, Heath stressed a new tone to the Tory Party after he took charge. The rejection of past collectivism was to be a series of specific steps; but with them, underlying them, was the new theme of the Tory leader as middle-class businessman, decisive in action and opposed to inefficient lack of competition.[24] Even when the rejection proved difficult in practice, the tone remained.

This Liberal innovation, in style and substance, was seen and credited by the press, especially during the 1964 election period, when new and renewed Liberal proposals had been in circulation for some time. Press remarks indicate the extent to which the journalistic community recognized the Liberal contribution and its adoption by the major parties:[25]

> The Liberals have carried their thinking on the reform of government further than either Labour or the Conservatives; and they are now seeing their wardrobe of political ideas being freely raided by their opponents. This they may find exasperating, but it demonstrates the usefulness of an active Liberal Party, even when there are only half a dozen Liberal MPs and a handful of Liberal peers. Parliament would be a more vigorous place if there

24 A brief portrait of Wilson is given in David E. Butler and Anthony King, *The British General Election of 1964*, p. 23; a sketch of Heath is found in Anthony Sampson, *The Anatomy of Britain*, pp. 77-8.

25 Quotations are from: the *Guardian*, 24 February, 1964, p. 8; *The Times*, 14 October, 1964, p. 13; the *Guardian*, 13 October, 1964, p. 10; *The Times*, 1 February, 1964, p. 9.

were more Liberals in it ... The strength of the Liberal scheme for regional government is that it is conceived as the way to regenerate the life of the regions outside London, and not merely as a better instrument for speeding up decisions at the regional level. [*Guardian.*]

... everyone who has liberal instincts and a Liberal candidate to vote for should vote Liberal. Such a vote is not wasted. The House of Commons would be better with more Liberal MPs and if all liberals voted Liberal it should get them. Even if it does not, every Liberal vote on Thursday can have an effect on the two other parties thereafter ... Britain needs a strong Government, not a weak one. It needs that Government ... to be committed to forthright and radical change. A competitive economy, a more sensibly articulated society, a Britain continuing in a new phase its historic role in Europe – the Liberals represent the views of millions of voters on all these things. [*The Times.*]

Will the Liberals be crushed between the two big parties on Thursday? We hope not, though it could happen. The Liberals deserve more seats in Parliament – not just the seven that they have had or a smaller number. They have been a stimulant to the big parties and a rich source of ideas. Their influence has been felt. [*Guardian.*]

... the two major parties have committed themselves to programmes of social reform of so monumental a character – whatever the differences in emphasis – that it scarcely seems possible to argue that the specification for the new Britain is not large enough ... The [Liberal] party may claim, justly and no doubt indignantly, that they thought of a good deal of all this first. [*The Times.*]

The *New York Times* recognized the same phenomenon in its editorial comment upon Grimond's resignation as leader of the party. The main accomplishment of the Liberals, ran the piece, was not Grimond's extraordinary personal impact or the modest party electoral revival. Rather, it was that the Liberals 'sowed for others to reap'. They had urged important ideas concerning regional development and devolution, industrial decentralization, and entry into Europe.[26]

For Liberals interested in political power, whose expectations had been raised by the party's gains under Grimond, little comfort could be drawn from intellectual success alone. It was this very abstract victory, in the sense of broader acceptance of Liberal ideas, which contributed to party political failure. Moreover, the major parties joined acceptance of Liberal ideas with lively efforts to crimp the party's advance. At the same time that the Conservative Party was moving in Liberal directions, it opened a heavy barrage of hostile anti-Liberal Party propaganda. Liberal Party documents and statements were carefully examined for inconsistency and implausibility. Conservative press releases adopted the tactic of quoting all sorts of unofficial statements by Liberals, in turn contrasting them with statements by other members of the party. Unofficial opinions were turned, by implication, into contradictory and confused party policy.[27]

The Nationalists

This big-party effort to close Liberal channels of access to national power was not the only competition faced by Grimond and his followers. Simultaneously, there were specific small-party challenges from the geographic hinterlands. While Liberal Party interest in devolution of some administrative and political independence to Scotland and Wales contrasted with conventional Tory and Labour positions, it has been matched in its concern – and surpassed in intensity of rhetoric and the degree of devolution advocated – by the Scottish Nationalist Party

26 *New York Times*, 18 January, 1967, p. 42.
27 *Liberal News*, No 836, 16 June, 1962, p. 1. The article states that Iain Macleod was appointed by Macmillan to organize a great anti-Liberal campaign to culminate in the autumn. Every pronouncement by a Liberal candidate, councillor or other leader was to be collated and compared for inconsistencies.

Table 5:1 The Nationalist Parties in General Elections

Year	Plaid Cymru			SNP		
	Total Vote	% Total Welsh Vote	Candids	Total Vote	% Total Scot. Vote	Candids
1929	609	0·0	1	3,313	0·1	2
1931	1,136	0·1	1	20,954	1·0	5
1935	2,534	0·3	1	25,652	1·1	7
1945	14,321	1·1	6	30,595	1·2	8
1950	17,580	1·2	7	9,708	0·4	3
1951	10,920	0·7	4	7,299	0·3	2
1955	45,119	3·1	11	12,112	0·5	2
1959	77,571	5·2	20	21,738	0·8	5
1964	69,507	4·8	23	64,044	2·4	15
1966	61,071	4·3	20	128,474	5·0	23
1970	171,583	11·5	36	299,969	11·4	65
1974 (Feb)	171,364	10·7	36	632,032	21·9	70
1974 (Oct)	166,321	10·8	36	839,628	30·0	71

(SNP) and the Welsh nationalist party (Plaid Cymru). Public attention was focused on the nationalist parties in two by-election victories in the second half of the 1960s – Gwynfor Evans of Plaid Cymru at Carmarthen in 1966, and Winifred Ewing of the SNP at Hamilton in 1967. Each of these seats was lost by the nationalists in the general election of 1970, even though the SNP compensated by winning another – and then another in a 1973 by-election.[28] In the two 1974 general elections, Plaid advanced to three seats and the SNP captured eleven – clear evidence of growing nationalist political support, especially in Scotland.

The first two nationalist parliamentary victories excited speculation about quick surges to power which was clearly premature. Nevertheless, the parties' victories reflected

28 David Butler and Donald Stokes, *Political Change in Britain*, p. 122; in the 1970 General Election, Western Isles went from Labour to the SNP, and Glasgow Govan was taken in November 1973.

growing pools of nationalist support. Table 5:1 illustrates this improvement in candidates offered and votes received. Neither of the two nationalist parties was able to build upon its tiny base of electoral support until the middle and late 1950s. The Scottish nationalists did manage to elect Compton Mackenzie, a party leader, to the Rectorship of Glasgow University in 1931 and to win the Motherwell by-election of 1945; but the university post was hardly a political victory, and the by-election result was reversed three months later in the general election.

Both of the nationalist parties have enjoyed their post-war increases in strength at approximately the same time that the Liberal Party has experienced its national revival. The nationalist advocacy of complete independence for Scotland and Wales is partially matched by the Liberal policy of devolution. While the Liberals may lack the specific geographic identification available to the nationalists, the party cannot be accused of lack of concern for these regions. After all, promoting devolution historically has carried a significant political price for the Liberals, yet it has been a cause to which the party has been notably loyal.[29]

But the Liberals have stood with equal consistency against devolution of responsibility for defence, Commonwealth and other foreign affairs. It is this crucial difference which has helped prevent a political reconciliation between the Liberals and the nationalists, even in the context of election tactics. Despite the efforts of some Scottish Liberals, including Jo Grimond in recent years, it has been impossible to work out an accord with the Scottish Nationalist Party. The majority of members in both parties find co-operation unacceptable. At the 1961 Liberal Assembly in Edinburgh, delegates declared in favour of self-government for Scotland, but also stated that nowhere 'is there a place in Liberal policy for any separatism of the extreme character advocated by the

20 At the 1962 Liberal Assembly, in an amusing but revealing incident, the delegates gave great applause to a Welsh speaker, even though he spoke entirely in Welsh and without translation; *Liberal Assembly 1962, the* Guardian *Report*, p. 11.

Scottish Nationalists'. In March 1964, John Bannerman, Chairman of the Scottish Liberal Party, declared that there was 'no place' in Liberal policy for Scottish nationalist 'extremism' and so there could be no arrangements between the two parties.[30]

Similarly, the nationalists have refused any possibility of a broad electoral pact with the Liberal Party. They consistently link the Liberals with Labour and the Tories, denouncing all three as London-oriented central government parties. A 1968 SNP publication linked the three parties together as long-standing deceivers who, 'divide Scotland against herself. These parties ask us Scots to give our prime loyalty to their out-dated Anglo-Scottish sectional and class interests'.[31] The situation between the Liberals and nationalists in Wales mirrors that in Scotland. One of the chief organizers for Plaid Cymru has remarked that the party was formed at a time when 'there was a complete disillusionment with Liberals'. The Liberal Party was not only in a state of decline from former greatness, it had failed to deliver on Home Rule. The Labour Party was also unsatisfactory in defining or taking steps to establish an independent Wales, 'and we were left with the conviction that the only pressure the English Establishment would understand would be that from an independent and radical Welsh Party immune from the temptation to sell out once in power'.[32]

Currently, the nationalists are especially unwilling to entertain the possibility of a deal with the Liberal Party. In earlier years, the parties rarely ran against one another in the same constituency. Starting in 1970, however, the growing strength of the nationalist parties has enabled them to challenge the Liberals in virtually every Celtic seat. Recognizing the danger presented by increasing support for the SNP, four of the five Scottish Liberal MPs attempted to establish electoral pacts with the nationalists. All were rebuffed. In the October 1974 general elections, the SNP established itself as the second party in Scotland, behind

30 *Liberal News*, No 928, 19 March, 1964, p. 2.

31 *SNP and You*, p. 5.

32 Correspondence, Spring 1970.

Labour but ahead of the Conservatives. This surge threatens both the Conservatives and Liberals with eclipse in Scotland. Plaid Cymru has been less successful in overcoming the Liberals as chief protest party, but it has clearly established a separate and distinct electoral base.[33]

Aside from basic differences on policy between Liberals and nationalists, their sources of votes appear to be generally similar. Since The Second World War, the Liberal Party's Scottish MPs have come from areas where the party historically was strong: the Highlands and Borders. Both regions are rural, agricultural, and in recent decades largely Conservative. The SNP initially developed strength in these areas, plus the small towns of central Scotland. During the second half of the 1960s, the nationalists also began to do well in the industrial midlands, long a stronghold of Labour Party support. Hamilton is part of this industrial belt. The SNPs progress in industrial areas during the tenure of a Labour Government naturally raised speculation that the party's new support represented temporary protest votes. Nevertheless, the SNP's strength has continued to grow during the Conservative and Labour regimes of the 1970s.

Some evidence indicating different sources of basic core support for the two parties is available from the few contests during the decade before 1970 when Scottish or Welsh nationalists and Liberals clashed. For example, in Greenock's 1966 local elections, Liberals took control of the city council despite the presence of Scottish nationalist candidates. In East Aberdeenshire, a seat the Liberals did not fight in 1959, they garnered 23 per cent of the vote in 1964 and 28 per cent in 1966, even though a Scottish nationalist also fought the constituency in these elections.

Voting in Wales in the 1960s was also characterized by different geographic centres of support for the Liberals and the nationalists. Elections during this period witnessed the Liberals offering most of their candidates and receiving their best results in non-industrial seats of middle and north Wales (e.g., Montgomery, Brecon & Radnor, Cardiganshire

33 The *Economist*, 19 October, 1974, pp. 36-8.
34 See Chris Cook, 'Election Surprises by Scottish Nationalists', *New Outlook*, No 61, February 1967, pp. 21-4.

and Denbigh); while Plaid Cymru has entered contests
mainly in industrial south Wales (e.g., Aberdare,
Caerphilly, and Rhondda East and West). In Montgomery
and Merioneth, Plaid voters appeared to come from Labour
and Tory ranks as much as from the Liberals. In Anglesey
and Llanelli in 1966, and Conway in 1964, the Liberal
candidates stood down, giving the nationalists a 'clear run';
but the Plaid vote increased only slightly, not as much as
might be expected if both parties were competing for
essentially the same constituency.[35]

Developments in the 1970's, however, indicate that in
fact the nationalists and Liberals in Scotland and Wales are
competing for votes from overlapping constituencies. The
nationalists may generally do better than Liberals in
industrial areas; nevertheless, they also have powerful
appeal in the sort of rural fringe areas which have
traditionally been centres of Liberal strength. The three
Plaid Cymru representatives elected to the House of
Commons in 1974, and eight of the eleven Scottish
nationalists, are from such areas.

As these electoral trends indicate, nationalist fortunes
have a bearing on the Liberals. The nationalists provide an
important challenge to the Liberal Party in Wales and,
especially, Scotland. Although the Liberal position is small
and insecure, it nevertheless has been significant for the
party. During the Liberal nadir of the 1950s, the party's
residual strength in the 'Celtic Fringe' was still great
enough to supply four of six Liberal MPs in the House of
Commons. Should the nationalist parties further broaden
their support, this traditional Liberal base might well be
eliminated. Clearly the SNP, rather than the Liberals, now
has the forward momentum in Scotland.

Less hypothetically, both the Liberals and the
nationalists seem to represent the same underlying
phenomenon: popular hostility to central institutions, and
to the two major parties with which they are associated,
over a period of relative economic distress. The economic
malaise of Scotland and Wales has been both persistent and

35 *Liberal News Commentary*, No 60, 21 November, 1967, p. 3.

measurable. In these areas, a significant amount of activity is concentrated in sectors which are declining or only growing slowly. These include fishing and forestry, mining and quarrying, textiles, and shipbuilding and allied engineering trades. Moreover, in recent years, there has been a substantial cut in railway employment. Unemployment has been constantly higher than the British average for decades. Additionally, hard-core unemployment is comparatively serious. Those out of work tend to remain so longer than in more prosperous parts of the country. Population loss has also contributed to discontent. Actually, migration to the south-eastern area in and around London helps Scottish and Welsh unemployment problems by bringing distribution of people and jobs more in line with each other. However, Liberals and nationalists are concerned primarily with the preservation of local cultures and societies, and find in these population shifts further cause for complaint.[36]

The discovery of very substantial oil deposits in the North Sea off the coast of Scotland has provided added economic incentive for political protest. Scotland's weak economy is one source of discontent; the desire to exploit the new resources directly without leaving their control to London is another. The SNP has always emphasized economic issues, and has been particularly insistent that the new oil discoveries belong to Scotland. The party's February 1974 election manifesto, for instance, stated in part: 'Do you wish to be rich Scots or poor British? ... The enormous wealth of the oil and gas fields off the Scottish coast, allied to our other vast resources, offers ever-improving standards to the people of Scotland when they demand a Scottish government.' The SNP has done particularly well recently in seats on the east coast of Scotland, close to the North Sea and most strongly affected by the oil finds. Four of the seats won in February, and two

36 'spokesmen for development areas complain of high rates of unemployment and of outmigration in the same breath; of such conditions are Scottish and Welsh nationalists ... bred.'
Richard Caves and associates, *Britain's Economic Prospects*, p. 378; Cavin McCrone, *Scotland's Future – The Economics of Nationalism, pessim.*

of the four new ones taken in October, are located there. Oil prosperity is already beginning to percolate through the Scottish economy; wage levels are rising to rival those south of the border, and labour shortages are increasingly common.[37]

Nevertheless, while North Sea oil promises dramatically to improve Scotland's economic conditions, the fact remains that the 'Celtic Fringe' generally has lagged the economy as a whole for a long period of time. Liberals and nationalists argue that this reflects neglect by central government. Actually, the picture is more complex, though there is still clearly evidence for a case that the Celtic periphery has not been helped. A significant regional development programme was begun by the National Government after the Second World War. Quite substantial aid was given to Scotland and Wales when they began to fall seriously behind the rest of the economy in the late 1950s. During that decade, the total spent on regional development was generally less than £10 million annually for the entire UK. By 1967-8, it had risen to £250 million each year, with 40 per cent of this going to Scotland alone.[38]

The real problem is that direct-grant and other aid programmes have still not prevented comparatively slow growth and high unemployment in the Celtic regions. This basic dilemma has been compounded by lack of general consistency in central government policy, giving an impression of tinkering rather than careful long-term planning. Tories have tended to favour indirect tax incentives, notably through depreciation allowances; Labour prefers direct grants. The borders of development areas are constantly being expanded and contracted. Moreover, regional aid policies have existed beside other national economic plans, such as that of Beeching, which have benefited the overall economy at the expense of the Celtic periphery. Finally, the two major parties have not so far been willing to consider significant devolution of political power to Scotland and Wales, as both the Liberals

37 The Times, Guide to the House of Commons 1974, p. 326; the *Economist*, 2 November, 1974, pp. 79-80.

38 McCrone, *op. cit.*, p. 45.

and nationalists advocate. All of these factors have hampered Tory and Labour efforts to respond to Scottish and Welsh concerns, despite the particularly prominent regional development and devolution efforts which began in the 1960s, and were outlined earlier.[39]

The primary question for this analysis is why the nationalists have been able to rise up beside the Liberals, and in Scotland clearly overshadow them, despite long-standing Liberal sensitivity to the problems of these regions. This issue becomes especially interesting in light of the proposition that the Liberals should have at least two strong advantages over the nationalist parties. First, the Liberal Party's specific policy on devolution, in contrast to those of the SNP and Plaid Cymru, is probably more in tune with the actual wishes of typical Scottish and Welsh voters. On Scotland, for instance, historian H.J. Hanham has written:[40]

> It is, indeed, a curious fact that the party which has thought most about Home Rule, and whose policy most reflects the views of the Scottish electorate as shown in public opinion polls, should be the least capable of doing anything about implementing it.

Table 5:2 provides some of this evidence.

Second, the nationalist parties' case for independence is objectively very difficult to defend. While both Scotland and Wales are wealthier than many independent nations, and theoretically at least could credibly survive in total independence from England, both are very dependent on British markets for their goods. This means that economic reality would still limit freedom of action, even in the event that political independence was won by either Scotland or Wales. Money, credit, fiscal and other economic policies would have to be co-ordinated with England. Scotland and

---

39 By 1967, more than half the passenger stations which Beeching had advocated abandoning were in fact closed, and local freight depots had been cut from 6,000 to about 1,800. See Caves, *op. cit.*, p. 408; A.J. Brown, *The Framework of Regional Economics in the United Kingdom*, p. 342.

40 H.J. Hanham, *Scottish Nationalism*, p. 192; David Butler and Michael Pinto-Duschinsky, *The British General Election of 1970*, p. 456.

Table 5:2 Attitudes Toward Devolution in Scotland and Wales

Attitude	Scotland	Wales
	%	%
No change	10	25
Minor devolution	21	31
A regional government for domestic affairs	46	26
Complete independence	17	13
Don't know	7	5

Source: Market Information Services, 1968, cited in Richard Rose, *Strathclyde Occasional Paper Number 6*, p 8.

Wales could attempt economic autonomy, but in that case firms which had located there because of access to the wider British market would lose that incentive. Nationalists often recognize that Common Market agreements with England would be necessary in the event of independence, but they also tend to brush over the reality that such agreements would have to be acceptable to the English. The eighteenth-century accord to link Scotland and England, for example, effectively resulted in a subordination of Scotland to England; but the other side of this situation has guaranteed economic access for the Scots into English markets. To break the political union would leave the English free to end those economic aspects of the former union which they found unprofitable. North Sea oil alters this situation but does not reverse it. England's economy is becoming less important to Scotland, and central government leaders now have a powerful incentive to be more forthcoming towards demands for devolution. But the fact remains that a Scottish break from England would require enormous adjustments.[41]

With these political and economic advantages over the nationalists, the Liberals have nevertheless not been able to eliminate the nationalist challenge or strengthen their own

41 McCrone, *op. cit.*, Chapter 4.

position. There are several possible explanations for this. One is the old Liberal hostility to organization, which has worked to limit the party's revival generally in the nation. Doubtless this national factor has had some role in these regional failures. An observer wrote of Liberal fatigue and lack of effort in Wales in 1964, for example: 'What has failed has been the lack of real constituency work.'[42]

Additionally, there is the difficulty that the Liberal Party is, as nationalist accusations stress, a *national* party, even if weak and thinly spread. The party has its history of concern for and advocacy of devolution, but in practical terms it is a party with a history also of association with the central governing institutions of Britain. Hence, to the angry voters of Wales or Scotland, the Liberal Party at best presents a blurred image – favouring forms of devolution, but also favouring national government for all of Britain. Liberals talk about devolution in a variety of regions, thus diluting their impact in any particular region. It is as though their breadth of advocacy of this reform hobbles the intensity of their emotional appeal. In contrast, as single-issue parties, the nationalists are able to focus attention on the goal of devolution from London to their particular regions. Though most Scottish and Welsh voters may intrinsically agree with the Liberal position, the more sophisticated Liberal case is more difficult to present, less exciting to hear, than the emotional, simplistic messages of the SNP and Plaid Cymru. If a voter is interested primarily in registering anger and frustration, why go half-way?

Emlyn Hooson, Wales's senior Liberal MP, has argued that Plaid's votes are primarily a reflection of general frustration rather than support for the specific goal of independence.[43] While he is probably not an entirely objective witness, it is also true that Plaid Cymru has not been unaware of the potential advantages of toning down the actual content of their message while maintaining the fervour for representing Welsh interests. At the 1968

42 Jeremy Rhys, 'Welsh Liberalism: How Green Were the Valleys?', *New Outlook*, December 1964, pp. 29-34.

43 *Liberal News Commentary*, No 82, 23 April, 1968, p. 3.

Caerphilly by-election, Plaid received a very high vote while the Liberals did poorly. In the campaign, the nationalists played down their policy of total independence and stressed general themes of neglect by the Labour government in London. In the same year, the SNP began an effort to moderate and tone down its image. Advocacy of complete freedom from London was muted, and it was emphasized that the party was an important representative of Scottish concerns generally. 'Cranks were expelled, including the semi-secret society which concentrated on romantic nationalism, the 1320 Club.'[44]

A third possible explanation for the rise of the nationalist parties, potentially the broadest in significance, relates to class. The point has been made that the Liberals and nationalists have drawn their support in the past from generally different geographic areas. Carrying the argument further, this difference may reflect a positive Liberal bias against encouraging working-class participation in the party. This basic phenomenon, which explains the demise of the Liberal Party from national power in Britain and its replacement by Labour, can also be used to understand the inability of the Liberals to prevent the recent growth in support for the nationalist parties. Liberal Party activists from Scotland and Wales frequently speak of their party as restrained and middle-class, in contrast with the nationalist movements, which they view as rowdy in spirit and simplistic in policy. This relates to another Liberal belief – that the nationalist parties are more working-class in composition. In fact, research on the nationalist parties indicates that they contain professional and other middle-class people among their activists. Nevertheless, they also appear to be more open to working-class people than the Liberals. Some concrete data supporting this argument is presented in Table 5:3, which reveals a noticeable difference between the Liberals and nationalists in the proportions of working-class candidates they have offered in general elections.[45]

44 Butler and Pinto-Duschinsky, *op. cit.*, p. 456.
45 These comments reflect interviews and correspondence with Liberal and nationalist activists. See for more rigorous, microscopic

Table 5:3 Proportion of Working-Class Candidates Offered by the Scottish and Welsh Liberal and Nationalist Parties, 1964-74 General Elections

Candidates' Class	Scot Lib.	SNP	Welsh Lib.	Plaid Cymru
Working Class	3	36	0	14
Middle Class	176	236	109	149
Totals	179	272	109	163

Source: *The Times Guide to the House of Commons.*

In sum, viewed in terms of the general position of the Liberal Party on the national political battlefield, the party has been caught between two different types of opponent, each possessing special advantages. The major parties have enjoyed greater financial and organizational resources, larger constituencies and consequently greater political credibility. With the revival of the Liberal Party, each of them in its own way moved to adopt Liberal style and policies for its own. Whether this was a direct or indirect response to the Liberal advance, it separated the party from a prime psychological asset in the struggle for revival – the advantage of being a fresh force confronting, and contrasting with, two major parties tied to the status quo. The nationalist parties have specific appeal and distinct electoral bases enabling them to pick up voters who might otherwise be Liberals. Additionally, in a nation where class differences still have an important bearing on electoral politics, the nationalists are apparently more open and receptive to working-class participation than the Liberals.

Yet, British history has seen a dramatic instance of a party growing from weakness to great strength, despite

research on the composition of the SNP, Richard Mansbach, 'The Scottish National Party: A Revised Political Profile', *Comparative Politics*, January 1973, pp. 188-9.

numerous handicaps: the rise of the Labour Party to national status. Why has the Liberal Party been unable to do the same, to catapult a rising vote into a surge to national strength and power? Liberalism's philosophical hostility to strong central organization is one factor acting as a drag on efforts to make the most of revival. Presumably, however, a strong thrust in electoral support could have overcome this. Liberals themselves stress that they are handicapped by Britain's electoral system. The single-member district, first-past-the-post method of electing MPs does restrict small parties by 'wasting' their votes in large numbers if they lack, as the Liberals do, a very strong regional centre of support. A proportional system of representation, which is part of Liberal Party policy, would pick up such neglected votes and doubtless would have resulted in more MPs elected in recent general elections, particularly in the two which took place in 1974.[46] At the same time, were there a truly great surge in national support from the electorate, it presumably would overcome this barrier just as the Labour Party was able to conquer the same handicap.

The Liberal Electorate

This is the key to the differences in the situations of the new Labour Party in the early years of this century and the renewed Liberal Party of Grimond and Thorpe. When it was growing, the Labour Party was propelled by the support of a great mass of newly-enfranchised working-class voters. In contrast, there is no indication that the Liberals, at any time in their recent revival, had the same sort of solid support, even in potential form, from a constant, loyal, large sector of the electorate. There are pockets of Liberal strength, but no broad base. The Liberals have had an anchor of sorts in the 'Celtic Fringe', but this base is in modern Britain strong enough to elect

46 See, *e.g.*, David Butler, A. Stevens and D. Stokes, 'The Strength of the Liberals Under Alternative Electoral Systems', *Parliamentary Affairs*, Winter 1968-9, pp. 10-15.

only a few MPs and is seriously menaced by the nationalists. The conception of a 'new middle class' which is white collar, technically trained, and not class-conscious – and thus is open to Liberal appeals – seems to have some basis in fact. Survey research indicates that the Liberal Party's electoral revival under Grimond was more visible in the suburbs, where this new type of voter is presumably most numerous, than it was elsewhere. Similarly, the party did particularly well in the Greater London suburbs in the February 1974 advance. But the Liberal impact in suburbia under Grimond was only very marginal, and London was the scene of particularly heavy Liberal losses in October 1974.[47]

Not only has the Liberal Party's electorate been rather small even during the peaks of revival, but it has been and remains a constantly changing one. Table 5:4 illustrates a point made by David Butler and Donald Stokes in their study of the British electorate – much of the Liberal Party's vote seems to consist of temporarily disaffected voters who normally support one or the other of the two main parties. When either of the two major parties is in power, the differential between promise and performance inevitably breeds disillusionment and discontent. Some of the discontented group moves to support the Liberal Party. Psychologically, this is doubtless easier for many than travelling all the way over to the 'enemy camp', be that enemy, in partisan Britain, Tory or Labour. During the 1964 peak of Liberal support, there were other, more positive factors working in the party's favour; but the fact that the Tories had been in power since 1951, and that Liberals tend to run in Tory-held seats, cannot be underestimated as a cause of the surge in Liberal Party fortunes. Similarly, the February 1974 peak in Liberal support occurred after four years of Tory rule. In the context of the stable British party system, the Liberals have played the role of 'safety valve', enabling some voters to release steam without having to support parties or

47 H.B. Berrington, 'The General Election of 1964', *Journal of the Royal Statistical Society*, vol. 128, 1965, pp. 17-66; *Economist*, 19 October, 1974, pp. 18-35.

Table 5:4 Circulation of Liberal Strength

Changes of Liberal Strength, 1959-1963			
Source	% To Libs.	% From Libs.	% Net Change
Exchanges with Conservatives	3·3	−0·2	+3·1
Exchanges with Labour	1·5	−0·4	+1·1
Circulation of non-voters	1·9	−0·2	+1·7
Replacement of electorate	0·3	−0·2	+0·1
Totals	7·0	−1·0	+6·0

Changes of Liberal Strength, 1963-1964			
Source	% To Libs.	% From Libs.	% Net Change
Exchanges with Conservatives	1·1	−3·2	−2·1
Exchanges with Labour	1·5	−1·7	−0·2
Circulation of non-voters	2·2	−2·1	+0·1
Replacement of electorate	0·3	−0·2	+0·1
Totals	5·1	−7·2	−2·1

Changes of Liberal strength, 1964-1966			
Source	% To Libs.	% From Libs.	% Net Change
Exchanges with Conservatives	0·8	−1·8	−1·0
Exchanges with Labour	1·1	−1·3	−0·2
Circulation of non-voters	0·6	−1·6	−1·0
Replacement of electorate	0·1	−0·1	+0·0
Totals	2·6	−4·8	−2·2

Source: David Butler and Donald Stokes, *Political Change In Britain*, pp. 318-319.

movements which threaten the basic stability of the system. In the context of hopes for Liberal Party revival, this role of importance for stability but distance from power is disappointing; and raises doubts about the long-term viability of even dramatic electoral revival.

This electoral situation is reminiscent of the profile of the Liberal vote during the party's years of collapse from national power. Liberal voters during the inter-war period were interpreted earlier as substantially fickle and

Table 5:5 *Liberal Support for Party Policy*

	educ.	cost of living	nuclear bomb	modernisn. of Britain	health	full employ	foreign aff.
Question: Which party do you think has the best policy on:							
	%	%	%	%	%	%	%
Cons.	40·4	33·4	38·9	40·0	36·2	35·9	46·4
Lab.	35·0	44·8	24·9	32·6	45·3	47·2	23·2
Lib.	3·8	3·8	3·1	3·4	2·7	2·7	2·3
Don't know	20·8	18·0	33·1	24·0	15·8	14·2	28·1
1 Conservative voters alone:							
Cons.	72·6	71·7	70·0	71·8	73·3	75·2	80·4
Lab.	8·4	9·0	5·5	6·2	11·7	12·0	1·1
Lib.	1·0	1·4	1·1	1·6	1·2	0·5	0·4
Don't know	18·0	17·9	23·4	20·4	13·8	12·3	18·1
2 Labour voters alone:							
Cons.	16·1	6·9	16·8	18·1	9·5	7·4	20·6
Lab.	62·7	81·2	45·8	59·6	79·2	82·8	46·9
Lib.	2·1	1·1	1·2	0·6	0·6	0·5	0·6
Don't know	19·1	10·8	36·2	21·7	10·7	9·3	31·9
3 Liberal voters alone:							
Cons.	34·4	17·8	30·0	32·8	30·0	30·6	46·7
Lab.	23·3	29·4	15·0	19·4	27·2	32·8	6·1
Lib.	25·6	28·9	20·0	25·6	22·2	23·9	20·0
Don't know	16·7	23·9	35·0	22·2	20·6	12·7	27·2

'Liberal voters are not people convinced of the merit of Liberal policies. In every case, the numbers of Liberal voters preferring the Liberal policies is smaller than either those who prefer the Conservative policies, or those who prefer Labour.'

Source: National Opinion Poll Bulletin, December 1963, pp 4-5.

temporary by nature, with the result that the party's national constituency was always in flux. During the Grimond revival, the situation appears to have been much the same – the Liberals lacked a consistent body of loyal voters, except of the smallest sort. Their statistically small base was itself not constant through time; it was endlessly shifting, unstable, unreliable.

This point is made more dramatic by the implications of Table 5-5 that Liberal voters during the period of the party's significant policy redefinition were nevertheless striking in their comparative lack of strong support for that policy; and by Table 5-6, which indicates that Liberal voters apparently are not very intense in their commitment to the party (though the growth in Liberal support implies a *general* decline in party loyalty, an important point to be pursued later). Clearly, the party elite of the Grimond revival period, for all its impressiveness and all its planning, was a surface visible on the national stage without any equally substantial, loyal voter support. This makes the role of the party's elite all the more important; it makes the possibility of dramatic *lasting* national electoral revival much less likely.

In final summary, this sort of structural, rather mechanical analysis of party affairs serves to present several important reasons for Liberal frustration in recent years, elements which restrict and box in the party from several directions. The Grimond Liberals were confronted with very large and solid major parties which nevertheless were able to show some flexibility through adopting parts of the Liberal Party's policies and general approach. Simultaneously, the Liberals were attacked from another direction by minor parties with specific appeals to discontented voters in the 'Celtic Fringe'; minor parties which were able to draw support because the Scottish and Welsh Liberal Party organizations seem to have been class-conscious in a *de facto* sense. Finally, the Liberals have been undercut across the national electoral board through having an electorate which has been largely a shifting one.

Yet, Liberal failure to attain large-scale national electoral victory under Grimond does not alter the party's

Table 5:6 Intensity of Support by Party

Question: How strongly do you support the Conservative/Labour/Liberal Party very strongly, quite strongly, not very strongly, or not at all strongly?				
	All %	Cons. %	Lab. %	Lib. %
very strongly	38	37	41	23
quite strongly	36	37	35	44
not very strongly	20	21	19	22
not at all strongly	6	5	5	11
Results for same question asked November 1968:				
		Cons. %	Lab. %	Lib. %
very strongly		26	29	20
quite strongly		34	38	27
not very strongly		31	25	38
not at all strongly		9	8	15

Source: National Opinion Poll Bulletin, March 1966, p.9, November 1968, p.2.

success in surviving at all and in gaining renewed support under Thorpe. An examination of this continuing ability to survive and revive requires a closer look at the motives of Liberal loyalists, and the changing patterns of behaviour among voters and political activists in contemporary Britain.

The Liberal Party lacks the common touch.
A Liberal Party trade unionist

In addition to Liberal Party structure and policy, there is the issue of the motivation of Liberal Party activists. What are the incentives guiding people into work for a party which is so far from national power? Grimond was a clear source of inspiration; but his assumption of party leadership was preceded by a notable flow of new, often young, activists into the party. Moreover, it is doubtful that his personality is the entire explanation for the energy within the party during his tenure. Thorpe was a less prominent and dramatic leader, but the party drew even more electoral support under him. This issue of political motivation is a subtle one, not as clearly defined as the phenomenon of Liberalism addressing the weaknesses of collectivism on the policy level or encouraging weak party structure and lack of party unity. It is extremely important, however, not only to an analysis of the Liberal Party itself, but also as a possible device to explore the nature of forces adjusting collectivist attitudes and policies, and forms of political activism, in new directions.

The answer given by some to the question of Liberal motivation is *poujadism*. The party's small size; the free-wheeling, extremist atmosphere which has often dominated Liberal assemblies and is never entirely absent from them; emphasis on small units of government, in part to aid forgotten minorities – all these are reminiscent of the style and issues of the French extremist movement of the 1950s. The resemblance is apparent; condemnation is implicit in the term *poujadism*, which has come to imply that those so named are odd, crackpot, left behind by progress.

Seymour Lipset, in *Political Man*, lumps the British Liberals with the French Radicals and the American Taft Republicans, all representatives in his eye of the resistance of small business interests to the growth of large-scale industrialism. Given the fact that these small businessmen are being shunted to the economic periphery, it is to be expected that 'under certain conditions' such groups will turn to extremist political movements – 'fascism or anti-parliamentary populism'. The Liberal Party is not put into this category by Lipset, but he does place them into a related one. They are neither fascist nor anti-parliamentary, but they are 'irrational': 'To be against business bureaucracies, trade-unions, and state regulation is both unrealistic and to some extent irrational.'[1]

Certainly Liberals have been irrational and unsophisticated in the intensity and simplicity of some of the expressed dislike of large organizations. But Liberal hostility to collectivism has also been intellectually and politically significant in Britain. To point out the oversights of an excessively central perspective in planning, to stress the sectors which are overlooked by the dominant universality of the welfare state, to argue that Britain is more characterized by producer-group power in government than true 'regulation' of the former by the latter – none of these is irrational on the surface, and in fact the Liberals have been useful in highlighting the shortcomings of the collectivist *status quo*.

Moreover, the little research which has been done on the attitudes of Liberal Party activists indicates that they are not typically extremist, emotionally alienated or otherwise appropriate to being labelled either '*poujadist*' or 'irrational'. Jorgen Rasmussen, an American political scientist who has studied the contemporary Liberal Party in detail and interviewed a large number of members,

1 Seymour Lipset, *Political Man*, pp. 133-4.

searched for evidence of *poujadism* but found virtually none.[2]
M.P. Kochman, a British political scientist, conducted a
survey of letters to the editor in the party newspaper for the
years 1951-3, 1957-8, and 1963. He found, on the basis of
this uncertain and incomplete but not invalid tool, that
Liberals tend in this forum to be decisively more interested
in non-partisan civic or academic issues than in extremist
ones. He concluded that they do not seem, in this context,
to be notably more extremist than either their Conservative
or Labour counterparts.[3]

Broader themes of British politics suggest a double
explanation for activists joining the Liberal Party. First, the
particular ways in which the class factor interacts with the
Liberal Party make it highly attractive to a certain type of
middle-class activist who is strongly – if in too many cases
only theoretically – opposed to the class system. At the
same time, class influence on voters and activists has
handicapped the party's efforts to create broad-based
support for its cause. Second, the party apparently has had
a strong appeal for a certain type of activist interested in
local social and community service, normally regardless of
personal political gain from such work. The party put
increasing emphasis on such local work during Thorpe's
tenure as leader. Again, this factor has assisted the party
only to a degree, while in larger terms it has served as a
handicap.

Class Bases

It is not surprising that class should play a significant role
in analysis of the Liberal Party's fortunes. Academic
research has reinforced the common observation that class
has been the basic determinant of how the British electorate
votes. It has been the foundation-stone of the stability

2 Jorgen Rasmussen, *Retrenchment and Revival*, pp. 188 ff. He does find
some evidence that Liberals are 'alienated from society', notably in
various party statements which show hostility to big government and big
unions; but he notes that only 10-12 per cent of his interviewees seemed
'truly alienated from society and less than five per cent could fairly be
termed anomic'. [p. 193.]

which has characterized voting patterns in the Collectivist Age. The small, shifting 'floating vote' has been for some decades almost the only really unreliable element in a nation where Tory and Labour have been able to rely on large masses of automatic support in any election. And the term 'floater' does not refer to movements so slippery as to be totally unpredictable; rather, floaters have distributed themselves almost entirely within the boundaries of four possible choices: Conservative, Labour, Liberal or abstention. A consequence of this electoral constancy is that most House of Commons seats have been safe for one major party or the other, no matter what candidates have been put forward.

It is not easy accurately to define a concept as diverse and subtle as class without resorting to limiting simplification. In his notable analysis, T.H. Marshall defined class as simply the process of social interaction, the manner in which a person is treated by others – and not the attributes or possessions which create that treatment.[4] Yet characteristics of personality, reinforced by possessions, can encourage a certain type of treatment even if, in the complex of social reality, x qualities and x possessions only imperfectly correlate with the sort of treatment an occupant of category x might theoretically expect. The safest definition of class, in the broad sense, should include the things which, in shifting ways, go into determining class position –e.g., occupation, income, power, personality, family background. Status or lack of it may tend to correlate with having capital in each of these categories, but in any fairly complex social universe the combinations of degree are obviously vast.[5]

Sheer economic position seems to count for less, and other qualities for more, in Britain than in some other milieux such as the United States, where there is a more

3 M.P. Kochman, 'Liberal Party Activists and Extremist', *Political Studies*, June 1968, pp. 253-7.

4 T.H. Marshall, *Citizenship and Social Class*, p. 7.

5 Like most concepts which are important in a variety of separate social contexts, class is not only difficult to define completely, but is used in different senses by analysts concentrating on particular cultures or cross-cultural comparisons.

favourable attitude toward business wealth. This quality of British social life has led to a lack of synchronization in which the nation's progress in economic and political equality has travelled far more rapidly than its progress in social equality.[6] Thus, the British place greater importance on speech and background, style and culture, than on the bank account when measuring social position. The intangibility of these kinds of determinants makes the whole class phenomenon in Britain difficult to analyse and measure.

Similar problems arise when class is related to British politics. As various scholars note, the effort to analyse the political impact of class raises a series of difficult questions for students of the subject. Academic analysts and British political participants are able to see class as both a divider and a unifier, both a necessity to social order and a protector of inequality, both a useful element of social life and an evil to be abolished.[7]

In political practice, class has not only determined the philosophical natures of what Beer terms Socialist Democracy and Tory Democracy, the integrating ideas of the two main parties in his modern Collectivist Age; it has also broadly divided the electorate into the consistent supporters of those two main parties. The Labour Party, historically more pristinely and clearly based upon class-consciousness, has been linked to the working class not only in voting patterns, but in party doctrine as well. The situation in the Conservative Party has been more ambiguous, since Tory philosophy is implicit in history rather than explicit in ideology. Yet here, too, there has been a detectable class base, a mixed electorate of deferential working-class sectors plus most of the middle class, for both of whom social hierarchy is naturally ordained. Less clear and reliable than it was in agrarian Britain, compromised by the rise of industrialization and by the rationalization of science and technology, the

6 Robert Alford, *Party and Society*, p. 125, cites both T.H. Marshall and Leslie Lipson as notable holders of this view. He clarifies that both are referring to equality of opportunity, not absolute equality.

7 Samuel Beer, *British Politics in The Collectivist Age*, pp. xi-xii.

ancient class link between uppers and lowers – each of which has obligations to the other – has been mitigated but it has survived. The sensitive inferences of Beer's reflective analysis have been mirrored in more concrete behavioural research. In his 1963 study of the relationships between class and politics in four English-speaking democracies, for instance, Robert Alford discovered Britain to be the most class-based in its voting patterns.[8] While he also found that class seemed to be declining as a determinant of voting, its overwhelming importance at the time of his study (1964) would imply great difficulty in any effort to increase the Liberal electorate. Just as class seems to have been a crucial element in the sudden and steep electoral collapse of the Liberals in the 1920s, so it seems to have served more recently as a restraint upon gains by the party. The electorate of the modern Liberal Party has been not only small but highly volatile, very similar in this respect to the electorate of the collapsing Liberal Party in the 1920s.

Fluidity of the Liberal Vote

Yet it was precisely during the period of Alford's research that the Liberals were experiencing considerable forward political momentum. While the Liberals have been consistently hurt in a large way by the fact that they are formally anti-class in a nation of great political class-consciousness, the class factor may be used to assist with explanation of why the party has continued to draw sectors of the electorate and why it continues to enjoy periodic increases in support. The Liberals have been described as a safety valve for voters who normally support one of the two main parties but become unhappy with it in power. Expansion of this point will reinforce it. Butler and Stokes concerned themselves not only with the volatility of the Liberal vote, but also with the channels in which that volatility has moved. They found that voter-flow to and from the Liberals, during the period of their research, ran Labour-Liberal-Labour and Tory-Liberal-Tory (aside

8 Alford, *op. cit.*, p. 133 and *passim*.

from new-voter and non-voter circulation). They did not find Labour-Liberal-Tory patterns or the reverse.[9] An important related notation is that the Liberal Party has enjoyed its three revivals since its great collapse (i.e., in the late 1920s, the Grimond period, and currently) during years when the Tory Party has been in power. Doubtless this is related to the fact that Conservative voters have tended to mistrust Labour more than Labour voters have mistrusted the Conservatives.[10] This Liberal role as haven for the unhappy, disappointed former supporter of the party in power is aided by the fact that the Liberals seem to have had no clear class image in the mind of the electorate.[11] This seeming neutrality of the Liberal Party has made it acceptable to a class-conscious voter unwilling to vote for a party with clear-cut class ideas different from his own. The party's point of sharpest definition in recent times was probably during the months after the Liberal victory in the 1962 Orpington by-election, when for a brief time the Liberals led both Tories and Labour in the opinion polls. The Liberals were clearly characterized at that time, however, only by Grimond's constant message of strong *opposition* to class as an undesirable relic in modernizing Britain.[12]

In practical electoral fact, the lack of clear Liberal Party personality has led to a vote profile in which the party is represented fairly evenly all across the class spectrum, while failing to have a major impact in any particular sector. As various researchers have discovered, the Conservative Party's hold on the middle class and the Labour Party's hold on most of the working class contrast with the Liberal Party's small but consistent appeal all up and down the class ladder.[13] Thus, the Liberal Party was decisively damaged by the growth of class voting in Britain.

9 David Butler and Donald Stokes, *Political Change in Britain*, pp. 337-8.

10 See, e.g., Richard Rose, ed., *Studies in British Politics*, pp. 138-9.

11 Jean Blondel, *Voters, Parties and Leaders*, p. 83.

12 Grimond stressed the need for drastic reform consistently in his two books (*The Liberal Challenge* and *The Liberal Future*, cited earlier), his pamphlets and his frequent speeches. See the discussion in Chapter 3, above.

13 Butler and Stokes, *op. cit.*, p. 79.

The political importance of class has in the recent past served as a heavy weight restricting and limiting party efforts at revival, while simultaneously making the Liberals politically functional in terms of providing a separate but relatively moderate home for unhappy voters in the Tory and Labour ranks. Later discussion will argue that class is generally losing its earlier strong hold on the British electorate; but this again does not imply new Liberal strength, only greater insecurity for all parties.

Liberal Class-Consciousness

Voting populations are distinct from party activists, though class is constant in influencing the directions of activists' efforts. Again, as with the electorate, Liberals suffer because of the manner in which the class factor influences their activist core. In this case, however, the nature of the class impact is notably different from what it appears to be in the case of the electorate. The Liberals make small electoral gains; yet they suffer big losses because of their lack of association with a particular class doctrine. They appear to have attracted a kind of middle-class activist who agrees with the party's formal rejection of class-consciousness. At the same time the Liberal Party has suffered a great loss of potential members partly because it is class-conscious in a *de facto* sense, in the reality of its internal practices. Even in the Liberal Party, Britain's pervasive class system has had a discriminatory impact.

This is not to suggest that Liberals have been generally conscious of this discrimination. They have tended rather to be insensitive to class barriers within the party, and going beyond doctrinal classlessness, have taken action to try to broaden the class base of party activists. The strategy of the Grimond élite in the party included an effort to woo trade unionists to the Liberal cause. This was not the kind of effort which had been notably successful in the past; indeed, the 'doormat incident' (see p. 74) was a crucial event in helping to alienate working-class support from the old Liberal Party. Nevertheless, the Grimond planners devoted time and resources to several programmes oriented toward trade unionists. First, the party gave support to a short-lived newspaper, *United*, aimed at boosting trade-union membership in the party. Second, it worked to increase membership in the Association of Liberal Trade Unionists (ALTU), and in 1960 a trade unionist was appointed as the party's full-time trade union officer. Third, as discussed earlier, the party's old commitment to industrial co-partnership – uniting workers and managers within each industry – was reaffirmed, as efforts were made to define that policy concretely in a fashion likely to achieve broad approval within the party. Fourth, the party made an effort to win support within 'breakaway' trade unions, i.e. unions and union factions in trouble with the major union coalitions.[14]

This last effort was perhaps the most ambitious project the Liberals attempted, with its prime example the case of the 'blue union'. In the early 1950s, many thousands of unhappy dock workers from the Transport and General Workers Union (TGWU) moved over into the rival, much smaller National Association of Stevedores and Dockers (NASD). The migration, concentrated on Merseyside and at Hull, led the TGWU to accuse the NASD of 'poaching' before the Disputes Committee of the Trades Union Congress. The Committee backed the TGWU charge and ordered the NASD to return the 20,000 members in the North who were defectors from the TGWU, whether or not they wished to return. One NASD member took the issue to court; the TUC decided to fight the case through; and the NASD lost again. Nevertheless, there were no simple choices open to the NASD. If it returned its recent recruits to the TGWU, it would still leave itself open to court action from northern members who decided to sue it for surrendering. On the other hand, there was the threat of heavy penalties if the NASD did not return the members. There was a finale of sorts to the episode when the NASD was expelled from the TUC in November 1959. During the controversy, the Liberal Party took a clear interest in the problems of the NASD, with Mark Bonham Carter – then Liberal MP for Torrington – as

14 See, e.g., *United*, No 21, July 1960, p. 3.

chief party investigator in the case. He raised questions in the Commons, pursued particular issues submitted to him by the Hull and Liverpool branches of the NASD, and generally worked to show Liberal concern with the case.[15]

In a similar manner, the Liberal Party took up the cause of another breakaway union, the Aeronautical Engineers Association, which had been launched during the Second World War by aircraft mechanics who found their relatively new occupation refused recognition by the regular craft unions. After its formation, AEA found itself strenuously opposed by a coalition of the TUC, the Air Ministry, the Ministry of Labour, BOAC and BEA – with most of these organizations taking their positions in response to pressure from unions already in the TUC.[16]

Despite such efforts, reflecting a powerful desire to gain a foothold within the phalanx of Labour trade unions, and despite, too, the Liberals' traditional advocacy of industrial partnership schemes which would effectively increase the power and influence of the shop-floor worker, the party still dismally failed to attract notable defections either from trade-union ranks (in terms of affiliation with the party), or from working-class ranks (in terms of voter trends). What were the reasons for this failure? First, inevitably, there is the basic Liberal Party handicap of lack of credibility as a significant political force in the nation – a dilemma doubtless not mitigated by the fact that the party, which already suffered from a reputation as an odd and peripheral segment of the political scene, was making alliances with odd, peripheral, atypical elements of the labour movement. Second, the party's co-partnership schemes, though consistently a part of party policy since the 1928 Liberal *Yellow Book*, have never been politically profitable; their basic theme is out of tune with the nature of Britain's class relationships. Third, there is the testimony of the few working-class converts to activism in the modern Liberal Party that today's Liberals, like the old Liberals, are distinctly class-conscious, albeit unintentionally. Several pieces of evidence support this last contention.

15 *Ibid.*, No 8, May 1959, p. 1; No 20, June 1960, p. 1.
16 *Ibid.*, No 7, April 1959, p. 4.

Although some firms in Britain are run along co-partnership lines, often predictably because they were originally owned by a Liberal, the scheme has never proved especially profitable to the Liberal Party.[17] In fact, several prominent British concerns which have experimented with co-partnership or co-ownership ideas have suffered various forms of failure and frustration. Two very large industries which have tried workers' stock shares programmes are Imperial Chemical Industries Ltd and Rolls Royce Ltd. The former reports that, since the innovation was begun in 1954, only about 40 per cent of the stock distributed as a bonus to wcrkers has been retained. Rolls Royce has kept more detailed records. In this case, the contrast (in Table 6:1) between the increasing numbers of the company's UK employees between 1964 and 1968 and the constantly decreasing number holding workers' shares is striking. Yet another company reports that it has learned the following not very encouraging lessons from its own experience with a share partnership programme: '(1) continual maintenance of such a scheme is essential; (2) a continual internal propaganda campaign is needed; and (3) the scheme can cause anxieties amongst shop-floor workers who know they have a large sum of money and cannot afford to pay the gas bill'.[18]

Even when managerial hostility to such ideas can be overcome, there is the fundamental problem that the British working-class attitude toward management does not fit in well with the partnership concept. British working-class elements have tended to view such relations in terms either of sharp and hostile class *divisions*, or else in terms of vertical *integration* with working-class people in a clearly subordinate position. Neither concept assumes equality, but instead either hostility or subordination; each sees a community of sorts which is broad within society, not differentiated or distinguished by means of individual firms and businesses.

Additionally, there is evidence that the contemporary

17 George Goyder, Liberal big-businessman, has put his own conception of co-partnership into book form – *The Responsible Company*.
18 Correspondence with company official, Spring 1970.

Table 6:1 Rolls Royce and Workers' Stock Distribution

Employees			Year		
	1964	1965	1966	1967	1968
Number holding workers' shares	11,461	11,232	11,084	10,917	10,8
Number of UK employees	45,914	48,340	80,991	84,977	85,4

Source: Rolls Royce Ltd.

Liberals do not in fact practice equality between classes. Historically, the importance of class to British politics pulled the supports from beneath a great political party and sent it suddenly into collapse; more recently, that same middle-class exclusiveness within the party apparently has contributed to its inability to achieve a more substantial political revival. Those few working-class activists who were drawn to the party's individualism, its co-partnership ideas, its bright hopes of a decade ago, report that middle-class Liberal activists and leaders discriminate on class grounds. Other Liberals, whose background is not working-class, can be relied upon to deny this vehemently. Yet the more important and basic observation is that working-class party volunteers clearly feel a sense of unease and class bias. Consider, for instance, this extended testimony from a leader of the ALTU in 1968:[19]

> ... we need some plain speaking or we will never get on the right road. I believe the one most to blame for this state of affairs is Jo Grimond. Although years ago he spoke about realignment of the left, his ivory-tower lieutenants did not point out to him that this meant winning over a large section of the trade-union movement.
>
> And for the record, in twenty years mainly connected with the trade-union side of the party, I cannot remember Jo or the other leaders discussing current trade union issues with ALTU. Also for the record, our

19 *Liberal News Commentary*, No 88, 4 June, 1968, p. 3.

Industrial Panel has not met or considered a subject for over three years – and this at the time of prices and incomes with its far-reaching effects on the working man.

Small and ineffectual as ALTU is, we have at least studied Works Councils, Productivity Bargaining and Prices and Incomes over the past couple of years, but nobody has been interested.

The same sentiments were expressed by the editor of *United*, whose own career had included manual labour as well as journalism:[20]

In other fields, Liberals are so good at displaying the sympathetic imagination necessary to put themselves in other people's shoes ... that it comes as a blow to find they cannot so easily escape the shell of middle-class assumptions when it comes to the relations between master and man at work. They may succeed in bringing an enlightened eye to bear, but they focus it from *above*.

The lack of explicit clarity in some of these complaints does not make them invalid. Certainly, the party élite, most especially during the Grimond period of revival, was very concerned with trying to attract trade unionists to party membership. Union dissidents were doubtless selected because they provided an opening for recruiting activity. Good intentions, however, were clearly not enough. There was apparently an irreconcilable clash between the two cultures, middle and working, which Liberal doctrine and individualist ethos were unable to overcome. Indeed, as in the party's collapse after the First World War, the very lack of organic class conceptions in Liberal philosophy gives free rein to internal conflicts.

In personal interviews, some Liberal trade unionists – not all of whom were obviously working-class in their personalities or manners – testified that they felt either directly rebuffed or vaguely out of place at Liberal Party gatherings. One ALTU leader commented, nor without bitterness, that while Lady Violet Bonham Carter – Asquith's daughter and a party stalwart throughout her life

20 *Liberal News*, No 988, 14 May, 1965, p. 4.

– had always shown concern for the problems of the working-class person as an abstract part of mankind, she had never been willing to have much to do with him as an individual. Another noted frustration at being invited to a social function at the National Liberal Club in London, yet finding the people there 'on a different wavelength'. A third related a personal vignette concerning Lord Byers, one of the leaders of the Grimond revival, which speaks briefly but eloquently to the issue of the gulf between the classes, despite Liberal efforts both to bridge them and to deny their existence:[21]

> I was once asked by local party officials, the best time for Frank [now Lord] Byers to attend the Docks to meet and speak to Dockers. My experience led me to suggest either 7:30-8:00 a.m. or 12:15-1:00 p.m. ... [Finally] Frank Byers was persuaded to turn up at 5:15 p.m., a time when many men were home and the rest were interested in getting home!

The perceptions and experiences of working-class Liberals are reinforced by other pieces of evidence. A postal survey was conducted in 1970 in connection with this study of the Liberal Party, based on a list of speakers available at the Liberal Party Organization. Not one of those listed was a working-class trade unionist. The head of ALTU at the time, in fact, was a solicitor. A notable characteristic of the returns from the postal survey was a uniformly hard-to-read, at times almost illegible, quality. The ability to decipher such middle-class handwriting comes with practice, and helps differentiate middle and working classes. Middle-class exclusiveness was apparent in other ways as well – for instance, the Liberal who refused to answer the questionnaire at all but returned instead a long denunciation of people who ask prying questions by mail.[22]

Table 6:2, confirming the observation that the Liberals are notably class-selective, indicates that Liberal Party parliamentary candidates in recent general elections have

---

21 Correspondence with Liberal trade unionist, Spring 1970.
22 The criticisms ran to two pages, typed and double-spaced.

been markedly middle-class. The Tory Party has been able to rely upon deference, the Labour Party on its representation of the working class among its candidates, whereas the Liberals have had neither form of working-class support.

Table 6:2 Numbers of Working-Class Candidates in Recent General Elections

Year		Party				
	Lab.		Cons.		Lib.	
1974 (Oct)	112	(626)	7	(623)	25	(619)
1974 (Feb)	111	(627)	6	(630)	13	(517)
1970	101	(624)	8	(628)	1	(332)
1966	132	(621)	8	(629)	5	(311)
1964	152	(638)	11	(630)	11	(365)
1959	172	(621)	14	(625)	5	(216)
1955	175	(620)	19	(623)	4	(110)
1951	166	(617)	15	(617)	1	(109)
1950	92	(617)	7	(621)	13	(475)

The figure in brackets is the total number of candidates nominated by the party.

Sources: the Nuffield general election studies; *The Times Guide to the House of Commons*, 1970 and 1974.)

Paradoxically, there is also evidence to support and expand upon the argument that middle-class Liberal Party activists have a strong *philosophical* hostility to class conceptions. One high leader in the party explains ALTU's failure with the argument that it is a class-conscious body in a party where class is rejected: 'Within the Liberal Party, the class barriers disappear.'[23] To begin development of this theme, consider first the attitude toward class among the partisans of the two main parties. Butler and Stokes, in their exhaustive research into the beliefs of Tory and Labour supporters, predictably discovered that class conceptions were essential in maintaining party ties. They did find a distinction, however, between two types of class consciousness (aside from vague acceptance of the political

23 Interview, Spring 1970.

norms of one's class), with some voters (1) positively drawn to Tory or Labour because they felt it represented their class interest, combining these feelings with neutrality or near neutrality with regard to the other main party, while other partisans (2) were more conscious of a sense of opposition between the classes, with their own party seen as a protector of their class and the second major party as a hostile defender of other classes. Samples of remarks from each Butler-Stokes category include: '(1) (Likes about Conservatives): No, I don't take much notice; (Dislikes about Conservatives): No, I tell you I'm not interested in them; (Likes about Labour): Well, I think we'd be better off if they got in. They would do more for the working classes; and (2) (Dislikes about Conservatives): They are absolutely class biased. They have no room for the working class, and their whole attitude is in support of the capitalists; (Likes about Labour): They are 75 per cent for the uplifting of the working classes.'[24] Similar evidence of class-linked partisanship in the two main parties is visible in a variety of other indicators – the rhetoric of leaders, the resolutions of conferences, the pamphlets of party ideologues.[25]

A Survey of Liberal Activists

An effort was made in connection with this study of the Liberal Party to discover with some clarity the motivations of Liberal activists, especially as they relate to the class

24 Butler and Stokes, *op. cit.*, pp. 82-7.

25 The importance of class in holding the two main parties together has been stressed by a variety of analysts, in different ways. The most sensisitve and subtle analysis, rich in history, is probably Beer's. Alford and Butler-Stokes make many of the same points in a more statistical manner. A frequent observation by students of British politics holds that party leaders, in their comparative moderation, have more in common with the masses who provide them with their votes than they do with the very committed, but extreme, party activists. But Richard Rose has argued that this dilemma does not exist, that rather neither leadership nor rank-and-file activists are uniformly more or less extreme. See Richard Rose, 'The Political Ideas of English Party Activists', *American Political Science Review*, June 1962, pp. 360-371.

issue. The postal survey mentioned before was the
mechanism used. The responses to this survey (which was,
it should be stressed, extremely limited and hence only
suggestive in results) correspond with the basic
individualistic thrust of traditional Liberal philosophy, as
well as with the frequent impressionistic observations of
journalists and scholars that the Liberal Party is a home for
people who are highly individualistic and correspondingly
hostile to the political and sociological communalism of the
two main parties. The Liberal activists polled have a clear
tendency to lump both major parties together as equally
unfortunate giants – undemocratic prophets of a false
religion. In contrast to Labour and Tory Party voters in the
Butler/Stokes study, these activists seem normally to make
little or no distinction between the two big parties in broad
terms, and to express considerable hostility toward them.
Seventy-four of the 104 respondents made clear in
answering one of several questions that they felt the two
main parties to be twin evils. In replying to the single
question on how they saw both those parties, 43 per cent of
the Liberal respondents grouped them both together with
little or no distinction. Some of the blanket combinations
include:

> They both seek power for the few. Both tend to be rather
> arrogant with those who dissent from their views.

> Both concerned with looking after one section of the
> population not the population as a *whole*.

> Both 'class parties', tending to 'play the political game'
> with one another and relatively unimaginative in post-
> war politics.

> both are divisive factions where unity should be the aim.

> Blind followers of a party line.

> Basically 'class' parties.

Both in the pocket of vested interest.

Two questions immediately below this one asked for specific, separate statements concerning each party. The respondent was asked to note what he liked most and least about each. Among the diversity of responses, there were some streams of consistency, some partial patterns to Liberal sentiments. Dislike of the Tories tended to be personal, dislike of Labour ideological. Labour – despite Harold Wilson's years of trying to prove otherwise – was seen as a 'Socialist' party (49 respondents). Tories were condemned for their alleged self-esteem, snobbery, 'arrogance' (13 respondents). On the other hand, the mirror image of Tory arrogance was felt to be efficiency at managing government (38 respondents); that of Labour's undesirable Socialism, an admired humanity and concern for the less fortunate members of society (67 respondents). The problem with Labour's social conscience, in Liberal eyes, seems to be that members lack the competence to put it into practice.

Among specific comments were the following:

Conservatives: Have brains but no heart. Labour: Have heart but no brains.

Labour doctrinaire and lacking financial know-how. Government pressured by left wing into stupid policies through dogmatic approach. Conservatives more practical but less concerned with the individual unless [he is] one of them, and too class-conscious.

Conservatives: There is some chance that they will resist collectivism, which I like. They ignore basic justice ... and are not really sold on economic liberalism. Labour: I like their social conscience but not their solutions.

Conservatives: I like most its very occasional streak of honesty, least its snobbery and selfishness. Labour: I like most its ... social conscience.

Conservatives: Least – its arrogance. Labour: Most – its concern for the underdog. Least – its use of class distinction for social purposes.

Of those Liberals who would vote for another party if no Liberal were available, most would vote Labour (34 Labour, 6 Conservative, 29 not vote, 31 uncertain, 1 Scottish Nationalist, 3 no answer). This is no doubt a reflection of the fact that many of those polled felt the Labour Party to be admirably humanitarian.

Implicit in much of the Liberal response seems to be a rejection of the common-sense notion, clearly part of the electorate's general perspective, that the Liberals are a 'middle' party, between the left of Socialism and the right of Toryism. Liberals, on the other hand, seem to see their party at one end of a different spectrum – the individualist end – while Tory and Labour are grouped at the opposite collectivist pole, the reverse of Liberalism. This philosophical, and intensely emotional, individualism of the Liberals came out very strongly when they replied to the two most straightforward motivation questions on the original questionnaire, which asked respectively how they conceive of 'Liberalism' and why they devote time to such a small, weak party. Eighty-four replies stressed some variation of the individualism theme. Significantly, they often mentioned industrial co-partnership as an element of Liberal doctrine which was important in drawing them to the party. It is certainly the party policy which most directly rejects class ideas. A few mentioned the Suez crisis of 1956 as a specific spur for involvement in the Liberal Party, a vague but interesting bit of evidence for the proposition that there was a very real malaise after Suez, one which served as a politically useful if unpleasant background for the Liberal Party's revival.

Some of the reasons given for devoting time to the Liberal cause were:

I have a vision of society which is more likely to be achieved by Liberal industrial partnership proposals than by any proposals of the other two parties.

Several reasons, including support for Liberal emphasis on individual liberty.

I am a member of the Liberal Party because it represents the most feasible (if not the most hopeful) vehicle for eliminating 'class' as the basis of British politics.

A dislike of privilege.

Because I believe the Conservative and Labour Parties to be parties of vested interests, or parties of class, and so harmful to the nation.

Liberal policy still considers the individual.

Basically because I believe in individual freedom, in justice, in trying to solve problems rather than backing one class or group against another.

I agree particularly strongly with policies on Parliamentary Reform, Industrial Co-Partnership.

I feel the Liberal Party is more concerned with human values ... and that its policy of co-ownership is the only answer to industrial problems.

I was drawn to the Liberal Party by its independence of thought, its radical policies, and its non-class appeal. I like particularly their industrial policy which typifies these three facets.

Only group actively propagating liberal ideals in politics. Joined at time of Suez.

Suez ... Common Market ... Voting Reform ... Dislike of patronage and power of Labour and Tory Party Machines ... Anti-monopoly and free-trade policy.

I joined in active work at Suez, but the Liberal attitude to industrial affairs is a particular interest.

Its Freedom from big business and Trade Union domination. A great dislike of the Conservative party but a belief in private initiative and enterprise.

The flavour of such statements as these helps carry across the spirit of the party itself. It is a spirit of intensely pristine individualism, which rejects alike the collectivist politics of obvious party discipline, the big business and labour formations which are central elements of functional representation, and the organic collectivist philosophies seen as large in their domination of the two main parties.

Emotionally and philosophically, the reverse side of the party's individualism is an extreme hostility to the phenomenon of class, often indeed to the very *concept* of class. Several questions dealt with class, requesting the Liberals to note whether or not they saw themselves and fellow-Liberals as members of a particular class, if so which one, and how they felt about reducing class differences. Most of the respondents (63 of them) were, predictably, strongly in favour of reducing class differences. The great majority that answered the questions directly either claimed no class for themselves and others in the party, or listed a middle-class ranking. Sixty respondents, however, including some who answered and many who did not (often drawing angry lines through the questions to indicate their displeasure), felt moved to write down their hostility to class as reality, or to argue that it does not really exist, or even to express hostility to me for bringing up the topic. Some of the responses, varying in intensity, were:

I reject your premise but understand what you mean.

I do not believe in class.

I do not feel that class is a relevant word. Nearly everyone works ... Class is a lot of nonsense.

I guess I know people, not social categories!

I try not to be in a class.

Yes and no. What class is a bookmaker? or a dance band drummer?

I don't see myself in class terms.

I do not approve of this kind of class distinction.

I pity your approach! You must be an American!

classes are something I have never understood. ... Most Liberals I know are thoroughly decent people and this is their measure – not some artificial status.

I don't think there is any real class structure in this country except in the minds of certain politicians who use it for their own ends.

Liberals do not depend on class war for their existence.

Comparison of the class attitudes of these Liberal Party activists with the automatic, easy, positive acceptance of class conceptions on the part of the Labour and Conservative voters surveyed by Butler and Stokes brings home the Liberal Party's difference and the reasons for its appeal. In Britain's environment of class politics, a small minority of the middle class has not fitted in because it has refused to accept the class basis of modern collectivist parties and patterns of voting. Over one-third of the respondents to the postal survey felt they should make anti-class comments in space provided for answers to class-related questions. Virtually every respondent, in his reply to some question – concerning his own motivation, how he saw the other parties, how he defined Liberalism, how he viewed class – used some variant of the word 'individualism' to explain his attraction to the Liberal Party. In collectivist Britain, the party has provided the ideal home for the party activist who rejects collectivism.

The basic Liberal political dilemma is now more clear. There is a certain, mainly middle-class, element which has continued to reject class conceptions in politics, a small remnant of the vast Liberal tide of the nineteenth century. This residual pool of sentiment provides the kernel of Liberal Party activists. This kind of outlook is probably typical as well of many, if not most, of those who regularly vote Liberal in the midst of the rapid turnover in the party's vote as traced by Butler and Stokes. Conversely, the testimony of unhappy trade unionists who have tried working through the party, and the absence of working-class parliamentary candidates and activists, serve as evidence for the case that the Liberals have also been guilty of a type of class consciousness. The results of the survey indicate that a large number of the Liberals polled by mail (85 of them) do think working-class people play at least a noticeable role in the party's local associations. This could mean that local associations are more open than the national party élite, an argument which is no doubt true in some cases. It could also mean, more consistently with the trend of other points, that Liberals believe themselves to be open in class terms, while in reality the party has been rather closed.

The importance, in political terms, of this lack of working-class support for the Liberal Party can be stressed more emphatically by pointing out that those few districts in which the party has been able to elect MP's seem to be constituencies in which the Liberals have either retained distinctive working-class support or been able to win it. Colne Valley and several of the Celtic seats – notably Roxburg, Selkirk & Peebles – have active workingmen's Liberal Clubs, and in such Celtic areas there is often a lack of strong Labour tradition in the working-class vote. In Ross & Cromarty in Scotland, working-class support has been maintained by carefully including representatives of the working class in the constituency association, and in Ladywood there was a background of long years of slum social work.[26] The decisive loss of three of these four seats in 1970 is depressing testimony to the Liberals that overcoming class politics is a tenuous thing in Britain,

26 Information on the constituencies was gleaned mainly from interviews.

The spirit of service is in our people.
Lord Beveridge[1]

Class is an element of profound importance to an effort to
come to terms with the recent history of the British
Liberals. Simultaneously, it provides parameters which
explain limits on the party's revival, and a spur which
clarifies the motivations of certain types of voters and a
certain kind of activist who have been drawn to the party. It
is not, however, the only broad cultural explanation which
bears on why the Liberal Party survives and has been able
to revive, though only to a point. There is another element,
at least as subtle, equally double-edged. It gives deeper
significance to the Liberal Party's uneven odyssey in recent
years. Understanding it is a process which appropriately
begins with the city of Birmingham and the person of
Wallace Lawler.

Birmingham

Birmingham is removed, in ambience and spirit far more
than in distance, from the suburban affluence which is
typical of Orpington. Much of it is a grim, grey industrial
slum, with row upon row of squat, dirty brick residential
structures which are so much a feature of this sort of area in
Britain. Oddly, considering its history since that time, the
city was an important capital of nineteenth-century
Liberalism. The National Liberal Federation was formed in
Birmingham in 1877, and for a number of years after that
the headquarters of the Federation was located there. In the

1 Lord Beveridge, *Voluntary Action*, p. 151.

1880s, however, Joe Chamberlain bolted the Liberal Party, taking his Birmingham caucus with him. With the rise of the Labour Party, for which Birmingham was a natural centre of strength, a clear end was put to whatever faint hopes Liberals might have indulged of someday returning to power in the city. For decades later, the only trace in Birmingham of the once-flourishing Liberal Party was to be seen in some of the street signs of the city, which still retain the names of old Liberal leaders – Wright, Dixon, Muntz, Chamberlain, Bright; signs which conjure in their survival memories of a great past while at the same time symbolizing, perhaps better than any other relic could, the party's fall from greatness. The lifelessness and age of the old markers highlights the weakness and age of the party.[2]

It was in Birmingham, however, that a recent Liberal Party revival, centred in local government, began even as the party's national revival under Grimond was losing momentum. It paralleled similar Liberal growth in other urban areas, notably Leeds and Liverpool.[3] The Liberal advance in Birmingham, however, while among the most dramatic the party has accomplished in this sort of area, has never come close to reversing the near-total dominance of the local council by the Conservative and Labour parties. The council numbers 126 members, and Liberal strength in recent years has never risen above a total of 9 councillors. Even the peak of Liberal revival in this area – the capture of a parliamentary seat in a 1969 by-election – was frustrated in 1970 when the seat was retaken by Labour in the general election.

Yet the Liberal revival here, while relatively unimpressive in numbers in comparison with the strength of the two main parties, is clearly a significant happening in the context of what went before. From a position of quite literally no local councillors or MPs, indeed from a position of no party organization in the city deserving of the title, the

2 *Liberal News*, No 1014, 12 November, 1965, p. 7.

3 Birmingham is the only one of the three cities to have elected a Liberal MP during the revival. The Liberals however, as discussed later, did win a majority of seats in the Liverpool metropolitan district during the 1973 local elections.

Liberals grew to a point where they could elect several councillors and one MP. Given the difficulties automatically facing candidates who are outside of the two main parties, and the special problem of lack of established Liberal base in Birmingham, the party's accomplishment is notable.[4] A comparable Liberal advance has taken place in Leeds. The party took control of the Greenock council in Scotland in 1966. In Liverpool, the Liberal Party elected its first councillor in recent times in 1962, and as late as 1970 had only 4. Since then, however, the Liberal advance has given the party a plurality of seats – 48 against 42 Labour and 9 Conservative in the 1973 local elections – although the party has yet to elect an MP there.

Why have these gains occurred, especially since the party's advances in industrial areas have been somewhat out of synchronization with the more general rise and decline in the late 1950s and early 1960s, and the very recent growth in support in by-elections and the two 1974 general elections? There is the consideration that Labour was in office from 1964 to 1970, and this doubtless helped move some Labour voters into the Liberal column in conformity with the Liberal role as alternative for unhappy major-party voters. However, a more interesting and subtle phenomenon, connected with the Liberal Party and the significance of revival, is the spirit of service, defined specifically as a commitment to local social work and social service, often as an end in itself. To come to grips with this, it is necessary to move beyond the particular political situation in Birmingham, and the local Liberal association which functions there, and discuss this general theme in the context of Liberal Party history and Liberal thought.

Noncomformism

Class is the basic divider of British society and politics in the collectivist model, hence it is a key factor for an analysis attempting to explain modern British political behaviour. But it has not always been so, nor is class the only notable

4 William Shannon, 'A Letter from Brighton', p. 7.

causal element in voting even in modern British politics. Beneath class in importance in collectivist politics, but more decisive than class in the last century, is the religious factor. Controversy over the effect of the Balfour Education Act of 1902 on church schools, and later over Welsh Disestablishment, left marks which remain in the national political memory.[5] While the rise of class as a political issue brought about the fall of the Liberal Party, survival of religious influence on voting – in modern times, mainly nominal religious influence – helps explain the party's survival and limited success at political revival. It has worked to weaken the decline of the party, and defend areas of residual Liberal strength, in two ways. First, in very traditional Britain, old religious ties help to account for why some areas continue to vote Liberal. Second, and much more important, the atmosphere surrounding and themes present in Liberal philosophy and in the Liberal approach to politics, thanks partly to the nonconformist heritage, go far toward explaining why a certain type of activist has been drawn to the party in recent years – even though few of these new Liberals seem to have explicitly religious motivations.

It should not be surprising that such a traditional factor as religion should still make its weight felt in a nation as close to tradition in so much of its political and social life, and so habit-bound in voting, as Britain. Even in the comparatively unreligious modern age, old religious patterns of electoral cleavage leave their marks. The nonconformist 'Celtic Fringe' is still an area of comparative strength for the Liberals. The applicability of this point is broadened by Table 7:1, which indicates that nonconformist voters generally are more drawn to the Liberals than are members of other denominations. In addition, Butler and Stokes discovered that the nonconformists in their sample were more regular in their church attendance than were supporters of established churches, though they were less loyal in this regard than Catholics (see Table 7:2). This reinforces the point

5 David Butler and Donald Stokes, *Political Change in Britain*, p. 124.

concerning the relevance of nonconformist association to Liberal voting: nonconformists not only tend to be Liberals in a larger proportion than do other denominations, they also seem to be more committed to their religion than are many other groups.

Table 7:1 Partisan Self-Image by Religious Identification

	Cons.	Lab.	Lib.	Other, None	
	%	%	%	%	
Anglican	41	44	10	5	(n=1273)
Church of Scotland	39	48	6	7	(n= 187)
Methodist	23	55	19	3	(n= 140)
Other nonconformist	37	36	20	7	(n= 127)
Roman Catholic	24	62	8	6	(n= 169)
No religious pref.	31	52	8	9	(n= 64)

Table 7:2 Church Attendance

	At least once a month	At least once a year	Less than once a year
	%	%	%
Church of England	16	40	44
Church of Scotland	39	27	34
Nonconformist	45	32	23
Roman Catholic	73	11	16

Source: David Butler and Donald Stokes, *Political Change In Britain*, p. 125.

Religious nonconformity remains, as in the past, a diverse movement, its structural variety a function of its spiritual individualism. Much of its roots lie in the evangelical, revivalist spirit which swept Britain during the eighteenth century, moving vast throngs to attend the great open-air religious meetings of the time. One general theme which ran through the nonconformist movement, developing with it as the nineteenth century wore on, was that of reform combined with, and partly implemented through, an individualistic commitment to local social service and community improvement, the kind of orientation described by the general term, 'nonconformist conscience'.[6]

While localism was a basic theme in nonconformist literature and rhetoric, the movement lacked strategic political unity, thanks to the extremism of a variety of nonconformists who believed that only radical, direct local action was politically effective or morally acceptable. This breed clashed strongly with other, more moderate and pragmatic nonconformists, whose orientation was toward working through the Liberal Party of Gladstone. H.J. Hanham divides the nonconformists of the 1860s into three basic camps, on the basis of their degree of hostility to established institutions and conventional political methods. First, the strong and coherent group of nonconformists led by Samuel Morley, a member of Parliament and a newspaper owner, committed to Gladstone and his Liberal Party as a reform tool which was potentially more effective and long-lasting than the method of direct action outside the party system. A second nonconformist group, in the middle of the ideological road, was geared to social reform through comparatively moderate action. Unable to commit themselves to completely non-party direct militance, unable to join a Liberal Party which they felt was compromised by a commitment to practical politics, these nonconformists stood between the two wings of party work and non-party activism. To them, the Liberal Party was both too broad in its focus and too weak in its intensity. On one side, the party was concerned with a gamut of issues aside from local service; on the other side, to their eyes the commitment to local service was lacking in requisite fervour. A third faction consisted of those who were uncompromisingly committed to direct action, whether or not it injured the political position of the Liberal Party.[7]

Despite the disaffection of a faction of uncompromising

---

6 Hugh Tinker, *Re-Orientations: Essays on Asia in Transition*, Chapter 10, stresses the nonconformist tradition in the Liberal Party in the context of his fairly abstract reflections on the general election of 1964.

7 H.J. Hanham, *Elections and Party Management*, pp. 117-18.

purists among nonconformist activists, by the late 1860s there was a large nonconformist vote which was clearly Gladstone's. He was a shrewd and canny political operator, despite his religious feelings and personal morality, and both strains of his complex character combined in his appeals for nonconformist support. His speeches contained two general themes, both of which were designed to draw nonconformists to the Liberal camp. First, he stressed the need for reform of institutions, to include moral regeneration as well as structural change. The second constant Gladstonian theme was the need for economy and lack of extravagance in government. The reformism of the nonconformist ethic was joined with the faith in frugality so typical of Gladstone, nonconformists, and the sort of personally conservative people who generally are likely to be religious. His appeal was well-calculated, his success was great. As Hanham notes, 'it was by its nature almost the only appeal which could reach the mass of nonconformist electors, who became after 1868 his most numerous and effective supporters'.[8]

The identification between the party and the religion was never total, and could not by its nature be formal. Yet the mingling of the two could only be self-reinforcing, as themes common to both the political movement and the religious faith received support from two directions. The individualism, decentralization, and localism which characterized both party and denomination were strong currents in party policy through the nineteenth century. The nonconformist base of the party could only serve to assist in limiting the degree to which it moved in collectivist directions. Liberal policy, while it might be said to have edged somewhat in a collectivist direction during the early years of this century, has consistently emphasized decentralization of government, diffusion of power, and hostility to class orientations. The effort of the Liberal Government elected in 1906 to use voluntary societies to assist in the administration of new public programmes is an especially striking instance of a formal attempt to use both

8 *Ibid.*, pp. 204-5.

the voluntarism and the localism typical of the nonconformist, and the Liberal, approach.[9]

Because Liberal acceptance of collectivism was only partial, the nonconformist individualism of the party was never borne over by the large structures and communal attitudes which became dominant with the rise of the Collectivist Age. The Liberal Party was able, therefore, to retain an appeal for activists interested in the sort of local social service, on an individual or small-group basis, which is very much a part of the nonconformist ethic. The concrete presence of the nonconformist church, and the general attitudes it favours and encourages, both have provided support for candidates on the national and local levels, and for activists connected with the party.

A Liberal academic and parliamentary candidate, writing about this subtle but real connection between church and party, has this to say concerning its importance:[10]

> Perhaps one-third of the Liberal parliamentary candidates in 1964 were Dissenters, mostly having a more than nominal church membership ... Certainly, there was no attempt to utilize the local Free Church network for political motives ... However, the adoption of a Nonconformist parliamentary candidate did seem to bring about a certain transformation among many local Nonconformists from a passive to an active attitude to politics. Quantitatively this was not at first significant; but to an organization which was attempting to establish branches in areas where there was no known tradition of Liberal activity, it was important to be able to enquire along a known network.

Now we may see the interconnection of Nonconformity and Liberalism in practice. The individual Free Churches are local, self-governing, self-supporting

9 But these Liberal voluntary associations were not tied formally to the Liberal Party. The situation is developing in somewhat similar directions today, though with hardly certain prospects resulting for the modern Liberal Party.

10 Tinker, *op. cit.*, p. 160.

organisms ... to a political party which is weak in funds and in professional organization, this provides a vital means of creating grass-roots organization.

This nonconformist factor, in structure as well as in philosophy, provides a useful partial explanation for the party's ability to survive in a nation strongly committed to the two-party system and class-bound in its modern voting habits.

Local Work

The spirit of service, while it is a powerful element in the nonconformist church, transcends it as a general quality of the party. It seems to have been a necessary condition for much of the political success Liberals have enjoyed in recent years. The Grimond élite's decision to stress local elections was, therefore, shrewd. They rightly sensed that local government is more open than House of Commons seats to third-party candidates, and also that this tactic marries very well with propensities already present in the party. From the start of the really organized planning for revival, the theme of Liberal accomplishments on the local, personal level played a prominent part in the rhetoric of party leaders. Jeremy Thorpe's 1959 speech, which stressed Liberal interest in the kind of small-scale local problems which plague 'ordinary' people, was no isolated approach, but part of the broad effort to create a Liberal lever into political power through using the traditionally Liberal local theme. Factors of Liberal Party history joined with practical political considerations to draw the party's interest to local affairs. At a Liberal rally in Southport in March 1960, Grimond himself, stressing a point he would use often during the revival, declared that, 'The Liberal Party should be the party to which people look for reforms which affect their daily lives ... let us get things done and let us start in local government.'[11]

This commitment to local service, both within and

11 *Liberal News*, No 604, 7 May, 1959, p. 4; J.G. Bulpitt, *Party Politics in English Local Government*.

outside the avenues of local government, is the basic and most important explanation for the recent signs of Liberal revival in such places as Birmingham. Until his death after defeat in the 1970 general election, no Liberal personified this commitment better than Wallace Lawler, the leader of the Birmingham Liberal revival, a city councillor, and, briefly, Liberal MP for Ladywood during 1969-70. He was elected to the council in 1962, the first of the new Liberals to win a place there. In 1965, a major effort was made to unseat him, but he managed to win again, not only holding his seat but increasing his majority four-fold despite the fact that Labour assigned one of its most experienced and successful election agents to secure his defeat.[12]

Lawler's efforts in local social service preceded his electoral successes by a number of years. As early as 1954, he wrote an article for the party newspaper, urging Liberals to get active in and revitalize local government, to end the 'throttlehold' of the two main parties.[13] Starting well before his first election to the local council, he organized residents to protest against council planning of the city without consulting the desires and needs of the poorer residents. He also promoted the use of what is termed 'self-build'. The scheme entails approximately a dozen young married couples forming a self-build group, making sure that at least some of the men involved are skilled as craftsmen and tradesmen. They then apply to the city council for permits to be a self-build group and also for leases on land and for government aid in constructing their houses. A house for each couple is constructed by the group as a whole. Building costs are low, estimated at an average of £2,000 to £2,500 per house, with the possibility of selling a house in the future at a clear profit.[14]

His election to the council provided Lawler with a more visible platform for pressuring local government. In February 1965 he issued a strongly-worded denunciation of his 154 fellow councillors, accusing members of the two main parties of engaging in self-serving partisan fights

12 *Liberal News*, No 970, 7 January 1965, p. 2.
13 *Liberal News*, No 408, 2 April 1954, pp. 3-4.
14 Interviews with Birmingham Liberal activists, Spring 1970.

rather than trying to work in tandem to solve the housing problems of Birmingham. He declared that 'Sordid party strife over housing has contributed towards a major loss of some 2,000 municipal homes *annually* between 1952 and 1963.[15] In the same month, Lawler launched a petition which was designed to pressure the council to prohibit all office building in the city, which on estimates of that time was losing £800,000 per year in rates on buildings which had no occupants.[16] By the time the 1965 elections arrived, Lawler was able to claim that he had taken up the problem of industrial noise at night, had demanded a closer inspection by the council of the cleaning of the staircase windows of multi-story flats, had publicized the fact that three forgotten streets had been left out of the Birmingham redevelopment programme, had successfully negotiated to get more convenient access routes put into laundry areas for the use of housewives, and had agitated as well for protected play areas for children in housing estates. He could cite in addition his personal support and encouragement of a protection organization formed by tenants of 3,600 houses and shops to fight a take-over bid by the city corporation.[17] It was this sort of massive, concentrated, endless local work which enabled him to hold off the Labour effort to remove him from the council in 1965. In early 1969, Lawler began a charitable trust for local residents, not unwisely labelled 'The Wallace Lawler Friendship Fund', after securing contributions for it from local businessmen. Projects planned for the local-action trust included a study of the health hazards to old people who over-economize in home heating, and an old people's club in the centre of Birmingham.[18]

The result of this vast but very personal social work programme was that Lawler became personally known to almost every resident of the Ladywood area. Liberal Party workers who commuted to Birmingham to aid in the Ladywood by-election in 1969 testify that they were

15 *Liberal News*, No 975, 11 February, 1965, p. 8.
16 *Liberal News*, No 977, 25 February, 1965, p. 2.
17 *Liberal News*, No 990, 28 May, 1965, p. 5.
18 *Liberal News Commentary*, No 126, 25 February, 1969, p. 4.

amazed in their canvassing to find that people in house after house knew the Liberal candidate personally, and were planning to vote for him because he had fixed their door, repaired their roof, called the attention of the council to neighbourhood problems or had done one or another of a myriad of services for them. Other Liberals in Birmingham have followed in his footsteps, using similar tactics to build support and win votes. Each of the Liberal councillors was elected as a result of taking up local problems, frequently through residents' solicitation of help at one of the numerous Liberal 'advice centres'. Use of advice centres as a conscious means of winning Liberal support is common in wards which have been targeted for future efforts at capture. Advice centres, and follow-up personal assistance, remain important methods for maintaining voter support in those wards already won by the Liberals.

An important reason why the advice centres have been increasingly popular, in the theory of at least one Liberal councillor, is the fading of older methods of mutual assistance in communities. Neither the doctor nor the clergyman performs the local counselling functions he once did for the poor inhabitants of industrial centres – 'the doctor is too busy and the priest is out of touch'. This point may be broadened to explain the importance of individual Liberal volunteer workers as well as the more formal advice centres. As a result of this social change, the Liberal local activist is as likely to hear about problems of wife-beating or drinking as he is to find out about frustrations connected with income tax, housing, or pensions.

In addition to these activities, newsletters are sent around by some local Liberal organizations to selected wards. Each of these wards receives a somewhat different edition, designed to emphasize the local work of the relevant Liberal councillor or candidate. In a related tactic, Liberals make use of large bulk mailings to give residents a sense of involvement. One typical letter, from a council candidate to his constituents in Small Heath, reads:[19]

19 I am indebted to the Birmingham Liberal Party for making available a wide variety of local party literature.

Dear Friends,

I would like to thank very much all those people who signed my petition to get school warning signs on the approaches to Starbank School. This was presented at the last meeting of the City Council by Liberal Councillor Graham Gopsill and, as you will have noticed, the work has now been done.

Just to remind you, I hold my weekly Advice Bureau every Monday night at Starbank Schools, between 6:30 and 7:15. If you feel there is any way in which I can help on housing, rents, repairs, rates, pensions, etc. please look in and I will do my best to help you. Or, if you can't get along, you could drop me a line at the above address. If ever you need to get in touch with me in an emergency please phone. ...

It was this sort of intense local involvement which has been required for the comparatively minor Liberal political success in Birmingham. Similar work has preceded Liberal growth in other, similar urban areas — Leeds, Liverpool, and Greenock. Liverpool, in fact, has almost no Liberal tradition of any kind. Even in the striking national Liberal victory of 1906, the nine constituencies in the area returned only two Liberal MPs.[20] Greenock is worth noting thanks to Liberal capture of control of the council there. In spirit and problems, that city is comparable to the industrial poverty of Birmingham. It has a record of high unemployment, as well as overdependence on the traditional industries of shipbuilding and heavy engineering. It borders what used to be called the 'Red Clydeside', an historic bastion of Labour Party support. Despite a history of Liberal strength, the representation on the local council in 1960 was: 18 Labour, 8 Progressive (mixed Conservative and Liberal), 1 independent, no conventional Liberals. But by 1966, the Liberals had returned as a political force to take control of the council. By 1969, there were 20 Liberals, 7 Labour councillors, and no Tories at all.[21] Liberals in

20 *Local Government Newsletter*, May/June 1965, No 23, p. 5.
21 *Liberal News Commentary*, 128, 22 March, 1969, p. 7.

Greenock are representative of virtually all occupations and classes, but the Liberal success in Greenock is also an obvious function of interest in local problems. By 1968, the Liberal council could claim credit for constructing three factories, and for an unequalled record in the creation of new housing. Two years before Labour was ousted from control of the council, they had built 231 houses. In their final year of control of Greenock, they had constructed 294. Liberals constructed 833 in their first year as a majority, and increased this by 600 more in their second year.[22] The Liberals have not only built new buildings in Greenock, they also have seemed to take care in how the construction is done. The Liberal council's new buildings have won numerous civic awards. Planned urban development has also been undertaken, as it was under the previous Labour regime, but again the Liberals have exercised innovation in terminating an association which the council had with a London firm of developers and taking over more direct control of planning and construction themselves. This in itself might have been a political asset for the Liberals, given the ethos of Greenock, a city which is, in the words of the secretary of the Scottish Liberal Party, 'a fiercely independent place'.[23] This independence has also meant that Greenock, in its voting patterns, has never been identified with its populous and strongly pro-Labour neighbour, Glasgow.

The Liberal efforts in Leeds, Liverpool, Birmingham and Greenock may be especially dramatic and notable, thanks to the unusual environment in which they take place and the general lack of Liberal political tradition in most of these areas. But the political importance of the Liberal spirit of service seems to have considerably broader significance in explaining the party's recent history. The Birmingham pattern of local elections won on a basis of intense local service, leading in turn to more limited parliamentary election successes, has parallels in other English parliamentary seats where the Liberals did well in the 1960s. Table 7:3 shows the gains made by Liberals in local elections

22 *Liberal News Commentary*, No 86, 21 May, 1968, p. 1.
23 Interview, Spring 1970.

for both the four English seats won by the party in the 1960s and the five English seats where the Liberal candidate pulled close to the sitting Tory in the General Election of 1966.

Table 7:3 Liberal Local Gains in English Seats 1959-66

Divisions	Cllrs. on Borough and Urban Councils	
	1959	1966
Birmingham-Ladywood	0	1
Cheadle	15	22
Chippenham	3	10
Colne Valley	6	23
Eastbourne	1	11
Farnham	1	9
Orpington	0	8
Scarborough and Whitby	1	7
East Surrey	1	5
Totals:	28	96

Source: New Outlook, May 1966, p. 39.

In each of the English seats which elected Liberals in this revival period, success in local council elections was itself based on local community service. In Orpington, for instance, Liberal activists decided as early as 1955 to form local ward committees to fight local elections. From that time, the slow climb in the number of Liberal councillors was built upon local social work. The Liberals declared against a Conservative scheme to bring borough status to Orpington; for, as a party journal later put it, the 'hard-headed thousands of the new middle class' were in no mood to have their rates raised for an area in which they had no local roots. In one part of the constituency, Goddington South, considerable support was won from housewives by calling for more local shops and stores, notably a Marks & Spencers. A large part of this activity was supervised by Jack Galloway, Lubbock's predecessor as Liberal parliamentary candidate in the seat. It was because of this type of mundane, undramatic work that the Liberals on the council increased their numbers to a total of 12 in the 1961 local elections, the year before the publicized Orpington victory.[24]

Another striking case of Liberal activism leading to political success – though here only on the local level – occurred in Finchley, a northern suburb of London. Decades of Liberal absence from the area were ended in 1948, when a Liberal candidate contested a local election. From that beginning, the party climbed slowly in membership and council representation. In 1957, the first two Liberal councillors of the revival period were elected. Both of them were Jewish, reflecting a large Jewish constituency among the new Liberal activists in the area. The centre of their campaigns consisted of the charge that a local golf club, on which the council was represented, was practicing discrimination against Jews in its membership policy. The two Liberals lost a motion to withhold renewing the nomination of the council's representative on the club board, and were denounced for their efforts by both Tory and Labour councillors – but the golf club removed the religious belief clause from its membership form soon thereafter.[25]

The Liberals supplemented this major issue with the usual local social service approach. They devised a 'grumble sheet' on which local residents could describe problems to their councillor (they appear to have been the initiators of this practice, which was later taken up by the other two parties). They attacked the aldermanic system, which allowed the Tories to retain control of the council even after the Liberals had elected the most councillors. They protested an attempt by the Cotton-Glore firm's subsidy, Suburb Leaseholds, to buy a 2,000-year lease on the remainder of Hampstead Garden Suburbs, a development group already two-thirds under their control. In early 1963 they organized a popular protest to save County School and Christ's College, which were in danger

24 Donald Newby, 'The Orpington Story', *New Outlook*, March 1963, pp. 7, 11, 18.

25 John Irwin and David Crawford, 'The Finchley Story', *New Outlook*, August 1963, pp. 18-19.

of being replaced by a grammar school. It was, here as elsewhere, on the basis of this sort of constant effort that the party was able to take control of the council for a brief period in the local elections of 1963.[26]

The picture in the Celtic areas is not so clear, in part because the residual Liberal political tradition provides a pool of automatic support for the party. Also, there is a comparative lack of party-political activity in the more traditional rural areas where Liberals are strongest. The secretary of the Scottish Liberal Party has explained, for example, that the party has allowed local Liberal associations 'to pursue their own views' about standing for local elections. One important factor in this is that, 'we do not contest any seats at all in the Highlands or the Borders (where our MPs are elected) simply because there is very little Party label local government activity in these areas'.[27] Nevertheless, while the Celtic areas lack the clear outlines of Liberal local service leading to the election of councillors and MPs, it is clear that local work does play an important role in the efforts of Liberal MPs here to get and stay elected. Emlyn Hooson feels that the local work of his Liberal association has been an important element in his ability to retain his Welsh parliamentary seat.[28] In the Celtic areas, too, local issues become mixed with the broader regional issue, the charge that both Scotland and Wales are being neglected by a central government insensitive to their needs. James Davidson, Liberal MP for West Aberdeenshire from 1966 until he retired in 1970, notes:[29]

I think I was the first in this area to advocate a development authority for the North-East of Scotland and to speak out publicly for the small farmer. I have also emphasized constantly the importance of communications to this sort of area.

David Steel, M.P. for Roxburgh, Selkirk and Peebles from

26 *Ibid.*, pp. 22, 28, 30.
27 Correspondence, Spring 1970.
28 Correspondence, Spring 1970.
29 Correspondence, Spring 1970.

1965, and now Leader of the Party, has made the economic problems of the Borders area his own. One main task in the House of Commons has been agitation for the granting of development area status to the Borders. A special concern for him was the decision to close the Edinburgh-Carlisle railway route, despite his allegations against the Government that this seemed to be the sort of case for which the social clause of the Labour Transport Act had been designed. Russell Johnston, MP for Inverness, has used the regional issue frequently. He wrote in 1966, for example, that local government was failing to attract public participation even while failing adequately to meet its responsibilities. The situation was further complicated by immigration from some peripheral areas. In the face of this, he argued, 'the Liberal must advocate a single solution which will fuse the counter-attack. A regional pattern of administration offers this solution'.[30] The dramatic plea by Grimond, quoted earlier, in which he stressed in Commons debate the need to have concern for the special problems of his peripheral constituency, can be seen here as a theme of importance to the Scottish Liberals generally.

A similar approach to building support has been used by the West Country Liberals. Jeremy Thorpe has paid close attention to the particular concerns of the constituents of his North Devon seat, which he first contested in 1955 and won from the Tories in 1959. John Pardoe, Liberal MP for North Cornwall, draws upon a master list he has compiled of the occupations of the voters in his constituency. Using it, he sends constant questionnaires to constituents on issues before the Commons which might concern them.

This approach of local service is one which unites Liberals on both the right and left sides of the spectrum. Most Liberal seats are rural, hence conservative. Such right-wing Liberal MPs of the 1960s as Alasdair Mackenzie and Peter Bessell had ready-made issue-affinity with their seats from the start. For most of the new Liberals, however, who have been rather on the reformist, Grimond-Thorpe

---

30 Russell Johnston, 'Regionalism', *New Outlook*, February 1966, pp. 18-20. See also David Steel's article in *Liberal News Commentary*, No 48, 22 August, 1967, pp. 18-21.

left, the spirit of service (combined, at times, with appeals to the traditional nonconformist conscience) has been essential in winning their seats. These Liberals often nevertheless also represent rural fringe areas. Consequently, MPs such as Johnston, Pardoe, Steel, and Thorpe himself, must of necessity rely on tools other than their positions on national issues aside from regional and local devolution. The spirit of service, combined with pockets of traditional Liberal electoral support, can win a rural constituency for a Liberal even if he is on the political left. Conversely, the case of Roderic Bowen, who lost his Welsh seat in 1966, illustrates that even a well-established Liberal MP who is on the right, representing a traditional rural seat, can lose that seat if he does not organize and serve at the local level to create and maintain support for himself.[31]

The Liberal parliamentary by-election victories of the early 1970s have been generally but not uniformly related to issues of local service and community politics. The most striking example of success for the local approach was Cyril Smith's victory at Rochdale. He was first elected to the city's borough council in 1952, served as mayor during 1966-67, and has a strong local following as a result.[32] The theme of local issues has become a strong one in the Liberal Party and is normally given prominence in current by-election campaigns. On the other hand, the Isle of Ely victory had nothing directly to do with focused Liberal local activity; there was virtually no Liberal organization there, and the candidate had no history as a local activist.

The Service Ethic

Unfortunately, while local involvement has played an important role in most of the Liberal Party's political advances of recent years, it is far from being a sufficient condition for the election of Liberals. Even conscientious

31 Jeremy Rhys, 'Welsh Liberalism: How Green Were the Valleys?', *New Outlook*, December, 1964, pp. 29 ff.

32 The *Economist*, 4 August, 1973, pp. 19-20. Smith has served the council as a Labour and Independent member as well as a Liberal.

local work can lead to electoral frustration. The failure of the Liberals to elect an MP for Finchley is one instance of this. More examples can be culled from virtually all general elections. One of the more interesting cases is Baron's Court in the general election of 1964. There, the Liberal candidate caused the Labour Party considerable worry, and made the Tory organization uneasy. He had been a candidate for the borough council several times in Labour's Broadway Ward, with his campaign based on his energetic service to council tenants and others in difficult circumstances. He constantly attacked the local council for a variety of alleged shortcomings, represented the grievances of residents, and was able to make some gains in Labour territory. In the concrete general election returns, however, he received only 8·4 per cent of the vote. The major parties had their local activists too, and the handicap of being a Liberal in this case was not overcome by relatively intense and visible local work.[33]

Nevertheless, Liberal activists continue their involvement in local work, even though high investments of time and effort generally do not lead to electoral success, and at best bring only marginal improvement. One consideration is that such local work is usually essential to any political success the party does manage to achieve. Another, however, is that it seems to be a kind of end in itself for a large number of Liberal activists. Certainly, community involvement with this motivation makes more rational the work of volunteers in a party so far from power. Moreover, it conforms nicely with strains of the nonconformist ethic.

Interesting inferential evidence along these lines is available from the results of the limited postal survey of Liberal activists and leaders outlined in the Appendix. Table 7:4 provides a brief summary of the results of a question concerning local service by Liberals, with opinions expressed very top-heavily in favour of the proposition that there is a distinctive streak of the local service ethic in Liberal constituency associations. Typical replies to this

33 Robert T. Holt and John E. Turner, *Political Parties in Action – The Battle of Barons Court*, pp. 168-9; The Times, *Guide To The House of Commons 1964*, pp. 108-9.

Table 7:4 Liberals and Local Service

Responses to question asking how active the respondent's local Liberal Party association is in social service work	
Responses	Number
Yes, are active	80
No, are not active or are only slightly active	13
Don't know, not answered, or no Liberal organization in the area	11
Total:	104

question are also instructive. While it might be argued that the form of the question implies a biased response – i.e., people are unlikely to say their political organization is uninterested in the problems of the old, the poor, the unemployed – the specific nature of many of the replies, and the enthusiasm evidenced in more than a few, argue that the commitment to service is characteristic of a fair proportion of party activists:

Members are active in residents' association and in taking up local issues – e.g., road safety.

Sporadic campaigns on industrial reform, welfare rights etc. We use grumble sheets to get local complaints.

Not enough. Many are very active in the social field. So much so that it weakens political activity.

This is one of our troubles. They are so overworked in every form of social work that they haven't enough time for politics.

We have Liberals on most Councils in South Oxfordshire (though always in a minority!). Many are concerned with social, charity and Church organizations. Considering our numbers we are active within the community in many ways.

Yes – Shelter, Oxfam, citizens' advice bureaux, visiting old people.

Occasional 'special' public meetings, yes, help in Meals on Wheels, Friends of the Hospitals, etc.

Canvassing (by a few). Excellent literature distribution. Councillors take up local issues. Wymondham YLs visited the old. As candidate I speak frequently, write letters to the press, attend and speak at non-party meetings (local problems, church, UNA and other organizations).

An important complication of this portrait is the fact that the Liberals are far from alone in their commitment to local altruism. Unfortunately for an effort to make neat and simple distinctions between the Liberals and the two collectivist parties on the basis of the spirit of service, there is no simple, sharp dichotomy between them. Lord Beveridge, though a Liberal, chose to assign his compliment concerning the 'spirit of service' to the entire British people, not alone to his chosen party. Students of British politics have noted that the roles of MP and – even more – of local councillor tend to contain a large quantity of local social casework no matter what political party is involved.[34]

Nevertheless, despite the pervasiveness of the indicators of social altruism in British culture, there are several factors which make the spirit of service argument especially applicable to an analysis of the recent fortunes of the Liberal Party. No matter what the real situation may in fact be, a large number of Liberals seem to believe that their party is especially committed to local, comparatively informal social work.[35] The nonconformist conscience is an

34 See Anthony Barker and Michael Rugh, *The Member of Parliament and His Information*, pp. 196 ff. for discussion and defence of the proposition that local welfare work consumes large amounts of an MP's time regardless of his political party.

35 Along with the evidence already cited, this theme was constantly used by Liberals in personal interviews

historical element in the party, the spirit of service a constant theme of the recent revival. This belief that the Liberal Party is especially committed to social service can only be reinforced by the fact that party philosophy stresses localism, individualism, and decentralization in opposition to the basic themes of collectivism. In a sense, the Liberal's commitment to local service is undiluted and uncompromised by basic party ideas moving him in other directions. The Tory and Labour parties are based upon inclusive class conceptions of constituency, upon inclusive national conceptions of policy. Liberalism has had very different bases; its individualism is a strong opposite of class bias and class thinking. Hence, the Liberal outlook addresses particular local concerns and local styles of activism. In view of this, it is not surprising that the 1950s and 1960s witnessed a flow of new members into Liberal Party ranks as an indication of the increasing movement away from collectivist political concerns and activist styles.

More practical, structural political considerations reinforce this observation that the Liberal Party is more easily attuned to the spirit of service. Study of local councillors has indicated that they generally do not see their work as a stepping-stone to higher political office, but rather have one or more of several other motivations for doing what they do: (1) a sense of satisfaction from the approval they achieve from their council colleagues, (2) a commitment to local service as an end in itself, (3) being 'press-ganged' into service by their party.[36] For Liberals, both (1) and (3) would seem clearly to have generally little or no significance. Liberals on local councils are often treated as outcasts and pariahs by non-Liberal councillors, especially at the start of a local Liberal surge when they are an unaccustomed threat to other councillors. Because of the weakness of the Liberal Party, it is hardly in a position to 'press-gang' anyone into anything, let alone the time-consuming work of local council service. Again, the spirit of service is one factor among several for most councillors, but

36 Anthony M. Ress and Trevor Smith, *Town Councillors – A Study of Barking*, pp. 72-3, 78; see also A.H. Birch, *Small Town Politics*, p. 123.

for Liberals it would seem the prime consideration, especially during the period after the Grimond revival but before the current resurgence.

Absence of party discipline means that Liberals cannot be pressed to run for local seats, but also that members of the party have a flexibility not generally available to Tory and Labour activists. Liberal hostility to local council party whips means that representatives of the party continue to be able to act on their own after election. There is no large, cohesive party organization to impose caution and politically prudent restraint on local candidates. Liberals almost never have the inhibition of the electorate's memory of the problems and shortcomings of a council in which they had a majority. Moreover, the party normally is so far from power that the conventional fear of damaging future election prospects does not apply. The publicity given the housing problem in Birmingham by local Liberals has been possible partly because they need not fear embarrassing a large, ambitious party organization.

A number of Liberal parliamentary candidates interviewed in person stressed that they find satisfaction from involvement in local problems, whether or not the Liberals are a large presence on local councils or they themselves stand much chance for election. This was true of the candidate for Finchley, Margaret Thatcher's seat, during the period when Mrs Thatcher was Opposition spokeswoman on education, before the Tory victory in 1970. He argued that she was too busy and too safe to take an active interest in local problems. In reply to a Liberal campaign during this period to promote the party as the local social-service agency in Finchley – as the only party, for example, to run a local advice bureau – the Tory organization declared that the sitting MP was just as active as the Liberals (there is virtually no Labour organization in the constituency). A telephone call to the local Conservative headquarters, however, to ask for an appointment to see the MP, allegedly brought the reply that it would be necessary to arrange the meeting at Westminster. The Liberal candidate argued that few old people have the courage to travel what is, to them, a very long distance, to a very awesome and foreign palace.[37] Although Finchley was at that time represented by a member of the Shadow Cabinet, it was doubtless not unique in having an MP occupied and distracted by national considerations. The vast majority of parliamentary seats, after all, are safe for the party which holds them. The Liberals are not only free from philosophical restraints on individualism, their lack of presence in – or hope for – national office means that they are free from various practical restraints as well.

Another point should be introduced, as further evidence that the spirit of service must be no small motivation in encouraging Liberals to serve on local councils. Local constituency work is not only time-consuming in terms of the demands of constituents, it is also extremely complicated in the details of law and administration involved. Local services and issues are normally complex as well as mundane and boring as a steady occupation. American local government, by comparison, is more interesting because it is more independent, with wider scope for public policy innovation. To take up local problems means to become drawn into such issues as whether porterage, laundering, lighting, elevators and a myriad of other amenities and conveniences are covered by rules governing the landlord-tenant relationship, and whether the quality of services provided is up to the standards which are supposed to be maintained. Not even mastering the details of local rules is enough, for often the tenant complaint is that the rule book which governs them is out of date.[38]

To devote time to this kind of activity, given the political position of the Liberal Party in the nation, requires a commitment of considerable intensity. The religious convictions of a Gladstone, the religious altruism of a Cobden or Bright, are reflected in the ethos of individualistic social service – though not of a formally religious sort. In

37 Interview, Autumn 1969.
38 Interview. I am grateful to Councillor Simon Knott, who invited me to attend a revealing and educational rent hearing in late 1969 at which he represented some of his constituents in their complaint. See also the article by him in *Liberal News* Commentary, No 81, 16 April, 1968, p. 5.

practice, the moralism which accompanies the commitment of many Liberals often puts them at one pole, self-consciously denouncing both the Labour and the Conservative Parties. Sometimes, candidates of the other parties pick up the cue and respond in kind. In the 1964 general election, for example, one marginal constituency witnessed a particularly striking illustration of this. Both the Labour and Tory candidates, as the campaign progressed, 'tended to join forces in an attack upon their Liberal opponent who revealed a position, not at a point between the major parties, but on the moralistic end of the spectrum and somewhat on the periphery of British political life'.[39]

In serving to illustrate the partial crumbling of the earlier, more predictable Labour-Tory duopoly, the Liberal Party revival has been indicative of a new movement away from old patterns. The attraction of activists into the Liberal Party reflects at least some alteration of conventional national collectivist politics to an unconventional local Liberal politics which is at least partly removed from considerations of office and power. The irony for Liberals who have been interested in national political revival, however, lies in this very lack of connection between the spirit of service and national politics. If local service, in the collectivist parties, is compromised by national political work and party ambitions, the other side of the picture is that the spirit of service is not itself strongly connected to party. This is true in at least two senses. First, many voters seem to have sensed Liberal usefulness in handling local problems but, nevertheless, in national elections, have continued to vote on the basis of their prime commitment to one or the other of the two main parties. The *Economist* noted this in 1964. After first remarking on the fact that recent years had witnessed the installation of 'A fair number of Liberals on local councils', and observing that 'many have nursed their wards with great assiduity backed by Liberal associations who have regarded local government as their main practical political interest', the article continued that 'Liberals have paid perhaps more

39 Holt and Turner, *op. cit.*, p. 163.

attention than anybody else to strictly local issues, but have then found that the electorate invariably votes on national images.'[40] This implies the development of 'part-time' Liberal voters: people who are willing and anxious to vote Liberal in local elections, but do not transfer this loyalty to parliamentary elections, where the Liberal candidate is invariably less politically credible.[41]

Second, however, is the phenomenon that many Liberal activists themselves seem not to be motivated by real hopes for political office. An important explanation for the continuing survival, and the interesting revival, of the Liberal Party is that it has drawn people who have not been motivated by desire for political power. Service was their reward. This, to be sure, was hardly true of all the people drawn during the Grimond revival, and was not true at all of the ambitious Grimond élite. But it was and is a quality of many Liberals. The localism theme has been stressed by Thorpe and his colleagues in the current less colourful revival, and the point of this argument is that carrying it one step further means that party itself is not very important if local service is the motivation. Indeed, the fading of the Grimond revival brought hints that this was realized by some disillusioned Liberal Party supporters themselves. In 1968, for instance, there was a movement by some well-known Liberals, working in tandem with both Labour Party members and non-party activists, to create what was termed 'Radical Action', a coalition intended to draw people from a variety of sources, joined by their interest in local community action and local social service.[42]

In this context, the basic issue is whether the Liberal Party revival has itself been an early indication of a broader movement away from party in Britain, at least in the old sense of two massive coalitions with a virtual monopoly on significant political activity. To a good Liberal the structure of party is not itself central in the same sense that it is to a Tory or Socialist. This old sentiment, harking back to

40 The *Economist*, 16 May, 1964, p. 695.
41 The *Economist*, 12 March, 1966, p. 976.
42 *Liberal News* Commentary, No 78, 26 March, 1968, p. 1.

nineteenth-century individualism, implies both a lack of
strong commitment to party as an end in itself and a
willingness to put up with the inevitable frustrations which
accompany the effort to find room for manoeuvre outside of
the two main parties. A contemporary Liberal Party writer
and worker, Hugh Tinker, has written: 'One who protests
against the two-party system must be prepared to work for
long-term and not short-term objectives. This means a
politics of faith, rather than a politics of works.' Reflecting
on the 1964 general election, when so many votes for the
Liberals resulted in so very few MPs actually elected, he
finds some solace in the introverted reflections of an Indian
humanist intellectual, who rejects conventional
majoritarian democracy because he sees in party the
abrogation of popular sovereignty. The Liberal
Englishman, reaching the central point of his own
sentiments, quotes the rather-Liberal Indian at some
length:[43]

> When a man really wants freedom and to live in a
> democratic society he may not be able to free the whole
> world ... but he can to a large extent at least free himself
> by behaving as a rational and moral being, and if he can
> do this, others around him can do the same, and these
> again will spread freedom by their example.

To the Indian writer, party is not even a *necessary* evil; the
good individualist's alternative is to focus on his own
efforts, to celebrate his individual freedom by trying to
measure himself by and marry himself to moral behaviour,
to hope that one atom in the sea of society may change
others through example. Modern collectivism has its
normative bases, but they are bases of varieties of
sociological collectivism and communalism. Very different
is this highly individualistic moralism, finding a sense of
unity only in the most loose sort of abstraction. It is not
surprising that an English Liberal would find such a
perspective appealing; it fits well with the rejection of class
and the taste for individualist activism.

43 Tinker, *op. cit.*, p. 174.

The problem for those Liberals interested in the success of the party at the polls is that the doctrine implies rejection of party entirely. If party is conceived as a necessary evil, the perspective of party as unnecessary evil is less distance to travel than many party-oriented Liberals would care to imagine. Although the Liberal Party was able to move in collectivist policy directions in the period before its collapse as one of the two governing coalitions, modern party discipline and organization was generally viewed with antagonism. Party is, after all, inevitably a compromise of pristinely conceived individualism. Tinker himself comes very close to the Indian intellectual's own anti-party sentiment, or at least shows scant regard for the importance of party, in his own very rhetorical conclusion:[44]

> The writer of this essay found his understanding of the politics of participation from modern Indian thought. All the great problems of the world — racialism, fear of the other side, holding on to possessions, covetousness of others' possessions – all these problems exist within every man:
>> *They cease not fighting, East and West,*
>> *On the marches of my breast.*
> The Kingdom of God is within you; Hell is within you; and at a lower level, freedom or servitude is within you. The man who knows that in liberating himself and those around him he is helping to liberate mankind, does not need to fear the big battalions.

Has the revival of the Liberal Party in fact served as an early indication of a broader turning away from party? Certainly, Liberalism seems congenitally to lack the means of imposing large-scale institutional structures around Liberals. At least one writer sensed, indirectly, the surface of this quality when he criticized the Grimond Liberals of the early 1960s for addressing themselves admirably to the psychological consequences of change and reform for individuals, but neglecting to speak at length to issues of

44 *Ibid.*, p. 175.

change in institutions.[45] In one sense he was wrong, for the Liberals had detailed proposals at this time for a variety of alterations in the structures of government; in a more fundamental way, he sensed a basic orientation of Liberalism itself.

45 Birnbaum, *op. cit.*, p. 61.

8 Old Liberal Groups, New American Voting

People Count
Liberal Party campaign slogan, 1959

The underlying, broader significance of the Liberal revival proceeds from the underlying factors of class and social service. The intellectual, policy-related revival of the party may be slippery to trace, less simple and straightforward than the electoral and opinion-poll data; but it is traceable. Moreover, the drama and excitement connected with that aspect of the revival make for interesting – and comparatively clear and uncomplicated – research. The updating of policy was closely tied to other aspects of Liberal Party revival, and was explicitly conceived as a tool to further political advance. Hence, it is clearly relevant to a study of Liberal Party revival during the Grimond period. In addition, in pristine terms the opposition between liberalism and collectivism, as approaches to party and government policy, is so marked and sharp that highlighting differences, and the manner in which one replies to the problems of the other, is an exercise in clarity through opposition.

The broader themes of social changes within the electorate and among political activists is another matter. They are not easily defined with precision. Nevertheless, they are present, and important, and the Liberal Party revival's more general significance to British politics results from them. These themes help to explain the recent electoral gains of the Liberals, won in spite of the passing of the Grimond period's lively policy-drafting and organizational activity within the party. They also have important implications for more general structures of political influence and public policy, and the behaviour of the electorate, in modern Britain.

The structure of influence in contemporary Britain has

been dominated by party government and functional representation in terms of supports for public institutions and policy. The calculus engendered by these formations, in turn, tends to the creation of a welfare state which neglects certain sociological minorities, and a planned economy which emphasizes central and national perspectives and is resistant to political devolution. Beyond the administrative limits of central and universalist outlooks, there is the reinforcing political consideration that peripheral regions and the very poor have, in cold electoral terms, not been crucial to victory for either of the two main parties.

Role of Class

The electoral insignificance of these segments has been strengthened by the class nature of British voting behaviour. Class conceptions have provided the basic struts of party creed, which in turn have solidified the loyalties of the constant Labour and Tory electorates, giving a discipline to voting which has made most parliamentary seats safe and most MPs – for reasons of both practical party discipline and ideological solidarity – reluctant to break strongly with party leaders. Conversely, the basic solidarity created by class ideas has been maintained, and floating voters won, through the predictability of benefit by means of the planned economy and the welfare state. Economic planning ensures a necessary minimum of economic stability, plus representation for the large private-sector producer groups. The universalist welfare state provides payments and services to most of the needy population.

The entire structure, however, is fundamentally dependent on class conceptions of politics for stability. As has already been suggested, the collectivist electoral bases have rested firmly on the horizontal division of society explicit in Labour theory and the vertical integration of society implicit in Tory belief. If class is declining in intensity as a force defining British political life, a reasonable inference would be that both the structures of political activism and the patterns of voting behaviour would begin to change. With the decline of class, the collectivist model would begin to lose its twin roots in sociology and philosophy.

In fact, class seems definitely a declining force in British politics. The survey research of Butler and Stokes, as well as other scholars, indicates that younger middle- and working-class voters do not share the intensity of class feeling characteristic of their elders. Younger voters are much less likely to regard politics as a matter of class conflict or consider the two main parties to be separated by significant differences.[1] With the fading of this basic divider, and odd integrator, of British society, new divisions and tensions are free to increase in prominence. Their importance may be assumed to be a reflection both of new attitudes and expectations in the population, and of the decline of old time-consuming, emotion-consuming issues centred on class.

Potential candidates for new political divisions and emotional investments would include the peripheral minorities produced by the logic of the planned economy and the welfare state. Decline of the national class war would free the obviously deprived peripheries of Scotland and Wales to substitute their own sectional concerns and complaints for the previously encompassing national class division. Growth of general affluence would free newly prosperous, newly secure activists to concern themselves with the pockets of poverty which remain. As the economic level of the population in general continues to rise, the plight of the nation's stagnant economic backwaters becomes increasingly obvious.

Voluntarism

The nineteenth-century Liberal and Radical periods were times of strong voluntary reform and social service groups which operated independently of party. Moralistic, particular in focus, often very temporary, these Liberal

1 David Butler and Donald Stokes, Chapters 4-5.

formations were as much a part of the politics of the age as the Liberal Party was itself. Liberals saw such groups not as enemies of party, but as potential allies in the broad fight to install Liberalism in the working of government. The Liberal regime of 1906-14 tried to integrate voluntary associations, with their advantages of flexibility, into the administration of various reforms. The ultimate irony of politics for the party-oriented Liberal, which should never be far from the centre of any analysis of Liberal politics, is that to the pristine the Liberal Party is not of first importance. Establishing Liberalism is what occupies the centre of his mental stage. If this goal is not seen as best achieved through the Liberal Party, activists will turn elsewhere. For them, party is the compromise of individualism, not a vehicle for the realization of class interest and definition of class solidarity.

There are clear indications that the years of Liberal Party revival have also been years of increasing voluntary activity, disconnected from any particular political party. At the same time that the *structures* of collectivism have been undergoing the sort of arteriosclerosis which guarantees that powerful interest groups will oppose almost any dramatic policy shifts, less obvious social change – the decline of class – has released energy for a more fluid tableau of social and political activism.[2] To be sure, no recent period of British history has been without these voluntary groups. The spirit of service has age as well as depth in British culture. However, there are indications that these groups have proliferated markedly as the Collectivist Age has matured and begun to give way to new patterns. The handbook and directory of the National Council of Social Services, *Voluntary Social Services*, lists figures which indicate that the rate at which national voluntary service associations are formed has accelerated since the last century.[3] Before 1860, it has records for only

2 Samuel Beer, 'The Future of British Politics: An American View'; Samuel Beer, *British Politics*, pp. 391-434.

3 'A central link between different voluntary organizations and official bodies concerned with social welfare is provided by the National Council of Social Service.' [British Information Services, *Social Services in Britain*, p. 90.]

12 such organizations. Between the years 1860 and 1899, 31 were formed, a marked increase over the apparent tendency of previous years but not equal to the rate which followed: 46 groups were formed between 1900 and 1939, 23 each during the two periods 1900-19 and 1920-39. The rate accelerated further after 1939, with 31 groups created between 1940 and 1959.[4]

Recent years, when the Liberal Party has enjoyed new energy and support, have witnessed the birth of several large, very prominent, national voluntary reform and service organizations. The improvement in political support for the party generally paralleled the growth in energy of the Campaign for Nuclear Disarmament (CND, begun 1958). The Child Poverty Action Group (CPAG, begun 1965) and Shelter (begun 1966) are leading examples of the new welfare-oriented groups.[5]

There also has been a recent significant increase in the number of small, local voluntary associations, of the type which are less easily quantified. Significantly, the start of their proliferation again generally correlates with the beginning of the Liberal Party's revival. Perhaps the first of the new formations, notably ahead of the trend, were the Citizens' Advice Bureaux, local centres designed to handle enquiries from individuals concerning available public services and public assistance. Begun with government help by the National Council of Social Service in 1939, there were 430 such bureaux by the early 1960s.[6] In the mid 1950s, the new forms of social and political energy directed themselves into the formation of the National Spastics Society, the Association of Mentally Handicapped Children and the Muscular Dystrophy Group. Local branches of these, springing up across the country, were a vanguard for more of the same sort of neo-Liberal groups. In 1957, Duncan Sandys founded the Civic Trust, which

4 Kathleen Slack, 'Voluntary Effort', in James Farndale, ed., *Trends in Social Welfare*, pp. 36-7.

5 On the CND, see Norman Birnbaum, 'Great Britain: The Reactive Revolt', in Morton Kaplan, ed., *The Revolution in World Politics*, pp. 57-8; CPAG, *Poverty*; Shelter, *The Shelter Story*.

6 *British Information Services, Social Services in Britain*, p. 90.

led to the creation of the Civic and Amenity Societies, local planning groups. By 1966, there were 540 in operation. In 1960, the first Association for the Advancement of State Education was begun in Cambridge. Six years later, some 120 had been set up. In 1961, the Federation of Local Consumer Groups was formed, and saw its branches grow in the larger towns through the 1960s. Other groups, on the same model, were formed in connection with the hospital service. A very old form of the same type of organization, the Councils for Social Service, began to enjoy new life. By the middle of the 1960s, they had grown to 143 in the towns and 28 in the counties, all operating around the basic principle of serving as co-ordinating bodies linking other groups – the Citizens' Advice Bureaux, Marriage Guidance Councils, Arts Councils and old people's welfare organizations.[7]

These groups, large and small, have grown to such an extent that some see them as the wave of the political future, replacing old-fashioned political parties. This may be an extreme prediction, especially concerning a political system and culture where important change has been typified historically by slow motion and incrementalism. Yet the accretion of such neo-Liberal groups is striking. The Open Group, sponsored by the periodical *New Society*, published a pamphlet on social change in contemporary Britain which attempted to dramatize the potential policy importance of this style of activism:[8]

> government is now ringed by tens of thousands of organizations trying to influence it and each other. Civil rights were won in the eighteenth century, political rights in the nineteenth century and in the twentieth economic rights. But change has throughout depended on exercising the right to free association and combination. It has become more crucial than ever in this century.

On one side, groups are used in conjunction with formal public services to combat the welfare state's tendencies

7 L.J. Sharpe, 'Leadership and Representation in Local Government', *Political Quarterly*, April/June, 1966, p. 156.

8 *New Society*, 'Social Reform in the Contrifugal Society', p. 4.

toward rigidity and insensitivity. A British government publication outlining social services notes: 'Many voluntary social services surround and supplement the State services ... State services often work through voluntary agencies specially adapted to serve individual or special needs.' On the other side, other groups work independently of public agencies, which are considered inadequate to the task of aiding pockets of severe need. The same publication also observes categorically that State services and voluntary services are 'complimentary, not competitive'.[9] Clearly, this is true only very partially. A major incentive for the creation of voluntary associations has been the increasingly obvious inability of government to bring in the sectors excluded from the welfare state. In consequence, notable voluntary associations operate their own independent welfare activities and, additionally, attempt through agitation and publicity – through the power of embarrassment – to bend universalist institutions in selective directions.

In terms of service, the national scope of Shelter is testimony to its success. It was originally created by several voluntary societies in the housing field: the Notting Hill Housing Trust, the Catholic Housing Aid Society, the National Federation of Housing Societies, Christian Action, and the British Churches Housing Trust. While it acts as a publicity and pressure group, the primary accomplishment of the association has been in improving the housing of poor families through rehabilitating old housing and a little new building. By late 1967, there were over 70 affiliated Shelter groups. This total had grown to over 220 groups in England and Wales by the end of 1969. During the three years after the formation of the organization, over 4,700 families received improved accommodations.[10]

The picture is less clear in terms of moving public institutions themselves in the direction of reform. It is certain, however, that the publicity given to poverty of a severe sort, of a variety which was growing *worse* under the Wilson Government, resulted in victory for the Child Poverty Action Group when the government adopted their

9 *Social Services in Britain*, p. 89.
10 *The Shelter Story*, pp. 27, 33.

proposed 'claw-back' in an effort to provide aid for the very poor. This device increased both tax and child allowances, thus effectively increasing assistance for those too poor to pay taxes, even if by a procedure which was indirect but geared to political reality.[11] The fact that the Wilson Cabinet took this approach is mute testimony to the difficulty of urging universalist institutions in the direction of selective policy.

For the reform and service groups, motivation for activism derives from sources which are different from those of more conventional political work. The groups operate on the basis of a political calculus different from that of collectivism, responding to a view which contains the particular segments of the population which do not benefit from the general and majoritarian outlook of the central government's offices of planning and services. Also, however, aside from philosophy, their lack of large, formal structure and their sheer numbers mean that they have the flexibility to attack problems which are really a multitude of small, discrete issues of particular communities and sectors of society. The small size of so many of the groups and the loose organization of the larger ones are actually advantages.

The Liberal Party has grown increasingly conscious of the virtue of flexibility associated with voluntary social service. The party declared 1968 to be a year in which Liberal constituency associations should 'channel their energies into involvement in their local community'. In 1960-3, local government was stressed as part of a strategy to build a national political revival for the party. By 1968, 'the current state of disillusionment among voters' led the party to stress local social work. The party's most recent by-election victories and its exceptional, if temporary, climb in public support measured in opinion polls encouraged Thorpe and his colleagues to stress this approach even more, in turn reinforcing its normal appeal to liberals.[12] Even if local service has played a role in aiding the political revival of the Liberal Party, it is also true, however, that a considerable amount of local voluntarism has operated outside the

11 CPAG, *Poverty and the Labour Government*, pp. 14-15.
12 *Action and Feed-back*, No 68, 25 October, 1968, p. 1.

channel of that party. The Liberal ethic strongly contains both party and voluntary groups, and so it is not surprising that the party's revival should parallel the growth in voluntary associations. Nevertheless, energy which is devoted to group activity is effectively lost to the political aspirations of Liberal Party workers and leaders.

Regionalism

The maturing quality of the Collectivist Age has been reflected in sectionally based activism as well as these sectoral concerns. The most dramatic indication of the rise of peripheral regional sentiment has been the growth of the Scottish and Welsh nationalist parties in votes, activists, and resulting public attention. The inability of the nationalists and Liberals to co-operate and compromise with one another, to their mutual political benefit, would seem to imply a residual lingering class sentiment; but the fact that such a division is occurring between the parties in a clearly regional context indicates that *national* class sentiment has declined in importance. These new sectional concerns, above all, recall the types of cleavage which were characteristic of the pre-collectivist Liberal and Radical periods of British politics. It was after all the Irish question, a source of intense political conflict in the 19th century, which damaged the Liberal Party electorally, created intense political debate, and enabled Joseph Chamberlain to draw a large segment of the industrial working class from the Liberal Party to the Tories in the 1880s. Nevertheless, the Liberals never ceased advocating devolution throughout the United Kingdom or trying to define precisely just what workable policy along these lines might entail. While the recent growth in popular support for the nationalist parties may not prove permanent, it is also true that their gains (especially in Scotland) have persuaded the major parties to be at least somewhat more responsive to pressures for greater attention and practical devolution of power.

Electoral Change

The decline of the political force of class has not only

Table 8:1 Standard Deviations for British Gallup Polls

Year	Labour	Conservative
1947	6·86	4·91
1948	1·30	2·50
1949	2·33	4·07
1950	2·50	1·25
1951	6·02	2·27
1952	4·16	2·45
1953	1·25	1·45
1954	2·34	1·90
1955	0·74	2·24
1956	1·97	2·61
1957	2·36	11·34
1958	1·64	15·85
1959	1·46	6·47
1960	3·44	0·68
1961	1·80	4·72
1962	2·66	3·00
1963	1·81	1·35
1964	3·73	4·10
1965	8·04	6·24
1966	12·59	2·75
1967	14·48	6·39
1968	12·75	7·35
1969	14·90	4·53
1970	8·42	2·96
1971	6·97	10·35
1972	2·38	3·04
1973	3·90	5·60

Source: British Gallup Polls

encouraged the development of voluntary groups and regional parties, it has also undermined the predictability of broad national voter sentiments and election results. The 1970 General Election, in which an apparent last-minute swing in voter opinion handed victory to the Tory Party, is a dramatic indication of how far this uncharacteristic instability has progressed within the British electorate. A broader perspective making the same point is provided by Table 8-1, which measures the annual standard deviations from the mean of public support for both the Tory and

Labour parties, determined by use of Gallup Poll data. Clearly, there is evidence here that volatility is growing in the British electorate.

The Liberal Party's rising political fortunes are one indication of this general departure from previous habits of predictable conformity. One plausible explanatory hypothesis would be that, as old class solidarity began to decline, voters moved over into the Liberal camp with more frequency than had previously been the case. To some extent, however, the new strength of the Liberals was simply a reflection of the residual strength of class sentiment and traditional patterns of voting. Had class feeling been less strong, voters would have been more inclined to move all the way over into the other main party. Had conventionality declined more quickly, voters would have been less reluctant to select the more exotic and unconventional Scottish and Welsh nationalist parties. In the late 1960s, collapse of old constraints on voting patterns went much further. This can be seen not only in the growth in strength of the nationalist parties, but also in the abandonment of distinct class images by the two major parties. New Tory and Labour flexibility, added to the electorate's increasing willingness to go all the way over to vote for the other main party, deprived the Liberals of potential strength. As in policy, so in voter appeal: the two main parties reflected and restricted the Liberal Party's revival by capturing Liberal themes for their own.

But if the big parties managed to maintain their general supremacy, their security has been considerably diluted. Their supporters are not reliable as they once were. They must be constantly persuaded and re-persuaded, won anew at each election. Some inferential evidence for this dwindling popular commitment to party is given in Table 8:2, which lists non-trade union membership in the Labour Party since 1946. The general membership trend has been clearly downward in more recent years. The Liberal opportunity in this context is not to become solidly established within the electorate as Labour and Tory once were, but rather to take advantage of the greater room for manoeuvre present in a more fluid and variable situation.

Table 8:2 Non-Trade Union Membership in the Labour Party

Year	Number of Constituency and Central Parties	Total Indiv. Members	Socialist and Co-operative Societies: Number	Members
1946	649	645,000	6	42,000
1947	649	608,000	6	46,000
1948	656	629,000	6	42,000
1949	660	730,000	5	41,000
1950	661	908,000	5	40,000
1951	667	876,000	5	35,000
1952	667	1,015,000	5	21,000
1953	667	1,005,000	5	34,000
1954	667	934,000	5	35,000
1955	667	843,000	5	35,000
1956	667	845,000	5	34,000
1957	667	913,000	5	26,000
1958	667	889,000	5	26,000
1959	667	848,000	5	25,000
1960	667	790,000	5	25,000
1961	667	751,000	5	25,000
1962	667	767,000	5	25,000
1963	667	830,000	6	21,000
1964	667	830,000	6	21,000
1965	659	817,000	6	21,000
1966	658	776,000	6	21,000
1967	657	734,000	6	21,000
1968	656	701,000	6	21,000
1969	656	681,000	6	22,000
1970	656	680,000	6	24,000
1971	659	700,000	6	25,000
1972	659	703,000	9	40,000

Source: David Butler and Jennie Freeman, *British Political Facts 1900-68*, p. 108; also library of the Labour Party Headquarters, Transport House, London.

The present trend therefore does not involve the use of a new party to replace one of the two main ones, as happened when Labour rose to replace the Liberals as chief contestant of the Tories. Instead, it is a movement away from party entirely as that commitment was understood in earlier British politics. The recent Liberal by-election victories, the advance in the public opinion polls to a position which for a time rivalled support for the two major parties, and the impressive votes for the party in the 1974 General Elections are evidence for this. It is an historic fact that the Liberals, since dropping to third-party status, have normally had more support when a Tory Government has been in power. Doubtless the recent advance of the party from 1971 through to 1974 reflected lingering Conservative voter reluctance to move all the way to backing Labour. But growth of overall instability and volatility within the electorate has also played a role.

Liberal Politics

The Liberal Party's recent history reflects interesting and significant changes in the British electorate, as well as addressing dysfunctions of collectivist structures. The hypothesis presented here correlates with the observation of electoral analysts that third-party votes tend to increase in periods of basic party realignment and fundamental change in electoral behaviour. The Liberals have not only been performing the classic third-party role of promoting new approaches to public policy issues; they have also represented in their shifting vote broader changes in the electorate at large. Both of these functions historically have been performed by third parties in the United States. Britain has been generally less rich in third-party movements, even though the nineteenth and twentieth centuries have witnessed events of considerable domestic political trauma. The recent history of the Liberal Party seems then to represent a movement of British voting patterns in an American direction. US voters have been generally more willing than the British to move back and forth between the major parties and to support fringe movements.

Significantly, those American parties which have had the qualities of moralistic 'movements' have also generally represented various peripheral regions discontented with the central government.[13]

These similarities recall an observation of Samuel Beer concerning his personal reaction to a Liberal assembly he attended: the Liberals seemed reminiscent, in atmosphere and theme, of America's Republicans and Democrats, but hardly appeared to have much in common with Tory and Labour.[14] In so far as the two main parties have muted old class themes, old collectivist messages, in favour of a new classless message (or perhaps it might best be termed a new 'middle-classless' message), the Liberal Party's political revival has served to reflect a much broader change in British politics and society, in the ways in which the British view one another. The Americanization of Britain is a theme noted frequently, not without rancour, by Britons confronted with the spectacle of American language, folkways, advertising techniques, and business executives moving into more and more corners of British society. Traditionalism, restraint, understatement may remain paramount elements of British life; but the evolution of old ways cannot be denied. The American invaders just cited may be, in a way, superficial; but they reflect deeper and broader currents of modernization.

The replacement of position through birth with more open norms of achievement and competition in education and later in professional life is perhaps the most striking and profound change. But it is a reflection of the basic phenomenon of the decline of class in Britain. It is unlikely that a specific cause can be easily singled out for such a fundamental happening. The demands of modern industry and technology, recognized belatedly by the British, is one central consideration, inevitable in the observations of the interested scholar. The average man might cite another more readily: the impact of 'the war' – meaning the Second World War – and its influence in forcing the deterioration

13 See, e.g., Walter Dean Burnham, *Critical Elections – and the Mainsprings of American Politics*, pp. 27-31.

14 Samuel Beer, 'Liberalism and the National Idea', p. 149.

of horizontal class divisions in the face of the combination of horror at impending defeat and romantic unity in the struggle to fight on alone.[15]

As in areas of policy, addressing itself to the strictures and problems of collectivism, so in the area of social change, reflecting in electoral revival and decline the constant passing away of class as a central feature of British political life, the Liberal Party has served as a barometric indicator of change in Britain. The very success of the party in stressing non-class sectional and sectorial issues is a direct function of the decline of class as almost-total determinant of the ways in which the British voter decides on his party. The Liberal message of modernization and change was reflected, in different fashions, by Harold Wilson and Edward Heath. Specific policies and a more general tone associated with the Liberal Party were adopted by the two main parties, and in the area of regional devolution the nationalist parties have provided direct competition. The anti-class spirit of traditional Liberalism put the old party well in tune with the times, but the *de facto* class discrimination which is also endemic to the party limited the practical gains which could be made among trade unionists and other working-class activists. The electorate's diffusion from earlier discipline made class considerations themselves less important, but also made parties generally insecure in their positions. The movement of social change, in total, has made British politics more surprising and unpredictable than it has been through most of this century.

The Liberal revival continues therefore, in the sense that commitment to voluntarism and individualism is growing. Social service and reform groups operating outside of political parties increase in numbers, energy and impact. Electoral politics is more American, less certain. The basic irony for the Liberal Party is that a Liberal revival does not necessarily favour, and can clearly hurt, the Liberal Party.

15 Drew Middleton, *These Are The British*, p. 93, notes concerning the Second World War: 'This mobilization was the start of the social changes that have been going on in Britain ever since ... The mingling of classes began.'

The British electorate may be moving in American directions. The Liberal Party is the nation's most American party, in style, structure and internal culture. But current social and political change is undermining the security of parties generally, not reinforcing the position of a particular party. The British quality of this rests in the apparent ability of the society to accept and adapt to important social changes in the context of what remains a fundamental political consensus on the legitimacy of institutions.

Appendix: A Postal Survey of Liberal Party Activists.

Trying to secure a clear picture of the ideas and motives of Liberal Party activists is a difficult task. First, there is the problem of finding an adequate listing of such members. An accurate, extensive national list, or even regional lists around the nation, simply do not. exist. The party is generally very poor at keeping central records, and this situation is well reflected in the specific case of membership rolls. Virtually the only records of this type kept at the Liberal Party Organization in London are (1) a mailing list of constituency association officers throughout the country, and (2) a list of activists who have volunteered for service as speakers for the party.

I decided to use this second list for a postal survey. The first list had the disadvantage of containing only the membership of a particular sub-group of the upper-echelons of the party – a similar handicap attaches to using the Rasmussen approach of interviewing Liberal Party parliamentary candidates. Rather than contacting virtually 100 per cent of the membership of a very limited – therefore not necessarily representative – population, I decided to use a comparatively small sample of activists from the party at large, distributed both up and down the membership hierarchy (vertically) and across the nation (horizontally). Party officials, be they constituency officers or parliamentary candidates, lack the first spread. Insight into the views of all of the representatives of a fairly small party group was sacrificed in the hope of getting some handle upon the orientations of party members at large. The main uniformity connecting those sampled, aside from party membership, is that they were very active in party work –

outside of the fact that this quality would seem necessary anyway for a person to volunteer himself for party speaking, such involvement was a stipulation of LPO when the list was secured through a mailing to constituency associations throughout the UK.

Approximately 66 per cent (104 of 157) of those to whom questionnaires were sent filled out and returned them. The fairly high rate of response encourages confidence, at least, that the views expressed are representative of the population of party speakers surveyed. Beyond this, the highly individualistic, anti-class, pro- 'spirit of service' replies of so many of the respondents reinforces the evidence of other sources – my own more informal interviews with a large number of Liberal leaders and activists, the themes and emphases of Liberal Party philosophy and literature both past and present. Taken individually, none of these several pieces of evidence may seem decisive. Taken together, they form a persuasive case arguing that the Liberal Party provides a home for a kind of activist who is strongly opposed to class-consciousness and class politics; who is instead highly individualistic, with this manifested in part through a commitment to local social service.

A second basic issue concerned questions to be used in the postal survey. A variety of questions was asked, concerning both specific factual issues and – much more important – broad attitudes of those who were surveyed. Inevitably, arbitrary pruning of questions had to be done. Desire to secure a maximum amount of information on different subjects was balanced by a realization that the more questions asked, the less the likelihood of a large response by return post. The particular issue of individualism-class consciousness was sufficiently interesting to include an obviously leading question (No 4) to see if it would elicit any complaints. There were almost none, implying that the extreme nature of the question correlated well with the extreme individualism of almost all of the Liberals, and that they see the individualism of their party as a very important characteristic.

Below is a sample of the questionnaire.

Questions:

(1) Why are you a Liberal, rather than in the Conservative or Labour Parties, when the Liberals are so far from national power? Did any particular issue draw you to the Liberal Party?

(2) What do you suppose was mainly responsible for the Liberal revival of the late 1950s and early 1960s? How important was (a) the fact that people were reluctant to vote Labour because they did not trust the party, but were unhappy with the Conservative Government, (b) the growth of a 'new middle class' which rejected the class politics of the two big parties, (c) the impact of Jo Grimond on the electorate?

(3) Briefly, how do you conceive of 'Liberalism' as a philosophy, a set of principles?

(4) Would you agree strongly or somewhat or not at all with the proposition that the Liberal Party is a bastion for the 'individual' in a Britain which is becoming increasingly 'collectivist' with large and bureaucratic parties, interest groups, and government:
    agree strongly
    agree somewhat
    do not agree at all

(5) Were/are your parents Liberals? If not, in what political affiliation would you put them?

(6) Are you optimistic or pessimistic about future Liberal political prospects? Why?

(7) Why do you suppose the party is having so much financial trouble currently?

(8) Have the 'Red Guard' elements in the Young Liberals been, on balance, a political asset or a liability, both within

the party and within the electorate? Why?

(9) Do you feel the loss of Mr Grimond as Party Leader was:
  a disaster for the party
  a serious but not disastrous loss
  not a serious problem for the party

(10) How prominent would you say working-class people are in your own local Liberal constituency association?:
  Very prominent, holding important posts
  Active, holding some posts or at least doing a lot of volunteer work
  Somewhat active, doing some work for the party
  Not active in the party

(11) If you indicated that working-class people hold no offices in your local party association, why do you suppose this is the case?

(12) What sort of activities does your local Liberal association engage in to promote the Liberal cause? Do prominent Liberals in your area take an active interest in local problems and complaints, especially problems of the old, poor and unemployed? What exactly do they do along these lines?

(13) Aside from the Liberal Party, do you have any preference for one or the other of the two major parties, or are they both equally bad? If you could not vote for a Liberal for Parliament, how would you vote?:   Labour;
      Cons.;   Not vote.

(14) Did you ever consider joining one of the two major parties but not join? Which one? Why didn't you join?

(15) Were you ever in one of the two major parties? Which one? Why did you switch? When did you switch?

(16) Please describe, in a few words, how you see the

Conservative and Labour Parties.

(17) What do you like most and like least about the Conservative Party?

(18) What do you like most and like least about the Labour Party?

(19) What is your religion? When you were young, were your parents religious; and, if so, what is/was their religion?

(20) What is your occupation, and what is/was your father's occupation?

(21) Do you see yourself in a particular social class? If so, would you classify yourself as: upper class;   upper middle class;   middle class;   lower middle class;   skilled working class;   labouring working class.

(22) Would you say most Liberals fit into a particular class? If so, which one: upper class;   middle class: working class. If no particular class, why not? Do most of the Liberals *you know* fit into one of the above categories of class? Which one: upper; middle; working. If most of the Liberals you know do not fit into a particular class, why is this the case?:

(23) How do you feel about reducing class differences?:   strongly favour reducing;   agree generally with reducing;   no opinion;   disagree generally with reducing;   strongly against reducing them.

(24) Is there a trade union in your firm?   Yes;   No. If so, are you a member of it?:   Yes;   No. If not a member, why not?

(25) How do you feel, generally, toward trade unions?:   very favourable;   favourable;   no opinion;   unfavourable;   very unfavourable. Why do you feel this way?:

(26) How long have you been a member of the Liberal Party?

BIBLIOGRAPHY

I Books

ALFORD, ROBERT, *Party and Society*, London: John Murray, 1964.

ALLEN, A.G., *The English Voter*, London: English Universities Press, 1964.

AMERY, L.S, *Thoughts on the Constitution*, London: Oxford University Press, 1947.

ANDREWS, CHARLES M., *A History of England*, Boston: Allyn & Bacon, 1903.

BAGEHOT, WALTER, *The English Constitution*, London: Fontana Books, 1963.

BARKER, ANTHONY, and MICHAEL RUSH, *The Member of Parliament and His Information*, London: George Allen & Unwin, 1970

BEALEY, FRANK, and HENRY PELLING, *Labour and Politics 1900-1906*, London: Macmillan, 1958.

BEER, SAMUEL H., *British Politics in the Collectivist Age*, New York: Vintage Books, 1969.

—, and RICHARD BARRINGER, eds, *The State and the Poor*, Cambridge: Winthrop Publishers, 1970.

BEER, SAMUEL H., and ADAM ULAM, eds, *Patterns of Government*, New York: Random House, 1962 (2nd ed.) and 1973 (3rd ed.).

LORD BEVERIDGE, Voluntary Action, London: George Allen & Unwin, 1948.

BIRCH, A.H., *Small-Town Politics*, London: Oxford University Press, 1959.

BLAKE, ROBERT, *Disraeli*, London: Eyre & Spottiswoode, 1966.

BLEASE, W. LYON, *A Short History of English Liberalism*, New York: G.P. Putnam's, 1913.

BLONDEL, JEAN, *Voters, Parties and Leaders*, Harmondsworth: Penguin Books, 1963.

BLUMLER, JAY G., and DENIS McQUAIL, *Television in Politics: Its Uses and Influence*, London: Faber & Faber, 1968.

BONHAM, JOHN, *The Middle Class Vote*, London: Faber & Faber, 1954.

BOOKER, CHRISTOPHER, *The Neophiliacs*, London: Collins, 1969.

BROGAN, D.W., *The English People*, New York: Alfred A. Knopf, 1943.

BROWN, A.J. *The Framework of Regional Economics in the United Kingdom*, Cambridge University Press, 1972.

BULLOCK, ALAN, and MAURICE SHOCK, eds *The Liberal Tradition From Fox to Keynes*, London: Adam and Charles Black, 1956.

BULMER-THOMAS IVOR, *The Growth of the British Party System* (2 vols), London: John Baker, 1965.

BULPITT, J.G., *Party Politics in English Local Government*, London: Longmans, Green, 1967.

BURNHAM, WALTER DEAN, *Critical Elections – and the Mainsprings of American Politics*, New York: W.W. Norton, 1970.

BUTLER, DAVID E., *The British General Election of 1951*, London: Macmillan, 1952.

—, *The British General Election of 1955*, London: Macmillan, 1955.

—, *The Electoral System In Britain 1918-1951*, Oxford: The Clarendon Press, 1953.

—, *The Electoral System In Britain 1918-1951*, Oxford: The Clarendon Press, 1953.

—, *The Study of Political Behaviour*, London: Hutchinson, 1958.

—, and JENNIE FREEMAN, *British Political Facts 1900-1968*, 2nd ed., London: Macmillan, 1968.

BUTLER, DAVID E., and ANTHONY KING, *The British General Election of 1964*, London: Macmillan, 1965.

BUTLER, DAVID E., and ANTHONY KING, *The British General Election of 1966*, London: Macmillan, 1966.

BUTLER, DAVID E., and MICHAEL PINTO-DUSCHINSKY, *The British General Election of 1970*, London, Macmillan, 1971.

BUTLER, DAVID, and RICHARD ROSE, *The British General Election of 1959*, London: Macmillan, 1960.

BUTLER, DAVID, and DONALD STOKES, *Political Change in Britain*, London: Macmillan, 1969.

CARBERY, THOMAS E, *Consumers in Politics*, Manchester University Press, 1969.

CAVES, RICHARD E., and associates, *Britain's Economic Prospects*, Washington: The Brookings Institution, 1968.

CHAPMAN, BRIAN, *British Government Observed*, London: W.H. Allen, 1963.

CLINE, CATHERINE ANN, *Recruits to Labour – The British Labour Party 1914-1932, Syracuse University Press,* 1963.

COATES, KEN, ed., *Can the Workers Run Industry?*, London: Sphere Books, 1968.

COWIE, HARRY, *Why Liberal?*, Harmondsworth: Penguin Books, 1964.

CRAIG, F.W.S., *British Parliamentary Election Statistics*, Glasgow: Political Reference Publications, 1968.

CROZIER, MICHEL, *The Bureaucratic Phenomenon*, University of Chicago Press, 1964.

DAHL, ROBERT ed., *Political Oppositions In Western Democracies*, New Haven and London: Yale University Press, 1966.

DAILY TELEGRAPH, *Election '66*, London: *Daily Telegraph*, 1966.

DANGERFIELD, GEORGE, *The Strange Death of Liberal England 1910-1914*, London: Glanadu; New York: Capricorn Books, 1935, 1961.

DUVERGER, MAURICE, *Political Parties*, New York: John Wiley, 1963.

ECKSTEIN, HARRY, and DAVID APTER, eds, *Comparative Politics – A*

Reader, New York: The Free Press, 1963.

EPSTEIN, LEON D., *Political Parties In Western Democracies*, New York: Praeger, 1967.

EVANS, T.J., *Sir Rhys Hopkin Morris*, Llandyssul: Gomerion Press, n.d. (received Harvard University Library 1958).

FARNDALE, JAMES, ed., *Trends In Social Welfare*, Oxford: Pergamon Press, 1965.

FLEISHER, DAVID, *William Godwin — A Study of Liberalism*, London: George Allen & Unwin, 1951.

FORDER, ANTHONY, ed., *Social Services of England and Wales*, London and New York: Routledge & Kegan Paul, 1969.

FRIEDMAN, MILTON, *Capitalism and Freedom*, University of Chicago Press, 1962.

FULFORD, ROGER, *The Liberal Case*, Harmondsworth: Penguin Books, 1959.

FYFE, HAMILTON, *The British Liberal Party*, London: George Allen & Unwin, 1928.

GERTH, H.H., and C. WRIGHT MILLS, *From Max Weber*, New York, Oxford University Press, 1958.

GOYDER, GEORGE, *The Responsible Company*, Oxford: Basil Blackwell, 1961.

GRAUBARD, STEPHEN, ed., *A New Europe?*, Boston: Beacon Press, 1967.

GRIMOND, JOSEPH, *The Liberal Challenge*1, London: Hollis & Carter, 1963.

—, *The Liberal Future*, London: Faber & Faber, 1959.

GUTTSMAN, W.L., *The British Political Elite*, London: MacGibbon & Kee, 1963.

HANHAM, H.J., *Elections and Party Management*, London: Longmans, Green, 1959.

—, *The Nineteenth-Century Constitution 1815-1914*, Cambridge University Press, 1969.

—, *Scottish Nationalism*, London: Faber & Faber, 1968.

HARTZ, LOUIS, *The Liberal Tradition in America*, New York: Harcourt, Brace & World, 1955.

HAVIGHURST, ALFRED E., *Twentieth-Century Britain*, New York: Harper & Row, 1962.

HOBSBAWM, E.J., *Labouring Men*, New York: Doubleday, 1967.

HOLT, ROBERT T., and JOHN E. TURNER, *Political Parties in Action — The Battle of Barons Court*, New York: The Free Press, 1968.

HUGHES, H. STUART, *Contemporary Europe: A History*, Englewood Cliffs: Prentice-Hall, 1961, 1966.

JAMES, ROBERT RHODES, *Lord Randolph Churchill*, New York: A.S. Barnes, 1960.

JENKINS, ROY, *Asquith*, London: Collins, 1964.

KAPLAN, MORTON, ed., *The Revolution In World Politics*, New York: John Wiley, 1962.

KAVANAGH, D.A., *Constituency Electioneering in Britain*, London: Longmans, Green, 1970.

KINNEAR, MICHAEL, *The British Voter*, Ithaca: Cornell University Press, 1968.

KUENSTLER, PETER, ed., *Community Organization in Britain*, London: Faber & Faber, 1961.

LAKEMAN, ENID, and JAMES D. LAMBERT, *Voting in Democracies*, London: Faber & Faber, 1955.

LAPPING, BRIAN, *The Labour Government 1964-1970*, Harmondsworth: Penguin Books, 1970.

LASKI, HAROLD, *The Rise of European Liberalism*, London: George Allen & Unwin, 1936.

LEONARD, R.L., *Elections in Britain*, London: Van Nostrand, 1968.

—, *Guide To The General Election*, London: Pan Books, 1964.

LICHTHEIM, GEORGE, *The New Europe*, 2nd ed.; New York: Praeger, 1964.

LIPSET, SEYMOUR, *Political Man*, Garden City: Doubleday, 1960.

LOCKE, JOHN, *Two Treatises of Government*, New York: New American Library, 1965.

LOWELL, A. LAWRENCE, *The Government of England* (2 vols), New York: Macmillan, 1908.

LYMAN, RICHARD W., *The First Labour Government 1924*, London: Chapman & Hall, n.d.

McCALLUM, R.B., *The Liberal Party From Earl Grey to Asquith*, London: Victor Gallancz, 1963.

MacCORMICK, NEIL, ed., *The Scottish Debate*, London: Oxford University Press, 1970.

McCRONE, GAVIN, *Scotland's Future – The Economics of Nationalism*, Oxford: Basil Blackwell, 1969.

McKENZIE, R.T., *British Political Parties*, London: Heinemann, 1964.

MAGEE, BRIAN, *The New Radicalism*, London: Secker & Warburg, 1962.

MARSH, DAVID, *The Changing Social Structure of England and Wales 1871-1961*, London: Routledge & Kegan Paul, 1965.

MARSHALL, T.H., *Citizenship and Social Class*, Cambridge University Press, 1950.

MIDDLETON, DREW, *These Are The British*, New York: Alfred A. Knopf, 1957.

MILL, JOHN STUART, *On Liberty*, New York: Liberal Arts Press, 1956.

MITCHELL, B.R., and KLAUS BOEHM, *British Parliamentary Election Results 1950-1964*, London: Cambridge University Press, 1966.

MORLEY, JOHN, *The Life of William Ewart Gladstone* (3 vols), New York: Macmillan, 1963, 1909.

MORRIS, JAMES, *The Outriders*, London: Faber & Faber, 1963.

MORRIS, MARY, *Voluntary Work in the Welfare State*, London: Routledge & Kegan Paul, 1969.

MORRISON, HERBERT, *Government and Parliament*, London: Oxford University Press, 1954.

NICHOLAS, H.G., *The British General Election of 1950*, London: Macmillan, 1951.

NORDLINGER, ERIC A., *The Working-Class Tories*, Berkeley and Los

Angeles: University of California Press, 1967.

OSBORNE, JOHN, *The Entertainer*, New York: Criterion Books, 1958.

OSTROGORSKI, M.Y., *Democracy and the Organization of Political Parties* (2 vols), London: Macmillan, 1902.

PELLING, HENRY, *A Short History of the Labour Party*, New York: Macmillan, 1965.

—, *The Origins of the Labour Party: 1880-1900*, London: Macmillan, 1954.

PHILLIPS, HERBERT, *The Liberal Outlook*, London: Chapman & Hall, 1929.

PINE, L.G., *Ramshackledom*, London: Secker & Warburg, 1962.

POIRIER, PHILIP, *The Advent of the British Labour Party*, New York: Columbia University Press, 1958.

PULZER, PETER, *Political Representation and Elections*, New York: Praeger, 1967.

RASMUSSEN, JORGEN SCOTT, *Retrenchment and Revival*, Tucson: University of Arizona Press, 1964.

READ, DONALD, *Cobden and Bright*, London: Edward Arnold, 1967.

REID, ANDREW, ed., *Why I Am A Liberal*, London, 1885.

RESS, ANTHONY M., and TREVOR SMITH, *Town Councillors – A Study of Barking*, The Action Society Trust, 1964.

ROBERTSON, J.M., *The Meaning of Liberalism*, London: Methuen, 1912, 1925.

ROSE, RICHARD, *Policy-Making In Britain*, London: Macmillan, 1969.

RUGGIERO, GUIDO DE, *The History of European Liberalism*, Boston: Beacon Press, 1959.

SAMPSON, ANTHONY, *The Anatomy of Britain*, New York: Harper, 1965, 1966.

SCHAAR, JOHN, *Escape from Authority*

THAYER, GEORGE, *The British Political Fringe*, London: Anthony Blond, 1965.

THE TIMES *Guide to the House of Commons*, London: *The Times*, volumes for 1945-74.

TINKER, HUGH, *Re-Orientations – Essays on Asia in Transition*, New York: Praeger, 1965.

TITMUSS, RICHARD M, *Essays on the Welfare State*, 2nd ed.; Boston: Beacon Press, 1969.

TUCHMAN, BARBARA, *The Proud Tower*, New York: Macmillan, 1967.

VINCENT, JOHN, *The Formation of the Liberal Party*, London: Constable, 1966.

WARD, MAISIE, *Gilbert Keith Chesterton*, New York: Sheed & Ward, 1943.

WATKINS, ALAN, *The Liberal Dilemma*, Plymouth: MacGibbon & Kee, 1966.

WATSON, GEORGE, ed., *Radical Alternative*, London: Eyre & Spottiswoode, 1962.

—, ed., *The Unservile State*, London: George Allen & Unwin, 1957.

WEBER, MAX (see H.H. GERTH and C. WRIGHT MILLER).

WILSON, TREVOR, *The Downfall of the Liberal Party 1914-1935*, London: Collins, 1966.

WOLL, PETER, *American Bureaucracy*, New York: W.W. Norton, 1963.

II   Main Articles

BEER, SAMUEL H., 'The Future of British Politics: An American View', *Political Quarterly*, XXVI, January/March 1955, pp. 33-42.
—, 'Liberalism and the National Idea', reprint article.
BERRINGTON, H.B., 'The General Election of 1964,' *Journal of the Royal Statistical Society*, 128, 1965, pp. 17-66.
BREMNER, MARJORIE, 'Noblesse Oblige', *Twentieth Century*, October 1957, pp. 391-400.
BUTLER, DAVID, ARTHUR STEVENS and DONALD STOKES, 'The Strength of the Liberals Under Different Electoral Systems', *Parliamentary Affairs*, XXII, Winter 1968/69, pp. 10-15.
CHRISTOPH, JAMES, 'Consensus and Cleavage in British Political Ideology', *American Political Science Review*, LIX, September 1965, pp. 629-42.
CRANE, PEGGY, 'What's in a Party Image?', *Political Quarterly*, XXX, July/September 1959, pp. 230-43.
CYR, ARTHUR, 'Class in Britain through Liberal Eyes', *Comparative Politics*, V, October 1972, pp.
DAHL, ROBERT, 'Workers' Control of Industry and the British Labour Party', *American Political Science Review*, XLI, October 1947, pp. 875-900.
Encounter (special issue on malaise in Britain), XXI, July 1963.
EPSTEIN, LEON, 'British Class Consciousness and the Labour Party', *The Journal of British Studies*, No 2, May 1962, pp. 136-50.
FOTHERGILL, PHILIP, 'The Liberal Predicament', *Political Quarterly*, XXIV, July/September 1953, pp. 243-9.
GRIMOND, JO, 'The Principles of Liberalism', *Political Quarterly*, XXIV, July/September 1953, pp. 236-42.
HOLT, ARTHUR, 'The Liberal's Attitude to Contemporary Problems', *Political Quarterly*, XXIV, July/September 1953, pp. 249-58.
KOCHMAN, M.P., 'Liberal Party Activists and Extremism', *Political Studies*, XVI, June 1968, pp. 253-7.
LIPSET, SEYMOUR, 'Liberals: The Second Party?', *The New Leader*, XLIV, 6 February, 1961, pp. 16-19.
LORT-PHILLIPS, PATRICK, 'The British Liberal Revival', *Foreign Affairs*, XXXVIII, October 1959, pp. 121-31.
MANSBACH, RICHARD, 'The Scottish National Party: A Revised Political Profile', *Comparative Politics*, January 1973, pp. 188-9.
MARMOR, THEODORE and DAVID THOMAS, 'Doctors, Politics and Pay Disputes: "Pressure Group Politics" Revisited'. *British Journal of Political Science*, II, October 1972, pp. 421-42.
NOONAN, LOWELL G., 'The Decline of the Liberal Party in British Politics', *Journal of Politics*, XVI, February 1954, pp. 24-38.
NEUSTADT, RICHARD, 'White House and Whitehall', *The Public*

Interest, II, Winter 1966, pp. 55-69.
Political Quarterly (special issue on local government), XXXVII, April/June 1966.
ROSE, RICHARD, 'The Political Ideas of English Party Activists', *American Political Science Review*, LVI, June, 1962, pp. 360-71.
SHARPE, L.J., 'Leadership and Representation in Local Government', *Political Quarterly*, April/June 1966, pp. 150-66.

III   *Newspapers and Periodicals*

Economist.
Guardian.
New Statesman.
New York Times
The Times

IV   *Liberal Party periodicals*

Action and Feed back.
Current Topics.
The Liberal Way Forward.
Liberal Headquarters Bulletin (includes *Action and Feed-back*).
Liberal News (also, briefly, *Liberal News Commentary*).
Local Government Newsletter.
New Outlook.
United.

V   *Liberal Party pamphlets (and party-related pamphlets)*

There have been a vast number of pamphlets produced by the party over the last few decades. As far as I know, no central index of them exists. The following series were most useful in this study. Other specific titles of particular assistance may be reviewed in the chapter notes.
The Grimond policy panel reports.
New Directions.
The Unservile State Papers.
New Orbit.

VI   *Other Liberal Party material*

Annual Reports, Liberal Party Organization (LPO), 1937-69.
Britain's Industrial Future, Being the Report of the Liberal Industrial Enquiry, (Yellow Book), London: Ernest Benn, 1928.
Liberal Candidates' and Speakers' Handbooks 1959, 1964, 1970.
'Liberal Left-overs', (typed manuscript at LPO, dated 1966).

Local Government Handbook, LPO, 1960.
Minutes of the Liberal Party Executive and Council (excerpts supplied by a party activist).
Radical Reform News-Letter.
Resolutions of the Liberal Assembly.

VII Conservative and Labour Parties

The Campaign Guide, Conservative Central Office, volumes of 1955, 1959, 1964, 1966, 1970.
Fair Deal at Work, Conservative Party, 1968.
General Election Manifestoes.
In Place of Strife, Labour Party, 1969.
Twelve Wasted Years, Labour Party, 1963.

VIII Theses

BRIER, A.P., *A Study of Liberal Party Constituency Activity in the Mid-1960s*, (unpublished Ph.D. thesis, University of Exeter, 1967).
WALLACE, WILLIAM, *The Liberal Revival – The Liberal Party in Britain, 1955-1966*, (unpublished Ph.D. thesis, Cornell University, 1968).

IX Other Material

Great Britain, *Parliamentary Debates* (Commons).
British Information Services, *Social Services in Britain*, ID 780 (revised), HMSO, 1963.
Report of the Royal Commission on Local Government in England *Local Government Reform* (short version), HMSO, June 1969.
Child Poverty Action Group, *Poverty*, 1969.
—, *Poverty and the Labour Government*, 1970.
Shelter, *The Shelter Story*,
SNP and You, Scottish Nationalist Party, 1968.
Your Part in the Life of Wales, Plaid Cymru, 1969.
Imperial Chemical Industries Ltd, *Profit Sharing*,
Rolls Royce Ltd, *Workers' (1955) Shares Explanatory Booklet*, 1969.
Guardian Report of the Liberal Assembly, 1961.
Guardian Report, *The Liberals and the Government*, 1965.
SCARROW, HOWARD, 'Policy Pressures and Initiatives by British Local Government: The Case of Regulation in the "Public Interest" ', (paper prepared for delivery at the 2970 Convention of the American Political Science Association).
SHANNON, WILLIAM, 'A Letter from Brighton', (typed manuscript).
YOUNG MICHAEL, *The Chipped White Cups of Dover*, London: Devonport Press, 1960.
WALLACE, WILLIAM, *Co-Partnership Re-Examined*, London: Industrial Co-Partnership Association, 1955.

INDEX

INDEX